AF730504

Social Protection and Cash Transfers to Strengthen Families Affected by HIV and AIDS

Michelle Adato and Lucy Bassett

RESEARCH
MONOGRAPH

INTERNATIONAL FOOD POLICY
RESEARCH INSTITUTE
sustainable solutions for ending hunger and poverty

IFPRI®

Supported by the CGIAR

International Food Policy Research Institute
2033 K Street, NW
Washington, D.C. 20006-1002, USA
Telephone +1-202-862-5600
www.ifpri.org

DOI: http://dx.doi.org/10.2499/9780896292017

Library of Congress Cataloging-in-Publication Data

Adato, Michelle.
Social protection and cash transfers to strengthen families affected by HIV and AIDS / Michelle Adato and Lucy Bassett.
p. cm.—(IFPRI research monograph)
Includes bibliographical references and index.
ISBN 978-0-89629-201-7 (alk. paper)
1. HIV infections—Economic aspects—Africa, Southern. 2. HIV infections—Economic aspects—Africa, East. 3. HIV infections—Economic aspects—Latin America. 4. AIDS (Disease)—Economic aspects—Africa, Southern. 5. AIDS (Disease)—Economic aspects—Africa, East. 6. AIDS (Disease)—Economic aspects—Latin America. I. Bassett, Lucy. II. International Food Policy Research Institute. III. Title. IV. Series: IFPRI research monograph.
RA643.86.A356A33 2012
362.19697'92—dc23 2012003982

About IFPRI

The International Food Policy Research Institute (IFPRI©) was established in 1975 to identify and analyze alternative national and international strategies and policies for meeting food needs of the developing world on a sustainable basis, with particular emphasis on low-income countries and on the poorer groups in those countries. While the research effort is geared to the precise objective of contributing to the reduction of hunger and malnutrition, the factors involved are many and wide-ranging, requiring analysis of underlying processes and extending beyond a narrowly defined food sector. The Institute's research program reflects worldwide collaboration with governments and private and public institutions interested in increasing food production and improving the equity of its distribution. Research results are disseminated to policymakers, opinion formers, administrators, policy analysts, researchers, and others concerned with national and international food and agricultural policy.

About IFPRI Research Monographs

IFPRI Research Monographs are well-focused, policy-relevant monographs based on original and innovative research conducted at IFPRI. All manuscripts submitted for publication as IFPRI Research Monographs undergo extensive external and internal reviews. Prior to submission to the Publications Review Committee, each manuscript is circulated informally among the author's colleagues. Upon submission to the Committee, the manuscript is reviewed by an IFPRI reviewer and presented in a formal seminar. Three additional reviewers—at least two external to IFPRI and one from the Committee—are selected to review the manuscript. Reviewers are chosen for their familiarity with the country setting. The Committee provides the author its reaction to the reviewers' comments. After revising as necessary, the author resubmits the manuscript to the Committee with a written response to the reviewers' and Committee's comments. The Committee then makes its recommendations on publication of the manuscript to the Director General of IFPRI. With the Director General's approval, the manuscript becomes part of the IFPRI Research Monograph series. The publication series, under the original name of IFPRI Research Reports, began in 1977.

Contents

Tables

Figures

Foreword

IFPRI's research in social protection stems from evidence that policies and programs focused on reducing vulnerability and risk and increasing resilience to shocks are an essential component of growth and development strategies. One of the types of assets that households draw down in times of shocks is human capital—including vital investments in the nutrition, health, and education of children—a process with irreversible consequences that perpetuates the intergenerational transmission of poverty. Few shocks have been more devastating to Sub-Saharan Africa than that of HIV and AIDS, with approximately 22.5 million people living with the virus in 2009, and an estimated 13–17 million children having lost one or both parents to the disease. The long-term threat to the human capital of these children, combined with strong evidence of the vicious circle between food insecurity and HIV, makes social protection an essential part of any strategy to address HIV and AIDS. IFPRI has conducted research on safety nets and social protection for over 20 years, and on AIDS, food security, and livelihoods for nearly 10 years. This monograph is based on work that IFPRI has done to bring together these themes, joining many international organizations, including UNAIDS, to bring social protection into the arsenal of approaches to reduce the prevalence and impact of HIV.

This monograph reviews the impacts of 20 cash transfer programs globally. Our findings show that conditional cash transfer programs have thus far demonstrated significant impacts on poverty, education, health, and nutrition in countries with low HIV prevalence, and that unconditional programs in East and southern African countries with high HIV prevalence have also shown promise with respect to impacts on food consumption and human capital.

In light of the evidence of a vicious circle among HIV/AIDS, food insecurity, and the drawing down of household assets, including human capital, the monograph concludes that social protection must be a critical part of the global response to AIDS. The vast literature review undertaken for this monograph also yielded important findings related to designing social protection programs: they should target poor households in areas of high HIV prevalence, but not HIV-positive households or orphans; and that conditionality should be carefully tested and not yet assumed to be appropriate in Sub-Saharan Africa. It also concludes that cash transfers are not the only relevant social protection response to the challenges of HIV and AIDS—other approaches may be appropriate to the conditions and capacities of beneficiaries. However, cash transfers have thus far demonstrated the greatest potential to directly affect poverty and human capital, and they can be scaled up rapidly to achieve greater coverage than alternative approaches.

Shenggen Fan
Director General, International Food Policy Research Institute

Acknowledgments

This research monograph was originally prepared for the Joint Learning Initiative on Children and HIV/AIDS (JLICA), though it has since been re-peer reviewed and substantially revised and updated. JLICA was an independent, interdisciplinary network of policymakers, practitioners, community leaders, activists, researchers, and people living with HIV that is working to improve the well-being of HIV-affected children, their families, and communities. This review formed part of the work of JLICA's Learning Group on Strengthening Families (LG 1), co-chaired by Linda Richter and Lorraine Scherr, with other LG 1 lead authors, including Mark Belsky, Upjeet Chandan, Chris Desmond, Scott Drimie, Mary Haour-Knipe, Vicky Hosegood, José Kimou, Sangeetha Madhavan, Vuyiswa Mathambo, and Angela Wakhweya. JLICA's founding partners and donors are UNICEF, the Bernard van Leer Foundation, FXB International, the Government of the Netherlands, the UK Department for International Development, Irish AID, the Rockefeller Brothers Fund, and the FXB Center for Health and Human Rights at Harvard University. This review was jointly undertaken as a project of the Regional Network on AIDS, Livelihoods, and Food Security (RENEWAL) of the International Food Policy Research Institute (IFPRI) with RENEWAL's core support from Irish Aid, the Swedish International Development Cooperation Agency, the International Development Research Centre, and the U.S. Agency for International Development. The authors thank these donors, the LG 1 members, and the many program implementers and researchers who assisted us in accessing documents; there are too many people to name, but all are greatly appreciated.

Acronyms and Abbreviations

AIDS	acquired immune deficiency syndrome
AIN-C	Atención Integral a la Niñez Comunitaria
ART	antiretroviral therapy
ARV	antiretroviral drug
BDH	Bono de Desarrollo Humano
BMI	body mass index
CBO	community-based organization
CCT	conditional cash transfer
CSG	Child Support Grant
CWAC	community welfare assistance committee
DECT	Dowa Emergency Cash Transfer
DfID	UK Department for International Development
DHS	Demographic and Health Survey
DSD	Department of Social Development
ECD	early childhood development
EPRI	Economic Policy Research Institute
EPWP	Expanded Public Works Programme
FACT	Food and Cash Transfers Project
FAO	Food and Agriculture Organization of the United Nations
FCG	Foster Care Grant
FSSAP	Female Secondary School Assistance Project
GAPVU	Gabinete de Apoio à População Vulnerável
GDP	gross domestic product
GTZ	German Technical Assistance
HAZ	height-for-age z-scores
HBC	home-based care
HCBC	home- and community-based care
HIV	human immunodeficiency virus
HSL	Household Subsistence Level
IATT	Inter-Agency Task Team (on Children and HIV and AIDS)
IEC	Information, Education, and Communication
IFPRI	International Food Policy Research Institute
IHH	Integrated Household Survey
IMAGE	Intervention with Microfinance for AIDS and Gender Equity

JLICA	Joint Learning Initiative on Children and HIV/AIDS
KIDS	KwaZulu-Natal Income Dynamics Survey
LCMS	Living Conditions Monitoring Survey
LEAD	Linkages for the Economic Advancement of the Disadvantaged
LOC	location OVC committee
MFI	microfinance institution
MGLSD	Ministry of Gender, Labour, and Social Development
MiET	Media in Education Trust
MIS	management information system
MTCT	mother-to-child transmission
NAS	National Institute of Social Welfare
NGO	nongovernmental organization
NPA	National Plan of Action (for Orphans and Vulnerable Children)
OAP	Old Age Pension
OVC	Orphans and Vulnerable Children
PATH	Programme for Advancement through Health and Education
PLWA	people living with AIDS
PPP	purchasing power parity
PRAF	Programa de Asignación Familiar
PROGRESA	Programa de Educación, Salud y Alimentación
PSNP	Productive Safety Net Programme
RENEWAL	Regional Network on AIDS, Livelihoods, and Food Security
ROSC	Reaching Out of School Children Programme
RPS	Red de Protección Social
SAARC	South Asian Association for Regional Cooperation
SASSA	South African Social Security Agency
SCTS	Social Cash Transfer Scheme
SDA	Social Dimensions of Adjustment
SIDA	Swedish International Development Cooperation Agency
STD	sexually transmitted disease
SWS	social welfare services
TWG	Technical Working Group
UCT	unconditional cash transfer
UNAIDS	Joint United Nations Programme on HIV/AIDS
UNGASS	United Nations General Assembly Special Session
VCT	voluntary testing and counseling
WAZ	weight-for-age z-scores
WFP	World Food Programme

Summary

The global trend toward investing in social protection in poor countries has reached Sub-Saharan Africa, taking on a new urgency as HIV and AIDS interact with other drivers of poverty to simultaneously destabilize livelihoods systems and family and community safety nets. A new focus on the vulnerability of families and threats to the long-term human capital of children have accelerated international, regional, and national commitments to social protection programs in heavily AIDS-affected countries. Social protection in the form of cash transfers is receiving increasing recognition as an important part of a comprehensive AIDS response. The urgency of cash assistance for food purchases is underscored by emerging evidence on the interactions between nutrition and AIDS disease progression.

Based on a review of over 300 documents, this monograph examines how social protection can be used to protect children and families affected by HIV and AIDS. It reviews evidence on the impacts of 10 unconditional cash transfer (UCT) programs in southern and East Africa and 10 conditional cash transfer (CCT) programs in Latin America. The monograph also reviews key policy debates relevant to program design, including targeting, examining debates about directly targeting AIDS-affected individuals versus poor families and assessing alternative targeting methods, as well as debates around conditionality, considering the advantages and risks of conditioning benefits on participation in services in heavily AIDS-affected contexts. In addition to cash transfers, the monograph also considers the relative strengths and weaknesses of food transfers and nutrition programs, public works, and microcredit and livelihoods programs, as well as social services.

Globally, the vast majority of cash transfer programs have been designed and rolled out in contexts in which AIDS either was not a large-scale problem requiring differential attention in social protection policy or was not taken specifically into account. Under any circumstances, determining whether and which type of program should be undertaken requires policymakers to consider a web of issues related to the causes of poverty; the indicators most in need of improvement; the constraints on achieving those improvements; administrative, technical, and financial capacities; demographics; the structure of employment; and political economy, as well as natural disasters, political conflict, and epidemics. In addition to the global challenges of growing the economy, creating jobs, and improving living standards, countries in Sub-Saharan Africa face the added challenge of dramatic escalations in the number of adults and children whose livelihoods are threatened by HIV and AIDS. In 2009 an estimated 22.5 million people in Sub-Saharan Africa were living with HIV, 67 percent of the global total, and there were an estimated 1.3 million deaths. The number of newly infected adults and children stood at an estimated 1.8 million. Despite a modest decline in adult HIV prevalence globally in the past decade and increased access to treatment, the number of children who have lost one or both parents to AIDS increased, from approximately 14.6 million in 2005 to 16.6 million in 2009. Nearly 90 percent are in Sub-Saharan Africa (UNAIDS 2010). Most of these children are being taken care of by extended families and communities, but many of these families were already very poor and are now in even greater need of external support. In addition to orphaned children, millions more children are also affected by HIV and AIDS as illness in families and communities undermines livelihoods systems, human capital, and physical and psychological well-being.

There is growing evidence that HIV/AIDS is significantly intertwined with other sources of vulnerability; for instance, HIV/AIDS has a two-directional relationship with food insecurity and malnutrition. Articulations of the epidemic with forms of chronic poverty have made social protection a moral and economic imperative. While preserving basic levels of comfort and human dignity among the sick, social protection interventions may also be the only means of preventing the destitution of entire households, as well as irreversible health, nutrition, and education deprivation among children—with lifelong consequences.

CCT programs have demonstrated large, statistically significant impacts on poverty and on education, health, and nutrition outcomes, mainly for children. The research on this issue has been done in Asian and Latin American countries, where HIV prevalence is very low. However, the impacts of CCTs are reviewed in this monograph because they offer the best evidence to date of the potential of cash transfers to protect and improve the human capital of poor children. With respect to education indicators, most CCTs have significantly increased school enrollment and attendance, and some have affected other indicators such as grade progression and dropout rates. There has been less demonstration of impacts on achievement, calling for more attention to the quality of schools—a challenge that will be even greater when CCTs move to Sub-Saharan Africa. CCT programs have increased health service use and reduced the incidence of illness, although evidence of the latter is weaker. CCTs have achieved strong results with respect to increases in the quantity and quality of food consumption and improvements in nutritional status, although the latter varies considerably across countries and types of indicators. Again, health service challenges will be even greater in Sub-Saharan Africa.

At the time of this writing, only a few rigorous evaluations of UCTs in southern and East Africa had data available; other studies had smaller sample sizes or weaker control groups. However, several have demonstrated substantial positive impacts on the well-being of families and children. These results come from modeling using large national datasets in South Africa and empirical studies at the provincial, district, or subdistrict level in several countries. The main impacts demonstrated in South Africa have been on school enrollment. Significant gender discrimination in schooling decisions in some countries indicates that it is critical to pay attention to gender issues in designing programs. There may also be some impacts on schooling via the spending of cash transfers on school expenses. Grant expenditures on food could also have an indirect effect on schooling via nutrition and health improvements, although these studies did not examine this impact pathway. Old age pensions have also been found to support children's education and nutritional status. However, pensions will miss children in households without elderly residents. A grant for households with children will better ensure that children have grant access. UCTs have had some impacts on self-reported health status in several countries, and there is some limited evidence of impacts of UCTs on nutritional status, though they were not directly assessed in most evaluations. UCTs were largely spent on food; in most of the programs evaluated, grants were associated with self-reported reduction in hunger and an increase in the average number of meals per day, and in some countries they were associated with an increase in dietary diversity. Analyses of existing cash transfer programs and country simulations demonstrate that these programs have the potential to reduce poverty, particularly the poverty gap and the severity of poverty, if they are well targeted. The impacts on the poverty headcount tend to be smaller. No other social protection mechanism has yet demonstrated these impacts through well-designed impact evaluations.

Targeting transfers in the context of HIV and AIDS involves decisions around who most needs benefits—whether to target only directly AIDS-affected families or the broader population of poor families and what criteria and methods to use to best reach different target groups. Where cash transfers are not rationed and available to all who are eligible, poverty criteria alone are sufficient to reach AIDS-affected households. In countries such as Malawi and Zambia, where the grants are rationed to 10 percent of a given community, reaching AIDS-affected households requires overlaying poverty criteria with proxy indicators of AIDS-affected households, such as labor constraints, illnesses, and high dependency ratios. An alternative approach is to target the elderly as a means of reaching children, including orphans. However, this approach would miss adults and children in households without elderly members, who would be better reached through grants targeting children through their caregivers. An important process of political mobilization for social protection in the context of HIV and AIDS has convened largely around orphans and vulnerable children, but this has raised questions around how to define a vulnerable child, such as whether orphans are disadvantaged in relation to nonorphans—including children with ill parents as well as those suffering other forms of deprivation and trauma. Some studies find that orphans are disadvantaged with respect to human capital indicators; others find that they are not, with results contingent on variables such as the relationships between children and caregivers, their poverty or wealth status, and household demographics and structure. In light of these equity concerns and those around stigma, there is greater support for targeting cash transfers based on poverty and multiple vulnerability criteria rather than for targeting orphans or families living with AIDS. Given the evidence on the relationship between nutrition and disease progression, there are stronger arguments for targeting food transfers to people living with AIDS.

With respect to targeting methods, data-intensive national surveys tend to have low error rates but are often not practical or cost efficient in the context of low administrative capacity and sparsely populated areas and would also likely be politically problematic if there was no community involvement in decisions in which only a small percentage of the population was included. Application-based systems using means tests work reasonably well in South Africa as long as documentation requirements are not too burdensome; otherwise, large exclusion errors are likely. In Kenya, Malawi, and Zambia, community-based decision-making processes are reported to have performed reasonably well with respect to identifying AIDS-affected and poor households, although they miss some and involve a substantial amount of capacity building to implement. Best methods depend on local conditions and on the prevalence and severity of poverty. Other methods altogether may be needed to reach street children and child-headed households.

An interest in the ability of cash transfers to protect children is driven by the evidence on the interactions among early childhood nutrition, health, and education and the effect of these interactions on the long-term intergenerational transmission of poverty or emergence from it. Many children who are not protected from the effects of HIV and AIDS on their families now will never recover. For these reasons, we examine not only UCTs in southern and eastern Africa but also CCTs in Asia and Latin America, which are designed primarily to strengthen nutrition, health, and education. CCTs have shown much promise globally but also raise many concerns in the context of HIV and AIDS. Several issues emerge. First, it is important to design them to carefully address priority objectives and conditions rather than adopting a blueprint from Latin America. Second, there is a need to determine whether conditionality adds value. In Latin America, several studies have found significant impacts from conditionality; the one study in Africa did not. The third issue is whether conditional transfers will be more politically popular and thus fiscally sustainable than unconditional transfers. Fourth is whether a country has the administrative capacity, service availability, and budgets necessary to run a CCT. Given current evidence and the urgency with which cash transfers are needed, UCTs are likely to be more appropriate in severely AIDS-affected communities. However, conditionalities should be tested on a small scale to determine their impact on carefully selected outcomes and where appropriate services are available. Services and activities—from productive economic activities and early childhood development to adult education and health awareness—can be linked to cash transfer programs, with participation in these activities encouraged but not required.

A final policy debate addressed in this monograph concerns the relative advantages of cash transfers vis-à-vis alternative social protection interventions for families affected by HIV and AIDS. For a government-administered national system of social protection, cash transfers tend to require fewer capacities and inputs, are faster to scale up, and are more likely to achieve wider coverage than are alternative approaches. However, a mix of interventions is needed, appropriate to the priority needs and capacities of beneficiaries. Food and nutrition programs are likely to be particularly useful for subgroups of AIDS-affected families, for example, people on antiretroviral therapy and children in need of nutrition rehabilitation. Nutrition counseling is also essential to support critical behavioral changes such as appropriate food consumption, diarrhea treatment, and prevention of mother-to-child transmission of HIV. Another approach to AIDS-responsive social protection is to use economic strengthening approaches that include public works, microcredit, and livelihoods activities adapted to the conditions of affected households, such as public works that involve less physically demanding work or family-based work contracts. These will be more effective for families that are "less affected"—less labor constrained, less destitute, and possibly better off in terms of various asset endowments. Given the level of inputs and capacities required, these activities will not reach as many people as cash transfers. "AIDS-affected families" do not comprise a homogenous category; they embody many variations with respect to wealth or poverty, education, household structure, stage of illness progression, dependency ratios, social status, and access to assets. This argues for a mix of social protection approaches rather than a single approach. However, pursuing a mix does not conflict with a national strategy of scaling up cash transfers for the most vulnerable families.

Social assistance and social security are often seen as luxuries available only to rich countries; however, they can also be seen as necessities for poor countries. These are all issues relevant to a wider antipoverty and social protection agenda but require further analysis through an HIV/AIDS lens. Such analysis can be done in the course of action as part of the efforts currently under way to scale up cash transfer programs and political processes currently under way to work for social protection as an integral part of the response to HIV and AIDS.

CHAPTER 1

Introduction

The global trend toward investing in social protection in poor countries has reached Sub-Saharan Africa, taking on a new urgency as HIV and AIDS interact with other drivers of poverty to simultaneously destabilize livelihoods systems and family and community safety nets. A new focus on the vulnerability of families, along with threats to the human capital of children with lifelong and intergenerational consequences, has accelerated international, regional, and national commitments to social protection programs in heavily AIDS-affected countries. Social protection in the form of cash transfers—which provide support for food purchases, transportation, education, healthcare, and other expenses—is receiving increasing recognition as a critical piece of a comprehensive AIDS response. The urgency of cash assistance for food purchases is underscored by emerging evidence on the importance of good nutrition in slowing the progression of AIDS and on the effectiveness of antiretroviral therapy, with consequences not only for people living with HIV but also for their children, extended families, and communities.

More commonly a feature of social policy in wealthier countries, social protection has emerged as a political possibility for poor countries, with an increasing number experimenting with program options. Social protection enables individuals, families, and communities to reduce risk and vulnerability, to mitigate the impacts of stresses and shocks, and to support people who suffer from chronic incapacities—due to, for example, age, illness, disabilities, discrimination, or their position within the social and economic structure of their society—to secure basic livelihoods. If designed to do so, social protection can enable people to move out of structural poverty by building assets and by altering social relations.

Among different forms of social protection, momentum is gathering around cash transfers, now found from Cambodia to El Salvador to Kenya. In Sub-Saharan Africa, some countries already have cash transfers in place that reach tens of thousands to millions of people. In other countries in the region, governments, donors, multilateral agencies, and international and national nongovernmental organizations (NGOs) are cooperating to pilot and roll out programs intended to reach hundreds of thousands of people. More than a dozen countries in southern and East Africa currently have cash transfer programs, most at early stages, and more countries are planning or considering them. Questions are raised, however, with respect to their effectiveness in mitigating the impacts of HIV and AIDS, reducing poverty, and protecting human capital, as well as their affordability, sustainability, political support, targeting, and design.

This research monograph examines how social protection can be used to protect children and families affected by HIV and AIDS, and specifically, the potential of cash transfers to secure basic subsistence and reduce poverty while also strengthening the human capital of children, especially their education, health, and nutrition. We review evidence to date on the impacts of 10 unconditional cash transfer programs in southern and East Africa and 10 conditional cash transfers programs in Latin America, all with quantitative impact data. Table 1.1 provides an overview of the programs in the African countries, which are the main interest of this monograph, given that we are looking at how these programs can contribute to the prevention and mitigation of HIV and AIDS in this region. The monograph also reviews key policy debates that accompany decisions on program design and how to make programs responsive to the context of HIV and AIDS. In particular, it examines targeting systems, experiences and dilemmas, and the debate on conditionality, that is, whether cash transfers should be conditioned on beneficiaries' participation in services such as education and healthcare.

Cash transfer programs can take many forms. They can be provided to households as a unit because they meet poverty or vulnerability criteria, to an individual such as an elderly or disabled person, or to families based on the presence of individuals of interest, such as children, girls, or fostered orphans. Cash transfers can be unconditional—given without obligations—or conditional—tied to obligations of recipients to participate in work, training, education, health, nutrition, or other services or activities—or they can be linked to these activities but not contingent on them. Cash transfers help to meet current basic needs of adults and children such as food and clothing. They can also contribute to development processes by enabling or encouraging investment in assets that increase people's chances of breaking out of poverty over the long term. Cash transfer programs—depending on their design and people's ability to take advantage of that design—can also have additional benefits, such as increasing women's autonomy and capacities, or strengthening capacities of local organizations.

Globally, the vast majority of cash transfer programs have been designed and rolled out in contexts in which AIDS either was not a dominant factor requiring specific attention in social protection policy or was not taken specifically into account. Under any circumstances, determining whether a program should be undertaken and which type of program should be provided requires policymakers to consider a web of issues related to the causes of poverty; the indicators most in need of improvement; the constraints on those improvements; administrative, technical, and financial capacities; demographics; the structure of employment; and political economy; as well as natural disasters, political conflicts, and epidemics. In addition to the global challenges of growing the economy, creating jobs, and improving living standards, countries in Sub-Saharan Africa face the added challenge of dramatic escalations in the number of adults and children whose livelihoods are threatened by HIV and AIDS. In 2009, AIDS killed an estimated 1.8 million people globally, and an estimated 2.6 million became newly infected, bringing to an estimated 33.3 million the number of people living with the virus. Approximately 22.5 million (an estimated 21–24 million) of these people live in Sub-Saharan Africa (UNAIDS 2010). Furthermore, there is growing evidence that HIV and AIDS are significantly intertwined with other sources of vulnerability, including a two-directional relationship with food insecurity and malnutrition (Gillespie and Kadiyala 2005). Articulations of the epidemic with forms of chronic poverty have made social protection a moral and economic imperative.

Behind these cases of infection and illness are tens of millions of additional people who are affected by AIDS, most of them children. As of 2009, an estimated 13–17 million children under age eighteen in Sub-Saharan Africa had lost one or both parents to AIDS (UNAIDS 2010). Most of these children are being taken care of by extended families and communities, but many of these families were already very poor and are now in even greater need of external support. In addition to orphaned children, millions more children are also affected by HIV and AIDS as illness in families and communities undermines livelihoods systems, human capital, and physical and psychological well-being. While preserving basic levels of comfort and human dignity among the sick, social protection interventions may also be the only means of preventing the destitution of entire households and irreversible health, nutrition, and education deprivation among children, which have lifelong consequences. Cash transfer programs thus have the potential to reduce trade-offs between short-term household needs and the long-term well-being of individuals and the wider society (Adato and Gillespie 2006).

The rest of this monograph is organized in the following manner. Chapter 2 presents a profile of AIDS-affected countries and households, identifying characteristics to which social protection interventions respond. It then develops a social protection–assets framework for understanding the objectives that different types of interventions can achieve and explains why the monograph focuses on cash transfers and on human capital. Chapter 3 discusses

Table 1.1—Unconditional cash transfer programs with evaluation impacts reviewed in this monograph

Country	Program	Date of initiation (or expansion plan)	Conditional? (Yes/no)	Geographic coverage
Ethiopia	Productive Safety Net Program	January 2005-December 2006 (phase 1) January 2007 (expansion)	Yes/no (some public works requirements)	262 *woredas*
Kenya	Cash Transfer Program for Orphans and Vulnerable Children (OVC)	December 2004 (pre-pilot)	No	3 districts
Kenya	Cash Transfer Program for OVC	2007-2008 (expansion)	Yes/no	17 districts
Kenya	Cash Transfer Program for OVC	2009-2015 (full-scale)	Yes/no	74 districts
Lesotho	Old age pension (universal)	2004	No	National
Malawi	Mchinji Social Cash Transfer Scheme	2006 (pilot)	No	Mchinji District
Malawi	Social Cash Transfer Scheme	2007-2008 2009-2012 (expansion)	No	4 districts
Malawi	Dowa Emergency Cash Transfer	December 2006 (ended April 2007)	No	Dowa District
Malawi	Food and Cash Transfers Project (FACT)	January 2006 (ended April 2006)	No	3 districts
Mozambique	Gabinete de Apoio à População Vulnerável (GAPVU)	1990-1996	No	Provincial capital cities

Main target group	Transfer size	Number of beneficiaries	Administering agency	Implementing partner
Chronically food-insecure households	$17.00[a] per person per year (2005) + food (cereals)	8 million (2006)	Government of Ethiopia	Department for International Development (DfID), World Bank
Orphans and other vulnerable children	$6.50 per month	500 households	Government of Kenya	UNICEF
Orphans and other vulnerable children	$13.00 per month	30,000-50,000 households	Government of Kenya	UNICEF, Swedish International Development Cooperation Agency (SIDA), DfID, World Bank
Orphans and other vulnerable children	$22.50 per month[b]	2009-2015: 300,000 households	Government of Kenya	UNICEF, SIDA, DfID, World Bank
Elderly over age seventy	$25.00 per month	72,000 beneficiaries	Ministry of Finance and Development Planning	
Ultra poor, labor-constrained households	$13.00 per month	3,094 households	Government of Malawi	UNICEF
Ultra poor, labor-constrained households	$13.00 per month	25,000 households, 260,000 households 25,000 260,000	Government of Malawi	UNICEF
Poor households in affected area	Sufficient to purchase Missing Food Entitlement	11,000 households	Concern Worldwide	Concern Worldwide
Poor households in affected areas	Cash + food (equivalent to 25 percent of household food needs)	5,050 households	Concern Worldwide	Concern Worldwide
Elderly, disabled, chronically ill (not including those living with HIV/AIDS), malnourished pregnant women	$3.00-$6.00 per household depending on household size	30,000 (1997)	Ministry of Finance	UNICEF and Social Dimensions of Adjustment / German Technical Assistance (SDA/GTZ)[c]

continued

Table 1.1—Continued

Country	Program	Date of initiation (or expansion plan)	Conditional? (Yes/no)	Geographic coverage
Mozambique	National Institute for Social Action	1997	No	National (provincial capital cities of selected districts, expanding to rural areas)
Namibia	Social Pension (universal)	1965[d]	No	National
Namibia	National Pension Fund (universal)	1992	No	
South Africa	Child Support Grant	1998	No	National
South Africa	Foster Care Grant	Unknown	No	National
South Africa	Old-Age Pension	1944[e]	No	National
Uganda	Cash Transfer pilot program	2007–2010 (pilot)	Yes/no	6 districts
Zambia	Social Cash Transfer Scheme	November 2003–April 2004 (test phase)	No	Kalomo Central agricultural block
Zambia	Social Cash Transfer Scheme	May 2004 (pilot)	No	Kalomo District: 2 agricultural blocks (Kalomo Central and Kanchele)
Zambia	Social Cash Transfer Scheme	2007–2008 (expansion)	No	5 districts (possible scale-up to 72 districts by 2012)

Sources: Low, Garrett, and Ginja (1999); Samson et al. (2004); Schubert (2004a, 2004b, 2005, 2007); Devereux et al. (2005, 2006); Zambia, MCDSS/GTZ (2005); Croome (2006); Kenya, OVPMHA (2006); Palacios and Sluchynsky (2006); Schubert and Huijbregts (2006); Zambia, MCDSS/GTZ (2006, 2007); Campbell et al. (2007); Ellis (2007); HelpAge (2007); International Poverty Center (2007); Ortiz (2007); RHVP (2007); SASSA (2007); Schubert et al. (2007); Uganda, MGLSD (2007); World Bank (2007b).

Notes: Some numbers of beneficiaries and districts listed in this table are approximate because of conflicting sources based on changing targets and timelines for program implementation. All dollar amounts are US dollars. Blank cells in the far right-hand column mean that there are no implementing partners. n.a. = not applicable.

Main target group	Transfer size	Number of beneficiaries	Administering agency	Implementing partner
Same	$3.00–$6.00 per household depending on household size	69,095 (2005) 101,800 (March 2007)	Ministry for Women and Social Action	
Elderly over age sixty	$24.40 per month	96,767 (2001)	Government of Namibia	
Elderly over age sixty	$30.50 per month	96,767 (2001)		
Poor children age fourteen or under (fifteen in 2009)	$27.00 per month	7 million (March 2006)	South African Social Security Agency (SASSA)	n.a.
Children under age eighteen (twenty-one if still in school) determined by court to be in need of care	$84.00 per child per month	300,000 children (March 2006)	SASSA	n.a.
Poor men over age sixty-five and women over age sixty	$111.00 per month	1.9 million (2002)	SASSA	n.a.
Children, elderly, and persons living with chronic illnesses and disabilities	$10.00 plus $1.00 supplementary transfer (per child or elderly person meeting conditions)	2007–2010: 9,000 households[f]	Ministry of Gender, Labour and Social Development	DfID, UNICEF, World Bank, HelpAge International
Destitute, incapacitated households	$5.00 per month	169 households	Ministry of Community Development and Social Services	GTZ
Destitute, incapacitated households	$7.50 per month, (increased to $10.00 per month in April 2005) plus $2.50 (child bonus)	1,027 households	Ministry of Community Development and Social Services	GTZ
Destitute, incapacitated households	Same, but adjusted 5 percent for inflation	9,600 households	Ministry of Community Development and Social Services	GTZ/CARE

[a]Valued at the November 2007 exchange rate, 1 birr = US$0.011.
[b]Valued at the November 2007 exchange rate, 1 KES = US$0.015.
[c]GAPVU was a part of SDA (Low, Garrett, and Ginja 1999, 5, 12).
[d]Black Namibians became eligible only in 1973 (Palacios and Sluchynsky 2006).
[e]Open to all South Africans by law, but de facto expansion to different races occurred over time.
[f]Rollout had not yet started as of April 2008 as the program awaited cabinet approval.

the key issues and dilemmas inherent in targeting and discusses targeting systems and experiences with targeting in AIDS-affected contexts. Chapter 4 turns to the question of conditioning cash benefits on participation in services, exploring the many facets of this debate. Chapters 5–9 examine evidence to date on the impacts of unconditional and conditional cash transfers on poverty, education, health, food consumption, and nutrition and consider complementary activities that can be implemented in conjunction with cash transfers to increase their impacts. Chapter 10 draws conclusions on the evidence to date on cash transfer performance; the debates raised, including alternative social protection approaches; and conclusions about the potential of cash transfers to strengthen families affected by HIV and AIDS.

CHAPTER 2

Social Protection in the Context of HIV and AIDS: Preventing Destitution and Strengthening Assets

Poverty, Food Security, Human Capital, and HIV/AIDS

This chapter begins by outlining the characteristics of AIDS-affected families and then describes the relationships between poverty, food insecurity, human capital, and HIV/AIDS in order to explain why social protection is a necessary component of a comprehensive response to HIV and AIDS in heavily affected countries in Sub-Saharan Africa. Sub-Saharan Africa remains the region of the world most heavily affected by HIV. In 2009, an estimated 22.5 million people there were living with HIV, 67 percent of the global total, and there were an estimated 1.3 million AIDS-related deaths, or 72 percent of the world's total. The number of newly infected adults and children in Sub-Saharan Africa stood at an estimated 1.8 million. This represents a decline since 2001, when HIV incidence (the number of new cases) stood at 2.2 million. Southern Africa remains very hard hit, however. An estimated 11.3 million people living with HIV, approximately half the cases in Sub-Saharan Africa, are in southern Africa, and there are nearly a third more than the estimated 8.6 million people living with HIV in the region a decade earlier (UNAIDS 2010).

Although there has been a modest decline in adult HIV prevalence globally in the past decade, as well as increased access to treatment, the number of orphans—children (those ages 0-17) who have lost one or both parents to AIDS—has increased, from approximately 14.6 million in 2005 to 16.6 million in 2009. Nearly 90 percent of these children live in Sub-Saharan Africa. More than 9 million of these children live in six countries, most of them in East and southern Africa: Kenya, South Africa, Tanzania, Uganda, and Zimbabwe. Only one country, Nigeria, is outside the region. Botswana, Lesotho, and Swaziland in southern Africa also have high rates of orphans, who represent more than 12 percent of all children (UNAIDS 2010). Table 2.1 shows HIV prevalence by country in southern and eastern Africa. Note that most of the countries in this table are featured in this monograph because they have cash transfer pro-

Table 2.1—HIV prevalence in adults ages fifteen through forty-nine in southern and eastern Africa, 2009

Country	HIV/AIDS prevalence (percent)
Swaziland	25.9
Botswana	24.8
Lesotho	23.6
South Africa	17.6
Zimbabwe	14.3
Namibia	13.1
Zambia	13.5
Mozambique	11.5
Malawi	11.0
Uganda	6.5
Kenya	6.3
Tanzania	5.6

Source: UNAIDS (2010).

grams for the poor or the elderly, and many hope to reach AIDS-affected families directly or indirectly. These high prevalence rates underscore the need for social protection to cope with HIV and AIDS.

Within these countries, HIV and AIDS affect all social and economic groups. However, women and girls fifteen years of age and older are disproportionately affected by HIV and AIDS, accounting for 60 percent of HIV infections in Sub-Saharan Africa (UNAIDS 2010). Not only women's greater physiological susceptibility to heterosexual transmission but also the social, legal, and economic disadvantages they face increase their vulnerability to HIV, especially that of girls and younger women. In Sub-Saharan Africa, young women ages fifteen through twenty-four are as much as eight times more likely than men to be HIV positive (UNAIDS 2010).

Many studies have demonstrated AIDS-related impacts on food security, including those showing reductions in subsistence agriculture, income, and expenditures on food. Gillespie and Kadiyala (2005) review more than 150 studies examining linkages between HIV/AIDS and food and nutrition security. Of course, findings are contingent on economic and social variables at the individual, household, community, and country level to which policy responses must be attentive. Studies in Kenya, Swaziland, and Zimbabwe have documented strong associations between AIDS and substantial reductions in crop production (respectively, Yamano and Jayne 2004; Muwanga 2002; Kwaramba 1997). A nationally representative survey using recall data in Mozambique found that households experiencing deaths had lower levels of cash, livestock, assets, and income (Mather et al. 2004).

Poor families are at risk for greater deprivation due to the combined effects of decreased income, increased expenses, and higher dependency ratios. Families affected by HIV and AIDS have higher dependency ratios because the disease, unlike most other illnesses, affects the strong and able bodied, meaning that more people in the household depend on each able-bodied adult for survival.[1] Households with orphans tend to have higher dependency ratios, especially those caring for double orphans (mother and father deceased) and those headed by women. This is because female-headed households are more likely than male-headed households to take in orphans (UNICEF 2009). The presence of HIV-positive adults in the household who cannot contribute to the household livelihood also increases dependency ratios. Several studies have found that deaths due to HIV/AIDS have more severe consequences on dependency ratios than deaths from other causes. For example, in the Rakai District of Uganda, households that experienced the death of an HIV-positive member had higher dependency ratios than those that experienced deaths of an HIV-negative adult (Menon et al. 1998, as cited in Gillespie and Kadiyala 2005).

HIV and AIDS can also affect household labor supply through several channels. AIDS deaths can directly reduce the number of available workers, and the younger, less experienced workers replacing those who have died are often less productive. A study of the social and economic impacts of HIV/AIDS on households and farming systems in Uganda found that AIDS-affected households diverted healthy labor to tend to the sick (Barnett and Blaikie 1992, as cited in Gillespie and Kadiyala 2005), and a study in Mozambique found that the death of a household head increased the likelihood of using child labor (Mather et al. 2004, as cited in Gillespie and Kadiyala 2005). The combination of loss of productivity and increased cost of production reduces business profitability, which can threaten the survival of employment opportunities (USAID 2002). In agricultural areas, the loss of prime-age adults can signify the loss of critical expertise that may not be recaptured by the younger generation.

Changes in household composition and labor supply, combined with increased costs, limit the income generation potential within affected families. Several studies have documented the impoverishing effect of HIV and AIDS on affected households. As family members become ill, resources needed for care increase at the same time as the capacity to generate income decreases, resulting in

---

[1] *Dependency ratio* is defined as the number of children from birth through age seventeen plus adults ages sixty or older divided by the number of adults ages eighteen through fifty-nine.

fewer household resources. A number of studies document the loss of income associated with HIV and AIDS. In Free State, South Africa, per capita adult-equivalent income in affected households was 50–60 percent of the income in nonaffected households (Booysen and Bachmann 2002). In a five-year retrospective study in Zambia, an 80 percent or greater reduction in monthly disposable income was detected in more than two-thirds of the AIDS-affected families (Nampanya-Serpell 2000, as cited in Gillespie and Kadiyala 2005).

Income losses have adverse consequences on consumption patterns. In Limpopo Province, South Africa, HIV/AIDS-affected households spent more on transportation, healthcare, and funerals, but less on education, housing, and remittances, than unaffected households (Oni et al. 2002, as cited in Gillespie and Kadiyala 2005). In Free State Province, South Africa, the average monthly food expenditure of affected households was 70–80 percent of the expenditure in nonaffected households (Booysen and Bachmann 2002, as cited in Gillespie and Kadiyala 2005).

Food Insecurity, Human Capital, and HIV/AIDS: The Vicious Cycle

Poverty and food and nutrition security are critical concerns in HIV-prevalent areas because of their powerful and mutually reinforcing relationship with HIV. In a vicious cycle, food and nutrition insecurity increases susceptibility to HIV exposure and infection and lower resiliency to AIDS impacts, while HIV/AIDS intensifies vulnerability to food and nutrition insecurity. Poverty and food and nutrition insecurity can accelerate the spread of HIV by increasing exposure to the virus and heightening the risk of infection if exposure occurs. There are several reasons for increased exposure. The economic and educational disadvantages that often accompany food and nutrition insecurity can limit people's access to information about the disease and make it more difficult for them to act on information they do obtain. Poverty and food insecurity lead people to migrate to find work (increasing their risk of exposure to infection), and some, primarily women and adolescent girls, may resort to transactional sex to earn income for food. A recent review of the literature (Gillespie, Kadiyala, and Greener 2007) finds evidence to support this relationship between poverty and risk-increasing behavior, although with contextual caveats. Several studies have shown that migration is associated with risky behaviors and increased HIV transmission in Guinea-Bissau, Malawi, Senegal, Tanzania, and Zimbabwe and in cities in Benin, Cameroon, Kenya, and Zambia (respectively, Lagarde et al. 2003; Boerma et al. 2003; Bloom et al. 2002; Auvert et al. 2001, as cited in Gillespie and Kadiyala 2005, 14–15).

Another hypothesized, although less researched, causal pathway is one by which malnourished people are more likely to suffer weakened immune systems, which may increase the risk of HIV transmission in an unprotected sexual encounter (Gillespie, Kadiyala, and Greener 2007). Poor maternal nutritional status can increase the risk of vertical transmission of HIV from mother to infant (during pregnancy or delivery or via breastfeeding). HIV can suppress the immune system and increase oxidative stress, which lead to nutritional deficiencies, which in turn allow for increased HIV replication and accelerated disease progression (Haddad and Gillespie 2001). HIV can lead to insufficient dietary intake, altered metabolism, and malabsorption of nutrients—because opportunistic infections associated with HIV, which cause diarrhea, vomiting, and damaged intestinal cells, among other effects, can inhibit the absorption of nutrients that are consumed—accelerating the onset of AIDS (Semba and Tang 1999, as cited in Gillespie and Kadiyala 2005, 24). Weight loss resulting from the deleterious interactions between HIV and food intake and absorption has been shown to be a strong predictor of morbidity and mortality for HIV-positive individuals. As opposed to experiencing no weight loss, losing 5–10 percent of one's body weight increases the risk of infection by 61–176 percent, and losing more than 10 percent of one's body weight is associated with more than double the likelihood of death (Tabi and Vogel 2006).

All of these processes severely affect children, from their own risks of infection (for example, from mother-to-child transmission or risk-taking by adolescents) to the interactions of malnutrition with infection to the economic and psychosocial impacts of parents' and other relatives' illness and death. Children, before and following the death of parents, suffer from trauma, new workloads and responsibilities, abandonment, migration, fear, and stigma (Adato et al. 2005). Children living with ill parents may be more food insecure, or their foster families may not be able to afford, or may not prioritize, spending on them. There is evidence from some countries that orphans are more food insecure and malnourished, are less healthy (Ainsworth and Semali 2000; Lundberg and Over 2000; Gilborn et al. 2001; Deininger, Garcia, and Subbarao 2003; Rivers, Silvestre, and Mason 2004), and have lower school enrollment and attendance rates (Case, Paxson, and Ableidinger 2003; Case and Ardington 2006; Evans and Miguel 2007). But there is also evidence that orphans do the same or occasionally better on these indicators and do not always live with poorer families than nonorphans, because wealthier families may be better positioned to take them in (Ainsworth and Filmer 2006). The relationships between child and caregivers, economic status, household structure, and especially wealth can have more bearing on these indicators than orphan status alone (see Case, Paxson, and Ableidinger 2003 on education; Ainsworth and Filmer 2006 on education; Stewart 2007 on nutrition). In Chapter 3 we review this literature and debate further in discussing how best to target benefits—that is, how to reach people affected by AIDS while remaining fair to others with similar needs.

Social Protection and Assets: A Conceptual Framework

Social protection is increasingly seen as a critical new component of the mitigation response to these impacts of HIV and AIDS on communities and families and, in particular, on children (see JLICA 2009; UNICEF 2009). New possibilities for social protection in poor countries began to emerge in the 1980s. Strategies for reducing poverty through growth, as well as through targeted direct development programs, were not proving to be sufficient to provide even a basic level of protection against deprivation. Growing attention to the role of risk and vulnerability in casting people into poverty, or preventing people from investing such that they could move out of poverty, was underscored by new forms of vulnerability brought on by structural adjustment policies and contributed to a new role for social assistance as a legitimate component of development policy (Guhan 1994). By the early 1990s, social safety nets had become a component of the World Bank's strategy for poverty alleviation, seen as contributing to growth through reducing risk (World Bank 1990). Over time, the safety net approach came to be criticized as "residualist and paternalistic," and more sophisticated possibilities began to emerge (Devereux and Sabates-Wheeler 2004). Ideas around social protection gained momentum and became mainstreamed in development discourse throughout the 1990s as multilateral agencies, NGOs, and researchers focused substantial attention on how to operationalize it, even if governments that would need to undertake social protection policies were much slower to respond (Devereux and Sabates-Wheeler 2004).

Social protection includes safety net-type protective features but can also contribute to development processes in a more systematic, dependable, and integrated way. It is often advocated as a right rather than a reactive form of relief (Adato, Ahmed, and Lund 2004). There are many different perspectives on social protection, reflecting different positions on its scope, time frames, targeting, and the role of the state, as well as on poverty, vulnerability, development, and human rights.

Figure 2.1 presents an asset-based social protection conceptual framework for understanding what social protection can achieve and how different types of interventions fit within these objectives. In constructing this framework we draw on the conceptual categories devised by Guhan (1994, 38) in an effort to develop an "operational notion of social security within a comprehensive antipoverty approach."[2] These categories reflect different types of objectives: promotional measures to improve endowments, income, and consumption; preventive measures to avert deprivation; and protective mea-

---

[2] These categories were adopted in the International Labor Organization's framework for social protection.

Figure 2.1—An asset-based social protection framework

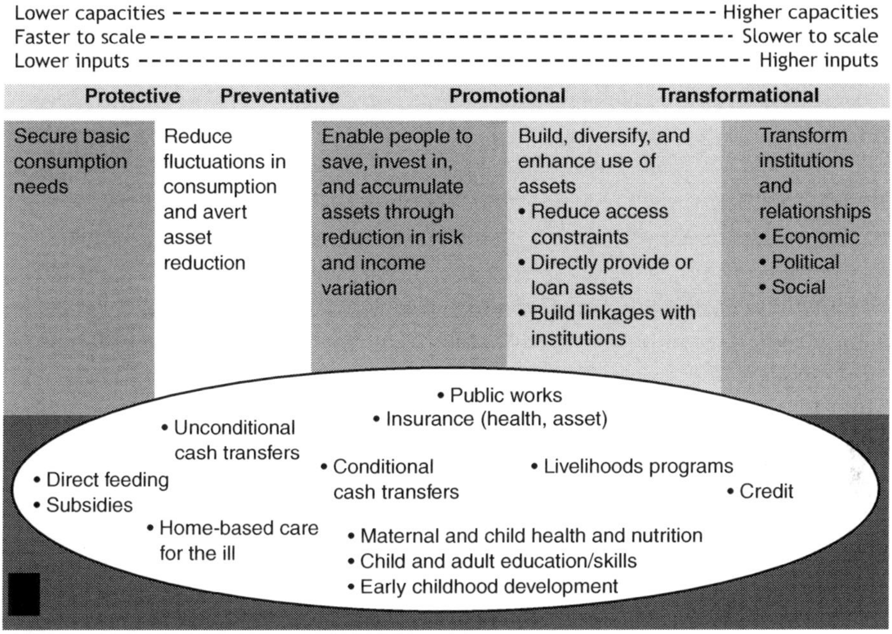

Source: Authors.

sures that even more directly avert deprivation (often associated with safety nets). We also add the transformational category developed by Devereux and Sabates-Wheeler (2004), who are concerned with adding a transformative dimension that confronts the power imbalances that create and sustain vulnerabilities.[3] The framework further draws on a continuum of "goals and means" around which people organize their livelihood strategies (Kabeer 2002, 593). Finally, we integrate an assets framework that uses the sustainable livelihoods framework's categories of financial, physical, natural, social, political, and human capital assets (Ashley and Carney 1999). Social protection can pursue the five types of objectives in Figure 2.1 for each of these types of assets.

In Figure 2.1, the different uses of social protection are seen as one moves from left to right: (1) securing basic consumption needs; (2) reducing fluc-

[3] Devereux and Sabates-Wheeler (2004, 9) come up with the following useful "working definition" of social protection: "Social protection is the set of all initiatives, both formal and informal, that provide: social assistance to extremely poor individuals and households; social services to groups who need special care or would otherwise be denied access to basic services; social insurance to protect people against the risks and consequences of livelihood shocks; and social equity to protect people against social risks such as discrimination or abuse."

tuations in consumption in order to avert the reduction of assets; (3) enabling people to save, invest in, and accumulate assets through reduction in risk and income variation; (4) building, diversifying, and enhancing the use of assets by reducing access constraints, directly providing or loaning assets, or building links with institutions; and (5) transforming institutions and economic, social, or political relationships. The programs in the oval represent a range of interventions that provide forms of social protection. They are loosely placed under the objectives with which they are most normally associated. For example, a direct feeding scheme is usually used to secure a basic level of subsistence; health or asset insurance is often used to reduce risk and enable investment; a livelihoods program is most often used to build assets; a credit program giving women cash and skills can transform social relations inside her household.

The programs are arranged loosely, however, to make a point: although programs have tendencies to be used to achieve particular objectives, each can be used to achieve any of these five objectives. Whether they can depends, first, on how they are designed (and, importantly, the ability to implement the design as planned) and second, on the capacities that people have to take advantage of these design features. So, for example, depending on their design, a public works program may be used to (1) pay people to dig ditches so that they can earn wages that keep them from going hungry when a drought has damaged their crops or where chronic high unemployment robs them of alternatives; (2) keep people from selling off their livestock; (3) build roads to help poor farmers get crops to market or build clinics in poor, underserved areas; and (4) transform the capacities of community organizations where projects are managed by or in partnership with these organizations. In the same way, a cash transfer program can assist AIDS-affected families by, for example, (1) securing their basic subsistence when illness prevents them from working to secure a livelihood, (2) keeping children from leaving school because of an inability to pay fees or because labor is needed at home, (3) enabling people to invest in a small income-generating activity, and (4) increasing the agency of communities where local organizations participate in targeting, monitoring, or service delivery.

Why a Focus on Cash Transfers?

Figure 2.1 also illustrates another point that speaks to the question of why this monograph focuses primarily on cash transfers and not livelihoods interventions, microcredit, or public works (although these are discussed in Chapter 9) in considering how to best support families affected by HIV and AIDS. Despite the potential of different program designs to achieve the range of objectives just stated, there are reasons that some programs are most often used to achieve certain objectives rather than others and are more likely to do so. These reasons are illustrated at the top of Figure 2.1, related to capacities, ease and speed of scalability, and quantity and quality of inputs required.[4] At one end of the spectrum, interventions intended to secure basic consumption, such as cash transfers designed with simple objectives to provide cash for food and other basic needs and avert the sale of assets, require lower capacities on the part of beneficiaries, for example, less physical strength and fewer physical and financial assets—significant constraints among many of the hardest-hit AIDS-affected families. They also require less of program administrators, for example, in terms of technical or financial capacities—which are low among many heavily AIDS-affected countries in Sub-Saharan Africa. Cash transfers will also be easier to scale up relatively quickly (even if not very quickly) and require lower inputs (for example, cash and an administrative and delivery system)—and speed is needed to respond to the needs for food, education, healthcare, and other basic needs of AIDS-affected families to avert the loss of life of adults and the human capital of children.

Also featured in Figure 2.1 and prominently in this monograph are conditional cash transfers (CCTs), programs that condition the cash transfers on a household's participation in education, health, and nutrition services. This is because CCTs have been demonstrated, with reasonable consistency although not universally, to increase children's school enrollment and attendance, reduce child labor, increase the use of preventive healthcare services, and improve children's nutritional status, as will be seen in Chapters 6, 7, and 8. However, concerns over shortage of services, the possibility that human capital investment is related more to supply than to demand constraints, and the urgency of cash for survival, call into question whether conditional programs are appropriate for AIDS-affected families in southern and East Africa. Still, if protecting the human capital of children is also an objective of the cash transfer programs and CCTs prove that they do this more effectively than unconditional programs, conditionality is worth exploring. Determining if this is so will involve research designed for this purpose, such as a study recently completed in Malawi (Baird, McIntosh, and Özler, 2010). Chapter 4 explores the issues surrounding conditionality in depth.

As Figure 2.1 illustrates, there are many different approaches to social protection, and each of these interventions potentially has a role to play in protecting the poor, including those affected by HIV and AIDS. A social protection strategy for AIDS-affected families cannot consist simply of cash transfers. Furthermore, there are synergies that can be built between cash and other types of support. For these reasons, this review discusses these other

[4] Note that this is a continuum and not a dichotomy, with ways to design programs with varying degrees of complexity.

approaches, in Chapters 6, 7, and 8, on education, health, and nutrition, respectively, and in Chapter 9, on complementary approaches. However, cash transfers are the primary focus of this review because of their particular advantages in protecting the human capital of the extreme poor and most severely AIDS affected, in large numbers, with the reliability required of a social protection system. Interventions intended to build physical and financial assets, such as livelihoods activities and microcredit (the latter normally intended to invest in the former), demand more capacities on the part of both beneficiaries and program implementers, are more complicated and take longer to scale up, and are more demanding with respect to inputs and institutions (materials, training, markets). They cannot reach as many people as quickly as can cash transfers, and they tend to benefit those who are better off because people with higher capacities are better able to participate and succeed.[5] Microcredit programs have been used successfully by many poor people, but they tend not to do as well in benefiting the extremely poor (Rahman and Hossain 1995, cited in Kabeer 2002; Hashemi 1997; Hulme and Mosley 1997; Halder and Hussain 1999), although some have managed to be better targeted than most (Sharma et al. 2000). Microcredit programs in highly AIDS-affected areas also involve high risks to borrowers and lenders. Families affected by AIDS are not just poor; they are also struggling with poverty and severe illness and are labor constrained, often headed by the elderly, the sick, or even children.[6] Furthermore, many countries with large AIDS-affected populations have low administrative and technical capacities. It is unlikely that they would be able to scale up livelihoods interventions for a large proportion of people who need them.

This is not to argue that livelihoods interventions or microcredit should not be undertaken for people affected by HIV and AIDS. They should. Numerous NGOs and community-based organizations (CBOs), as well as some government programs, are doing excellent work in these sectors, and they should be supported to scale these activities up at the pace that is feasible. This is not a question of either/or—different types of interventions should be used simultaneously. Some microcredit programs have been adapted to reduce risk in AIDS-affected contexts (see Chapter 9), for example, through mandatory loan

[5]Although programs involving graduated steps into microcredit, such as the Vulnerable Group Development Programme in Bangladesh, have been much more successful in reaching poorer people and offer valuable models, they are still more demanding than cash transfers.
[6]Parker, Singh, and Hattel (2000) argue that there is a tension between the scale of microcredit and the extent of services and that those who most need services are also those most likely to default. Barnes et al. (2001) found that HIV-affected households in Zimbabwe that started microenterprises had a decline in profits compared with nonaffected households.

default and death benefit insurance, legal services, and education trusts for children (Barnes et al. 2001; IMAGE 2002, cited in Gillespie and Kadiyala 2005). But these measures will remain small scale relative to need, and they do not resolve all the capacity constraints AIDS-affected families face. Those families with members who can take advantage of microcredit and livelihoods programs will benefit. The United Nations Capital Development Fund / Special Unit for Microfinance (UNCDF/SUM 2003) recommends that microfinance services be targeted to clients who are HIV positive but still productive, family members of HIV-positive individuals, and surviving family members. But credit and livelihoods programs will reach fewer families and are more likely to miss the most destitute and in need. In Malawi, where the government's cash transfer is limited to the poorest 10 percent of the population, those in the third and fourth poverty deciles would be more likely to take advantage of a livelihoods support program (see Malawi 2009 and the discussion in Chapter 10). If they are successful, they have benefits far beyond the cash transfer. However, their complexities are limiting, and they often tend toward "boutique" projects, ad hoc and scattered, supported by NGOs and donors or by local churches, organizations, or volunteers (Subbarao and Coury 2004), rather than ensuring broad, systematic, and reliable coverage.

Several other types of programs have been used to reach AIDS-affected families. One category is public works. Public works fall somewhere in the middle of the capacity-scalability-inputs continuum—exactly where depends on their design. This can vary widely, from conventional programs providing food or cash for physical labor to the Productive Safety Nets program in Ethiopia, which combines transfers with access to agricultural technologies, extension, and other services to the ambitious but smaller Community-Based Public Works Program in South Africa, which required CBOs to participate in project implementation, to South Africa's Expanded Public Works Programme, which provides training for caregiving activities (see Chapter 9). If conventionally designed as labor-intensive infrastructure or environmental projects, public works are not a way to help labor-constrained, severely AIDS-affected families. Creative ideas have been developed to adapt to AIDS-affected contexts, however, from reducing labor demands to providing needed services. Some are closer to livelihoods or food transfer programs than public works but may be undertaken as a subcomponent of a public works program. Innovations include the use of household contracts with flexible family labor arrangements so that well members can substitute for weak or ill members as needed, home-based activities such as small food gardens, free distribution of food or agricultural inputs for people unable to work, and programs of training and work in home-based care (HBC) for the ill and early childhood development (see more on these in Chapter 9).[7] These are also potentially important interventions that should be piloted and scaled up at the pace possible. However, public works, especially those involving more ambitious plans for skills certification in service provision, are not necessarily the best way to provide income support to the very poorest and most severely affected by AIDS (although they will benefit from the services).

The remaining intervention that needs to be considered seriously is that of food transfers and nutrition interventions.[8] These approaches have the same strengths as cash with respect to where they fall on the household capacity continuum. They do better on the scalability and inputs continuum in comparison with livelihood approaches but involve complexities in these dimensions. Food and cash have relative advantages and disadvantages in different contexts related to factors such as infrastructure, food markets, seasonality, logistical and administrative capacities, politics, gender relations, and the target group and the nature and urgency of their needs (Gentilini 2007).[9] These are factors that apply to food and cash comparisons in all contexts, not specifically that of HIV and AIDS. How these factors look through an "HIV/AIDS lens" is an important area for research.[10] Food-based interventions may be better than cash for specific groups of AIDS-affected adults and children under specific conditions, and these conditions need to be better understood. However, there are issues of logistics, economics, and political economy at the international and national levels that make it unlikely that food transfers would be scaled up as a national strategy of social protection. Cash has been gaining momentum in recent years in countries looking at national social protection systems for children affected by AIDS. Furthermore, many food transfer programs operate in conjunction with other livelihoods, health, nutrition, and education programs. Although some, like school feed-

[7] Although these provide services rather than income for AIDS-affected families, they can strengthen their human capital through ECD services and through HBC that frees up older children to go to school.

[8] Nutrition interventions are often food-based transfers or supplements that have the specific objective of improving nutritional status. These may include transfers of different types of nutritional supplements or fortified food.

[9] Interviews carried out on beneficiary preferences for cash versus food in four African countries found that beneficiaries preferred cash, mainly because of the choice it offered them in meeting a wider range of needs (Devereux et al. 2005). Interviews in Malawi revealed similar preferences, although the results were mixed, and the market had food shortages (Savage and Umar 2006). A comparison of cash versus food from a survey in Bangladesh also found that beneficiaries preferred cash and that cash and food transfers performed similarly with respect to targeting and school enrollment; however, food consumption was increased only by the food transfers (Ahmed 2005).

[10] The "HIV/AIDS" lens is a conceptual tool for reviewing situations and actions in the light of HIV/AIDS and how they may increase or reduce risks (Loevinsohn and Gillespie 2003).

ing programs, may compete for resources with a cash transfer program, others, such as those that operate as part of livelihoods, maternal health, or nutritional rehabilitation programs, should not have to.

Despite these reasons for our focus on cash transfers, the case for scaling them up ultimately depends on how they perform—the impacts they have on poverty and human capital. This monograph explores the evidence that currently exists to answer these questions.

Why a Focus on Human Capital?

This monograph focuses on human capital in two ways: first, we look at the impact of cash transfers on education, health, and nutrition, as well as how they could be designed to increase these impacts for AIDS-affected families and communities. Second, we consider CCTs, programs that, in addition to reducing short-term poverty, have increases in education, health, and nutrition as their primary objectives. CCTs make cash benefits conditional on household members' participation in education, health, and nutrition services. We give this attention to CCTs for two reasons. The first is that the vast majority of the global evidence to date on the impacts of cash transfer programs comes from evaluations of CCTs. This is because these programs have been undertaken in a large number of Latin American and other countries where complex impact evaluations, often involving experimental designs and large panel surveys, have been mandated by governments or donor agencies. The impacts, particularly with respect to human capital, are the strongest found in terms of magnitude, underscored by the rigor of the research and analytic methodologies. CCTs thus show us what can be achieved through cash transfer programs. The second reason we consider these conditional programs is that, given their demonstrated impacts, there is at least the possibility that they could have significant impacts on protecting and strengthening the human capital of children in AIDS-affected families. We do not know this yet—we do not know whether conditions would make a difference or whether they would work at all. Many arguments support and caution against conditionality in cash transfer programs, many contextual considerations arise in this debate, and there are reasons why conditionality may not be appropriate for the most severely AIDS-affected families, who need immediate unconditional assistance. One of the main concerns is the quantity and quality of education and health services available. The options for improving services, in or out of the context of a cash transfer program, deserve attention, as does the possibility that CCT programs might provide impetus for increasing the availability and quality of services. All of these issues are discussed further in Chapter 4.

Whether through conditional or unconditional programs, the need to achieve impacts on human capital is paramount and cannot be put off. Of course food security always will be a priority; without this, education and health will be sacrificed regardless. But the human capital of children must be a simultaneous priority, because any sacrifice now has lifelong and intergenerational consequences. There is extensive evidence of the interactions among early childhood nutrition, health, and education, as well as between human capital and long-term earning ability. During pregnancy and in the first two years of life, known as the "window of opportunity" for nutrition interventions, nutritional losses take their greatest toll, causing damage that is largely irreversible.[11] Children under two years of age are growing at a rapid pace and have high nutritional requirements. However, the foods typically provided to complement breast milk in low-income countries provide insufficient energy and nutrient content for optimal growth. Additionally, with weak immune systems and living in conditions of poor hygiene and sanitation, young children are highly susceptible to infection, which can exacerbate malnutrition. Approximately half of all deaths of children under age five in developing countries result from the interactions between common infections, such as diarrhea, respiratory infection, measles, and malnutrition (Behrman 2000, 7). Inadequate food supply and quality, poor hygiene and sanitation, and low levels of maternal education are all associated with child illness and poor nutritional status.

These nutritional impacts interact with education. Poor and malnourished children are likely to start school later and complete fewer years of schooling than are wealthier and healthier children. Cross-sectional studies in Uganda and Zambia showed that poor children were 10 times and 4 times, respectively, more likely than the richest children to enter school late (Grantham-McGregor et al. 2007, 64). Malnourished children were shown to enroll later than healthy children in Ghana, Nepal, the Philippines, and Tanzania (Behrman 2000, 9; Grantham-McGregor et al. 2007, 63). In Tanzania, stunted children were also less likely than healthy children to be enrolled in school at all (Grantham-McGregor et al. 2007, 63). Glewwe, Jacoby, and King (2001) find that better-nourished Filipino children start school earlier and repeat fewer grades. The authors conclude that an increase of 0.6 standard deviation in the height of malnourished children would increase the schooling they completed by nearly one year (Glewwe, Jacoby, and King 2001, 362–363). Alderman et al. (2001) find that malnutrition decreases the probability of ever attending school, particularly for girls. An improvement of 0.5 in the height-for-age *z*-scores (HAZ) of preschoolers would increase school initiation by 4 percent for boys and 18 percent for girls, closing the gender gap in enrollment by 20 percent (Alderman et al. 2001, 198). Tracking a cohort of Zimbabwean children over two decades, Alderman, Hoddinott, and Kinsey (2003) find evi-

[11] Martorell, Khan, and Schroeder (1994) note that growth lost in early years can be only partially regained during later childhood and adolescence when children remain in poor environments.

dence of delayed school initiation and fewer grades completed for individuals who were malnourished as children. The authors conclude that a median preschooler in the sample could have started school 7 months earlier, completed 0.7 additional grades, and grown 4.6 centimeters taller if she had attained the median height in a developed country (Alderman, Hoddinott, and Kinsey 2003, as cited in Behrman, Alderman, and Hoddinott 2004, 373). Behrman et al. (2003) find that Guatemalan children ages six through twenty-four months receiving a nutritional supplement experienced a significantly higher probability of attending school and of passing first grade (Behrman et al. 2003, as cited in Behrman, Alderman, and Hoddinott 2004, 373).

Additional evidence comes from a study of 79 countries with data on education and stunting, which found that every 10 percent increase in stunting was associated with a reduction of 7.9 percent in the proportion of children reaching the final grade of primary school. A similar study including 64 countries found that every 10 percent increase in the prevalence of poverty reduced by 6.4 percent the likelihood that children would enter the final grade of primary school (Grantham-McGregor et al. 2007, 63). A study in the Philippines found that an increase of 1 standard deviation in the stature of malnourished children would increase the schooling they completed by nearly 18 months and reduce their probability of repeating first grade by around 9 percent (Glewwe, Jacoby, and King 2001).

Beyond delayed school entry and reduced completion, malnourished children often experience a reduced capacity to learn. Stunted children (in Brazil, China, India, Jamaica, Malaysia, Nepal, the Philippines, Turkey, and Vietnam) and boys in Guatemala have been found to be more likely than healthy children to have lower achievement levels and poorer grades.

Stunting was also associated with lower scores on cognitive tests in Ecuador, Guatemala, and the Philippines (Pollitt et al. 1995; Martorell 1995, 1999, cited in Berman, Alderman, and Hoddinott 2004, 368; Grantham-McGregor et al. 2007). Stunted children were more likely to have lower achievement scores and poorer cognitive ability in Chile, Ethiopia, Guatemala, India, Indonesia, Kenya, Peru, and Vietnam. Stunting at twenty-four months was associated with lower cognition at age nine in Peru and with lower IQ at eight and eleven years of age in the Philippines (Grantham-McGregor et al. 2007, 63). In Guatemala, children exposed to a high-energy, high-protein nutritional supplement performed better on tests of knowledge, reading and vocabulary, numeracy, and information processing (Pollitt et al. 1995, 1116S).

Furthermore, according to studies from Barbados (Galler et al. 1983; Galler 1984), Guatemala (Pollitt, Gorman, and Metallinos-Katasaras 1991), and Jamaica (Richardson, Birch, and Ragbeer 1975), individuals who were severely malnourished as young children were less well liked by their peers and were unhappier than classmates who had been well nourished as children. Previously severely malnourished children more frequently exhibited immature behavior, had poorer relationships with classmates and teachers (in Barbados and Jamaica), and acted more withdrawn, solitary, or unsociable than their classmates (Behrman 2000, 9).

These human capital deficits, in turn, have long-term impacts on earnings, completing the cycle that transmits poverty through generations of families. One route is through a link between poor nutrition and physical productivity. Stunting at thirty-six months among Guatemalan children led to reduced body size and strength among adults (Behrman 2000, 13). Work capacity, defined as maximal oxygen consumption (or VO_2 max), was significantly greater among males who had received an energy- and protein-rich supplement as children than in those who had received a low-energy, low-protein supplement, albeit fortified with vitamins and minerals. The effect on the productivity of females was weak (Martorell 1995, 1134S). More recent research comparing these same groups years later found that exposure to the more nutritious supplement before age three—but not after—was associated (when the children had become adults) with a 46 percent increase in average wages, although for men only (Hoddinott et al. 2008).

Fewer years of education, poor cognitive development, and smaller stature in childhood reduce adult earning potential. Studies from 51 countries show that each year of schooling increases adult wages by 9.7 percent, on average (Grantham-McGregor et al. 2007).[12] Examining the relationship between cognitive skills and earnings for male workers in rural Pakistan, Alderman et al. (1996) find that a 1 percent increase in cognitive skills increases adult earnings by 0.233 percent (Behrman 2000, 18). Similarly, short adult height, resulting from childhood stunting, is associated with reduced adult earnings in 55 countries (Grantham-McGregor et al. 2007, 67). In Brazil, a 1 percent increase in height was found to lead to a 2.4 percent increase in adult male earnings (Thomas and Strauss 1997, cited in Behrman 2000, 18). If each year of schooling increases adult yearly income by 9 percent, the loss in adult income from being stunted but not poor is roughly 22.2 percent, the loss from being poor but not stunted is 5.9 percent, and the loss from being both stunted and poor is 30.1 percent (Grantham-McGregor et al. 2007, 67).

[12]Although some of the studies had methodological weaknesses, this average matches that of another more rigorous study, which reported that each year of schooling in Indonesia increased wages by 7-11 percent (Grantham-McGregor et al. 2007, 66).

CHAPTER 3

Targeting Families and Children Affected by HIV and AIDS: Key Issues, Dilemmas, Methods, and Experience

Targeting, in which resources are directed toward a particular group based on socioeconomic or demographic characteristics, has long been a feature of programs offering social assistance, from cash assistance to public works to certain forms of public subsidies. Whether and how programs are targeted are driven by global and national political economy, including revenues and access to grants and loans, the political climate, ideology, and mobilization; by social characteristics of communities; as well as by technical knowledge and capacities. In the 1980s and 1990s, targeting gained new prominence against a global backdrop of economic downturns, a growing neoliberal orthodoxy preoccupied with the efficiency of government expenditures and leading to dramatic reductions in poverty alleviation budgets, and a growing body of evidence that universal programs such as general food subsidies were benefiting the middle classes more than the poor. Social programs were reexamined for how to best allocate resources among a smaller group of beneficiaries, and "the extreme poor" became a new subset of "the poor." In Mexico in the 1990s, for example, targeted programs were directed to the 20 percent of the population living in "extreme poverty," although the government recognized a 40 percent poverty rate, leaving the other half uncovered (Yaschine 1999). In the early 1990s, Besley and Kanbur (1993) observed that targeting had come to be seen as a panacea in poverty alleviation; policymakers thought that improved targeting meant they could alleviate poverty with less expenditure.

Poverty targeting is based on an efficiency argument and an equity argument: for a fixed amount of resources, if the objective is to reduce poverty, a greater proportion of these resources should be directed at the poorest. Targeting is mainly justified based on two economic principles: first, that the social returns for a given level of transfers are higher for households at the lower end of the income distribution than at the higher end, so maximizing the welfare impact for a given population means targeting the poorest;

and second, that targeting saves budgetary resources, giving more of these resources to the poorest, who need them most, and avoiding more taxation (Subbarao et al. 1997). These economic, political economy, social, and technical issues are all relevant to cash transfer programs for AIDS-affected families. However, in AIDS-affected contexts, these issues are articulated with AIDS-specific issues to pose new dilemmas and design considerations.

Options for Targeting

Targeting normally takes one of four main forms, although in practice these are usually used in combination: categorical targeting, self-targeting, geographic targeting, and targeting based on individual or household assessment. Categorical targeting does not require a means test, instead directing benefits toward a group that is relatively easily identifiable, for example, women, the elderly, children, the disabled, the landless. Targeting resources toward people affected by HIV and AIDS could be a form of categorical targeting, although this is a harder group to delineate and identify and involves other problems related to equity and stigma (discussed later in this section). Categorical targeting is often designed to achieve similar objectives to those of poverty targeting in that demographic or other socioeconomic groups are often targeted to lift them out of poverty or keep them from falling into, or further into, poverty.

A second form, self-targeting, refers to a method whereby anyone may participate, but the program is designed with features that discourage the participation of people with better alternatives. A common example is a public works program with wages set at or below market wages, in which (at least in theory) the poorest people, who are willing to work for these wages (because they are less likely to get work in the better-paying private labor market), self-select into the program. Another form of self-targeting is used with subsidies, in which, for example, subsidies are put on types of food disproportionately consumed by the poor.

A third form is geographic targeting, in which a region is selected because of its poverty, demographic, or other characteristics, for example, a region where there is a very high proportion of people who are very poor, are affected by AIDS, or both. Complex processes of geographic targeting can develop indexes based on sets of variables.[1]

Although geographic targeting can mean that everyone in that geographic region is included, it is often followed by individual or household assessment

[1] In Mexico's CCT, for example, these indicators related to the share of the illiterate population ages fifteen or older; dwellings without running water, drainage, or electricity; dwellings with earth floors; the average number of occupants per room; and the percentage of the labor force in agriculture.

whereby individuals—but more commonly households—within that region are differentiated by some criteria and only those meeting the criteria are included. There are several methods for individual or household assessment. In the case of many Latin American CCT programs (for example, in rural Mexico and Nicaragua), a proxy means test through a detailed household survey is filled out in a visit to the household. Another variation is an application-based process (for example, in urban Mexico, South Africa, and Turkey) in which people go to centralized locations and fill out an application form that collects proxy means information. Program implementers sometimes then perform a random or systematic verification of information at the household. Application methods have tended to be used in urban areas where both household survey visits and community-based processes are not easy to implement well.

Both the household visit and the application processes use a proxy means test to collect data on variables that are proxies for poverty, vulnerability, or other targeted objectives. Proxies can be developed to capture variables signifying AIDS-affected households, such as dependency ratios (although these are not always correlated with poverty), illnesses, or the presence or absence of able-bodied working-age adults. For poverty or vulnerability targeting, quantitative data are collected on a set of observable characteristics, such as housing, durable goods, demographic structure of the household, education, types of work, expenditures, or reported income. Following the data collection, a statistical analysis is used to weight variables and calculate a score. In Mexico's Programa de Educación, Salud y Alimentación (PROGRESA), for example, survey data were used to construct per capita income and then compared to the Standard Food Basket, equivalent to an average aggregate income of approximately two minimum wages. A statistical technique was then used, separately for each geographic region, to identify the characteristics that best discriminated between poor and nonpoor households, and these variables were used to compute an index that represented the differences between poor and nonpoor households (PROGRESA 1997; Skoufias, Davis, and de la Vega 2001). Some countries follow this process up with a community assembly that reviews and comments on the list to reveal errors of exclusion (people who should be included but are not) and errors of inclusion (people who should not be included but are). There is variation with respect to the centralization of the targeting process (for example, in Mexico's CCT) and decentralization (such as in Brazil's CCT, which has a large role for municipalities).

A final method of individual or household assessment is community-based targeting, in which selection decisions are made locally. This often involves a community-based committee or general assembly, although it may also include local government officials, traditional leaders, or other elites, international NGOs, and local CBOs. Beneficiaries are selected based on some set of criteria determined by another community-based process or by program implementers. This method has been used in Africa, Asia, and Latin America. This is the method used in most of the new cash transfers programs emerging in southern and East Africa and will be reviewed later.

The trend toward more data-intensive systems has been motivated by, first, a history of political clientelism interfering in the distribution of resources and efforts to make this distribution fair and nonpoliticized and second, evidence that antipoverty programs have often not done well in reaching the poorest people. According to a review of 122 targeted programs by Coady, Grosh, and Hoddinott (2004), on average a quarter more resources go to those considered poor than would random allocations, but more than 25 percent of the programs had regressive outcomes. Methods that tended to perform best with respect to reaching the poor were self-targeting through work requirements, followed by means testing, categorical targeting based on age, and community-based methods (other forms of categorical and self-selection did worse). But there was less variation between these categories than within them, indicating that the way in which the systems are implemented is more important in determining performance than is choice of the method itself (Coady, Grosh, and Hoddinott 2004).

Proxy means test methods have been evaluated as largely successful in many of the Latin American CCT programs in which they have been used, although with qualifications. In Nicaragua's CCT, Red de Protección Social, in locations using geographic targeting, quantitative analysis found inclusion errors at 14 percent and exclusion errors at 3 percent. Where household targeting was used, inclusion errors dropped to 6 percent, while exclusion errors rose to about 10 percent (Maluccio 2009). In Mexico, Skoufias, Davis, and de la Vega (2001) found that PROGRESA's household targeting method outperformed alternative simulated methods in reducing the depth and severity of the poverty gap (not headcount), even accounting for cost. Once it had covered the extreme poor, however, it had a harder time distinguishing among localities and households in the middle. The reduction in higher-order measures of poverty accomplished by household as opposed to geographic targeting was relatively small, and the authors concluded that whether using household versus geographic targeting was worthwhile depended on the noneconomic costs (Skoufias, Davis, and de la Vega 2001, 1781), which were found to be significant in qualitative studies. Noneconomic costs refer to tensions between beneficiaries and nonbeneficiaries over who was included and who was excluded, with some cost to social capital, as well as to other stresses caused by a lack of understanding of or agreement with the exclusions (Adato and Roopnaraine 2010a).

Proxy means test methods have accuracy advantages due to the use of large quantities of data applied in a model. They also have several drawbacks. First, they can be costly, although these costs fall over time. In Honduras's CCT, the cost of targeting as a percentage of total program costs was about 23 percent (although this also included beneficiary incorporation costs). In Mexico's CCT, the cost of targeting as a percentage of program costs started out at a high of 61 percent in 1997, then fell to 47 percent in 1998, to 26 percent in 1999, and to 3 percent in 2000. In Nicaragua's CCT, targeting costs similarly fell from 20 percent in 2000 to 2 percent in 2002. This drop-off represents the fact that most of the targeting activities go on early in the program, followed by incorporation of the beneficiaries and then delivery of transfers (Caldés, Coady, and Maluccio 2006, 828). In this sense the first year's high costs can be seen as representative of the targeting process, but these can be averaged over a number of years, assuming that beneficiaries mostly remain in the program.

Second, the administration of a proxy means test with the accuracy found in the Latin American cases requires a high level of technical and administrative capacity, beyond what is likely to be available in many poor parts of the world. The formulation of a proxy means test model as normally used also requires the availability of a representative household survey dataset (at a national or regional level, depending on the geographic focus of the program) with a comprehensive set of variables (indicators of household welfare) that are highly correlated with household income or total consumption expenditures. However, depending on its objective, a proxy means test and its analysis can range from very complicated to very simple; a small survey uses a set of indicators chosen to be good proxies for poverty (or for AIDS-affected). The simpler end of the spectrum is often what is carried out by committees in a community-based targeting process (discussed later).

A third issue is that proxy means tests often use a generic measure of poverty based on an index from the field of economics. This method is considered state of the art and usually results in good targeting based on the indicators chosen. The problem is that these indicators and the formulas used for weighting them may yield results that differ significantly from local perceptions of relative need. Community-based targeting processes, on the other hand, draw on local people's knowledge of local norms and individual circumstances and reflect local priorities and perceptions of fairness, need, and entitlement, which can differ widely from what is captured through statistical measures (Adato and Haddad 2002; Zambia, MCDSS/GTZ 2006). In Nicaragua's CCT, for example, the quantitative evaluation of the proxy means test found "acceptably low" errors of exclusion (see the previously mentioned figures), but in the qualitative evaluation, 81 out of 125 households believed there were errors of exclusion in their communities based on their perceptions of relative poverty and fairness (Adato and Roopnaraine 2004). Both proxy means and community-based methods are likely to involve errors of inclusion and exclusion and can generate social tensions between neighbors and individual stress, particularly when the criteria and processes are not transparent. These problems are compounded where there is no reliable appeals process (Adato 2000; Adato and Roopnaraine 2010b). Any externally implemented method needs a reliable process for appeals and complaints so that individual cases can be reviewed and errors caught (see, for example, Oportunidades 2006a).

Community-based methods have also produced tensions, and are subject to the elite-influence that the survey-based approaches have been successful at avoiding. Where strong systems of patronage exist, or the target group has little representation, a categorical approach might be better (DfID 2005). Community-based systems can be designed with built-in reviews that strengthen transparency and accountability. In practice, targeting methods are most often used in combination; for example, data-driven geographic targeting can be followed by a community-based process involving some kind of household-level data collection.

In all of the methods described, there are risks of missing certain kinds of households and individuals: remote households living in difficult terrain, migrants, child-headed households, or street children.[2] Although community-based methods tend to be better at identifying some of these groups, they may still exclude others, such as people who self-exclude or face discrimination by other community members due to race, ethnicity, caste, severe disability, or other factors. Ways to reach these groups through eligibility criteria and targeting methods must be carefully designed into the process.

Targeting Poverty and Vulnerability or AIDS-Affected Families? Conceptual Dilemmas, Evidence, and Arguments

A number of global initiatives and forums have coalesced around the issues facing orphans and other vulnerable children affected by HIV/AIDS. These include, among others, the United Nations General Assembly Special Session (UNGASS) *Declaration of Commitment on HIV/AIDS* (2001), the US President's Emergency Plan for AIDS Relief's Orphans and Other Vulnerable Children Category, the US Assistance for Orphans and Other Vulnerable Children in Developing Countries Act of 2005, the Global Partners Forum on Children Affected

[2] Demographic and Health Survey data from 2000–04 in nine countries of Sub-Saharan Africa show that under 1 percent of households were headed by children (UNICEF 2006); still, these households are likely to be among those most in need.

by HIV and AIDS, the Inter-Agency Task Team on Children and HIV and AIDS, and the Joint Learning Initiative on Children and AIDS (JLICA).[3] There are also regional initiatives such as the National Plans of Action (NPAs) for Orphans and Vulnerable Children (OVC) and the South Asian Association for Regional Co-operation (SAARC) Draft Framework for the Protection, Care, and Support of Children Affected by HIV/AIDS, among others.[4] Apart and collectively, these have provided powerful opportunities for mobilizing strategies, resources, and action on behalf of children affected by HIV and AIDS. Although all allow room for OVC, they vary with respect to their focus on HIV/AIDS versus chil-

[3] The UNGASS Declaration of Commitment commits to "urge the international community, particularly donor countries, civil society, as well as the private sector to complement effectively national programmes to support programmes for children orphaned or made vulnerable by HIV/AIDS in affected regions, in countries at high risk and to direct special assistance to Sub-Saharan Africa" (UNGASS 2001). The Assistance for Orphans and Other Vulnerable Children in Developing Countries Act of 2005 amends the Foreign Assistance Act of 1961 to authorize the US president to provide assistance, including through nongovernmental or international organizations, for basic care for orphans and other vulnerable children in developing countries, including assistance for (1) community-based care, (2) school feeding programs, (3) education and employment training, (4) psychosocial support, (5) protection of inheritance rights, and (6) HIV/AIDS care. In 2004 UNICEF and the World Bank jointly convened the Second Global Partners' Forum for Orphans and Vulnerable Children Living in a World with HIV and AIDS. In 2006 this forum was hosted by UNICEF and the UK Department for International Development (DfID) and supported by UNAIDS, and it brought together senior representatives from 90 international NGOs and governments (World Bank 2004; UNICEF 2007c). Created in March 2001, the task force on children and HIV/AIDS was first called the Inter-Agency Task Team on Orphans and other Vulnerable Children. In 2004, to better reflect the challenges facing orphans and nonorphaned children made vulnerable by the AIDS epidemic, the name was changed to the Inter-Agency Task Team (IATT) on Children and HIV and AIDS. The IATT, composed of representatives from the Joint United Nations Programme on HIV/AIDS (UNAIDS) cosponsors, NGOs, donors, and other organizations involved in the international response to children affected by HIV and AIDS, promotes coordination and harmonization of programs and policies, encourages the development and sharing of technical and programmatic information, advocates for timely implementation of evidence-based interventions, and supports networking and collaboration among partners (UNICEF 2007d). JLICA, launched in 2006 and continuing through 2009, drew on interdisciplinary collaboration among policymakers, practitioners, and scholars to address the needs of children affected by HIV/AIDS. JLICA aimed to mobilize and generate evidence on operational, political, and public policy issues as well as programmatic experience and to produce actionable recommendations for policy and practice. JLICA also facilitated linkages among groups engaged in issues of children and HIV/AIDS (JLICA 2007).

[4] Many southern and East African countries have recently drafted NPAs for OVC, which prioritize a range of services for OVC including childcare, psychosocial support, child protection, access to basic health and education services, improved sanitation, birth registration, and social safety nets. Some NPAs also include advocacy and institutional capacity building, as well as legislative reform to protect orphans and vulnerable children. By late 2006, at least 20 countries had drawn up NPAs, and others were bringing theirs to completion (Sabates-Wheeler and Pelham 2005; UNAIDS/UNICEF/WHO 2007). The SAARC Strategic Framework for the Protection, Care, and Support of Children Affected by HIV/AIDS provides guidance to the eight member states on the protection, care, and support of children affected by HIV/AIDS. The regional Framework establishes a regionally consistent response to meeting children's medical, nutritional, educational, legal, and psychosocial needs in an age- and gender-sensitive manner within the context of the UN Convention on the Rights of the Child, which all member states have ratified (SAARC 2007).

dren vulnerable from other causes and the extent to which they are grappling with issues surrounding this focal dilemma.

This central targeting dilemma—whether to target AIDS-affected families and children or to target the most extreme poor households—involves (1) questions of equity and justice, because non-AIDS-affected families and children may be just as adversely affected by chronic poverty, illness, and death from other causes, war, or other forms of shocks or discrimination; (2) questions about accuracy, regarding whether AIDS-affected households or orphans are always the worst off and thus whether targeting them will reach those most in need; and (3) concerns about stigma, the effects of identifying "AIDS-affected" households or "AIDS orphans." Questions about equity and accuracy are closely intertwined, both requiring evidence of whether AIDS-affected families and children are worse off than those who are not.

The relationship between poverty and AIDS is not one of a clear, positive correlation. A recent review of the literature found that because HIV has different drivers across socioeconomic groups, poorer groups are not necessarily more at risk of HIV exposure than wealthier groups. What is clear, however, is that poor families are likely to be hit harder by the downstream impacts of AIDS. They are less able to cope, and HIV and AIDS are very likely to make them poorer. There are many reasons for this. Vicious downward spirals involve reduction and fluctuations in on-farm and off-farm income due to labor constraints from ill or deceased breadwinners; reductions in purchase and application of agricultural inputs and access to extension; increased expenditures on healthcare, transportation, funerals, expenses for fostered children, and food to replace that formerly accessed through subsistence agriculture; reductions in savings and selling of assets; and reduced access to credit or increases in debt at unfavorable terms. These are compounded by and compound other impacts on natural, physical, human, and social capital (Gillespie, Haddad, and Jackson 2001; Stokes 2002, cited in Gillespie and Kadiyala 2005; Harvey 2004).

Gillespie and Kadiyala (2005) review more than 150 studies examining linkages between HIV/AIDS and food and nutrition security. Many studies have demonstrated AIDS-related impacts on subsistence agriculture, income, and expenditures on food. A panel study of 1,422 households in Kenya found the death of a prime-age adult male household head associated with a 68 percent reduction in the value of per capita household crop production. It also found that the initial asset base helped to cushion this impact, another poverty-related determinant (Yamano and Jayne 2004). Other studies found crop output declines of 37–61 percent in Zimbabwe (Kwaramba 1997) and 54 percent in Swaziland (Muwanga 2002), labor reductions of 60–80 percent in Rwanda (Donovan et al. 2003), and labor shortages in 70 percent of the households in Malawi (Shah et al. 2001). In Mozambique a nationally representative survey using recall data found that households experiencing deaths had lower levels of cash, cattle, assets, and income (Mather et al. 2004). Several smaller studies in South Africa and Zambia demonstrated large AIDS-related impacts on incomes, including Booysen and Bachmann (2002) in Free State Province, Oni et al. (2002) in Limpopo, and Nampanya-Serpell (2000) in Zambia. As always, the findings are contingent on various economic and social variables at the individual, household, community, and country level.

The evidence is thus strong that targeting AIDS-affected families is likely to reach families that are poor and in need of social protection. There remain the problems, however, that first, many affected by AIDS are not poor, and second, many people are extremely poor due to other causes. Recent work, for example, has highlighted the importance of assets in explaining persistent structural poverty (Carter and Barrett 2006). In a study based on data from six southern African countries, Caldwell (2005) found that household asset ownership was a better predictor of food security than chronic illness, presence of orphans, and gender of the household head. Targeting on multiple criteria capturing poverty and vulnerability, including but not limited to indicators associated with AIDS, can capture AIDS-affected families but not exclude others.

Another case for targeting poverty rather than AIDS-affected households can be made based on evidence that not only does AIDS contribute to impoverishment but poverty is a driver of HIV infection. Poverty and food insecurity can lead women and older children into transactional sex or prevent economically dependent women from refusing unsafe sex. A recent review of the evidence (Gillespie, Kadiyala, and Greener 2007) finds a number of qualitative and quantitative studies that support this relationship between poverty and risky behavior (Kaufman et al. 2004; Brook et al. 2006; Bryceson and Fonseca 2006; Tladi 2006), although there are also contextual caveats and specificities (Kimuna and Djamba 2005; Nii-Amoo Dodoo, Zulu, and Ezeh 2007; Weiser et al. 2007). Another hypothesized, although less researched, causal pathway is one by which malnourished people are more likely to suffer weakened immune systems, which may increase the risk of HIV transmission in an unprotected sexual encounter. Gillespie, Kadiyala, and Greener (2007) review the evidence and conclude that this directional relationship between poverty and AIDS is not straightforward, in part because research on the association between socioeconomic status and the spread of HIV is still in a rudimentary stage and in part because of the complexity and context-specificity of pathways, including the influence of factors such as location, gender, age, mobility, and the social ecology of HIV transmission. Although the conclusion is that poor people are not necessarily more likely than wealthier people to be exposed to HIV, because different processes are at work in each case, the fact remains that poverty increases risk and that the poor are less resilient. In this light, interventions that target poverty can also reduce new cases of HIV and in turn reduce poverty.

The question of whether orphans are more disadvantaged than nonorphans is the subject of a large body of research, but the answer is also far from straightforward. Some research shows that orphans are more vulnerable and disadvantaged, and other research shows that they are not. These findings are not necessarily contradictory but rather are contingent on variables such as the relationships between a child and caregivers, their poverty status, and the household's demographics and structure. Ainsworth and Filmer's (2006) review of 102 datasets from 51 countries found mixed results on whether fostering households were poorer or better off than households without orphans. In about two-thirds of the studies, paternal orphans were more likely to be in relatively poorer households, whereas maternal orphans were in poorer households in only about one-third of the countries.[5] The results varied even more for double orphans; in 10 studies they were in poorer households, whereas in 22 studies they were in relatively richer households. This latter result probably reflects the facts that some deceased parents were from better-off families and that richer households may be better able to care for orphans and thus end up taking more in.

With respect to nutrition effects, orphans might be expected to be more malnourished than nonorphans because they came from households with very ill parents caught in the downward economic spiral described earlier or because their fostering households may discriminate against them. A number of studies have found that orphans are more food insecure and malnourished and less healthy than nonorphans (Ainsworth and Semali 2000; Lundberg and Over 2000; Gilborn et al. 2001; Deininger, Garcia, and Subbarao 2003; Rivers, Silvestre, and Mason 2004). To illustrate, a study in Tanzania interviewing 718 children in the early 1990s and again in 2004 found that children who lost their mother before age fifteen suffer a deficit of around 2 centimeters in final attained height and 1 year of final attained schooling and that the effect is causal. Another study in western Kenya of 1,190 children under age six (Lindblade et al. 2003), 7.9 percent of whom had lost one or both parents, found no difference in key health and nutrition indicators except in weight-for-height z-scores, particularly among paternal orphans and those orphaned more than one year. Mason, Musgrove, and Habicht (2003) found that drought in six southern African countries interacted with HIV/AIDS, contributing to a

[5] Paternal, maternal, and double orphans refer, respectively, to children whose fathers, mothers, or both are deceased.

rapid reduction in children's nutritional status. The Community and Household Surveillance system from six southern African countries (C-SAFE and WFP, cited in Greenblott and Greenaway 2007) found that households with orphans were not more food secure than those without orphans, although this analysis did not take into account how many orphans were in a household. An earlier review by Rivers, Silvestre, and Mason (2004) found evidence that households caring for one orphan were less food insecure than households without orphans but that 40 percent of households with more than one orphan were food insecure, with child hunger. Several other datasets collected by international NGOs also found that households with multiple orphans or those with orphans and other HIV and AIDS-affected children were more food insecure than households without orphans (Greenblott and Greenaway 2007). Hallman (2004) shows that, controlling for wealth and other factors, orphanhood confers an added risk of unsafe sexual behaviors.

New evidence based on analysis of Demographic and Health Survey (DHS) data from five countries (Stewart 2007), using sample sizes up to seven times larger than previous studies, found that orphans do not necessarily have poorer nutritional outcomes than nonorphans when age, sex, household wealth, and household demographics are controlled for. The main factor consistently and significantly affecting nutrition is wealth, and in some cases the relationship of orphans to the household head. The study did not find any pattern indicating that orphans were overrepresented in poorer households, but the evidence is again mixed. Within the poorest two quintiles, there is evidence of orphan disadvantage in Tanzania and Zambia, where orphans in blended households (those with orphans and nonorphans, where discrimination would be more expected) had greater evidence of stunting than did nonorphans. In Kenya, those in blended households had lower weight-for-age z-scores (WAZ) where they lived in grandparent-headed households, consistent with findings elsewhere that discrimination is affected by distance in kinship ties, where the de facto household heads may be aunts or uncles. Other findings further complicate the picture: nonorphans in blended households were better off than nonorphans in nonblended households, providing further evidence that fostering households may have greater capacity to care for children than households that do not take in children. These results are all for younger children who may be more easily assimilated than older children. Stewart (2007) notes that the probability of being an orphan and of suffering nutritional deficits that translate into anthropometric indexes increases with age.

If children are more easily assimilated at earlier ages, one might expect more evidence of discrimination with respect to education, especially because school expenses may be high, older children are needed to work or care for the ill, and education may seem more expendable than food. The question of whether orphans are disadvantaged with regard to schooling has received considerable research attention, but again the answer is not straightforward. Ainsworth and Filmer (2006) review 102 nationally representative datasets from 51 countries in Africa, Asia, the Caribbean, and Latin America, examining the relationships among parental survival, poverty, gender, and school enrollment. Comparing orphans to nonorphans, and controlling for enrollment differentials associated with economic status, statistically significant deficits in enrollment were found in 38 percent and 46 percent of the surveys for paternal and maternal orphans, respectively, climbing to 58 percent for double orphans. Associations between enrollment and the interaction of economic and orphan status have similarly varying results. There is a strong systematic association, however, between enrollment and economic status, indicating that wealth status is a much stronger predictor of enrollment than orphan status for paternal, maternal, and double orphans in most countries, although in fewer countries in the case of double orphans. Orphaned girls tend to be disadvantaged compared to boys, but not significantly different from girl nonorphans. The overall picture is one of a great deal of variation across countries, implying the importance of context-specific policy interventions. A UNICEF analysis of DHS and Multiple Indicator Cluster Survey data for 24 countries compared the school attendance of orphans and nonorphans and also found wide variation across countries (UNAIDS/UNICEF/WHO 2007). With respect to the question of targeting, the implication is that it makes more sense to work harder at reaching orphans in some contexts than in others. Countries with overall low enrollment rates among the poor can focus on the overall group and catch orphans in the process. In countries with overall high enrollment rates but large gaps among orphans, orphan-focused policies are more defensible, although these may require means other than unconditional cash transfers or other than cash transfers of any kind.

Case, Paxson, and Ableidinger (2003) find a different outcome than Ainsworth and Filmer (2006), particularly with respect to the importance of economic status, with somewhat different policy implications. Using 19 DHS surveys from 10 countries between 1992 and 2000, they find that paternal, maternal, and double orphans have significantly lower enrollment rates, in 8, 8, and 13 of the surveys, respectively. They also compare enrollment rates for orphans with those of nonorphans living in the same households, finding significantly lower enrollment rates for paternal, maternal, and double orphans in 9, 7, and 17 of the 19 surveys, respectively. Orphans tended to be poorer, on average, than nonorphans, but their enrollment rates were not explained by poverty or by gender differences, because orphaned girls were not disadvantaged compared to orphaned boys. Schooling outcomes were affected instead by the "closeness of biological ties"; enrollment outcomes depend on the degree of relatedness of the orphan to the household head. Children living in households headed by nonparental relatives were systematically worse off than those in households headed by parental relatives, and those living with nonrelatives fared even worse. Where intrahousehold discrimination exists, Case, Paxson, and Ableidinger (2003) recommend targeting orphans, because income support given to families may not benefit them.

Data from Kenya, Tanzania, and Zimbabwe show that orphans eleven through fourteen years of age are significantly more likely to be at a low grade for their age, and in Ghana and Nigeria, young paternal and double orphans are at a lower grade for their age, as are older paternal orphans (Bicego, Rutstein, and Johnson 2003). School and student surveys in Botswana, Malawi, and Uganda found mixed results, with orphans and nonorphans faring better, worse, or the same with respect to different measures (Bennell 2005). Country-level studies present more insights, with gender implications: using longitudinal data from the KwaZulu-Natal, South Africa, Demographic Surveillance Area, Case and Ardington (2006) find that maternal orphans are significantly less likely to be enrolled, have completed fewer years of school, and, if enrolled, have less money spent on their education than children whose mothers are alive. These results hold for younger and older orphans, but there were no differences between the outcomes of boys and girls. These disadvantages were not found for paternal orphans. Using a five-year panel study of 20,000 children in Kenya, Evans and Miguel (2007) found a substantial and highly significant drop in primary school participation following the death of a parent and a smaller drop just before death. The impacts are more than twice as large following maternal deaths as following paternal deaths. The effects are largest for children whose mothers have died, as well as for those with lower baseline educational performance. Panel data on 1,300 households analyzed by Deininger, Garcia, and Subbarao (2003) in Uganda showed that orphans were disadvantaged in primary and secondary education, but this effect was reversed after the introduction of universal primary education. New results from a panel survey conducted in Malawi in 2000 and 2004 found that maternal and double orphans tend to face higher mortality risks and lower schooling outcomes than paternal orphans and nonorphans, especially in the case of boys. As in Uganda, the effect on young orphans who enrolled following the introduction of free primary education in 1994 was less than that on adolescent orphans (Ueyama 2007). These studies show that programs reducing the costs of education can mitigate the effects of parental death.

Although many studies focus on orphans, these do not capture the experiences of children before they become orphans, which may be as bad or worse with respect to impacts on education and other areas. In a study in Uganda, Gilborn et al. (2001) found that older children (ages thirteen through seventeen) living with an ill parent had lower school attendance rates than did double orphans and that the former group had declines in school attendance due to parental illness, while the latter reported increased attendance following parental death. Adato et al. (2005) use qualitative research to focus on children before and after the death of parents, noting that orphaning in the context of HIV/AIDS is a process that begins long before the death of a parent. This involves the trauma and fear of imminent and—absent antiretroviral drugs (ARVs)—inevitable death, and often new workloads and responsibilities, withdrawal from school, abandonment, migration, fear, family dissolution, and stigma, the last of which may prevent parents and children from accessing resources that can strengthen the capacities of children to deal with these challenges. Another unique aspect of HIV/AIDS is multiple and serial deaths within households. All of this can contribute to the impacts on children, including their physical and mental health, and consequently their schooling attendance and performance. These unique disadvantages should be explicitly addressed, and cash transfers on their own will be an insufficient response. A focus on poverty status rather than orphan status does not necessarily need to apply to all interventions, such as, for example, mental health interventions that target children who are caring for or have lost parents or suffer from stigma. Haddad and Gillespie (2001), citing Parker, Singh, and Hattel (2000), suggest targeting for poverty but modifying interventions to meet the needs of HIV/AIDS survivors.

It may never be possible to completely unravel this picture of relative disadvantage, mapping out all permutations. Even if we accept that orphans or children living with ill parents face unique challenges, and may be worse off than other children in some cases, the evidence of their disadvantage with respect to poverty, health, nutrition, and education is not strong enough, from an evidence and equity standpoint, to justify assisting only orphans. There is also the consideration of stigma—negative effects that can come from the government or other institutions publicly labeling a child an orphan. Meintjes and Giese (2006, 423) found that in South Africa, local notions of vulnerability and orphanhood correspond poorly with international definitions. Local notions have negative connotations, derived in part from local translations of the term, associated with abandonment and destitution. These local terms are “steeped in stigma,” and the authors argue that labeling a child an orphan is stigmatizing for the child and an insult to those providing care and support to the child.

Furthermore, given the evidence that orphans’ disadvantage varies with factors such as poverty, demographic characteristics, household structure, and orphan-caretaker relations, targeting explicitly to respond to these variations would be operationally and ethically infeasible at a community level.

This research can help us contemplate, however, how AIDS-related specificities, articulated with other social and contextual specificities (based on region, gender dynamics, or household structure, for example), can inform the development of proxies, perhaps applied at a wider geographic level. These findings could also inform complementary programming.

In light of these concerns around accuracy, equity, and stigma, a consensus is building among researchers and program implementers around targeting cash transfers based on poverty and multiple vulnerability criteria, with attention given to the context of AIDS rather than to AIDS-affected or orphan status alone (see, for example, Subbarao, Mattimore, and Plangemann 2001; Harvey 2004; Slater 2004; Devereux et al. 2005; Greenblott 2007; Schubert et al. 2007). This is not a complete consensus (see, for example, Evans and Miguel 2007), which is not necessarily problematic in that it leaves room for caveats and context where needed. Organizations implementing food- and nutrition-based interventions see a more mixed picture, suggesting that school feeding and take-home rations be universal for all children (in poor communities) but that interventions such as prevention of mother to child transmission, HBC, growth monitoring, and nutritional rehabilitation services, as well as pediatric hospices and foster care programs, be used to improve the targeting of vulnerable children (Greenblott and Greenaway 2007; see also the later discussion on food transfers in the context of clinical treatment). Furthermore, a consensus among researchers and program implementers may take time to permeate international and regional institutions and policy forums in which *orphans* is still a key operational category and political rallying point.

Returning to questions of stigma and equity, lessons from food transfer programs are useful. Responding to evidence of interactions among HIV/AIDS, food security, and nutrition, including research suggesting that antiretroviral therapy (ART) is more effective for people who are well nourished because of increased caloric intake as well as decreased side effects that may reduce adherence (Paton et al. 2006; Zachariah et al. 2006), clinical care and treatment programs are teaming up with food aid programs.[6] A study in Kenya comparing 2,200 people receiving food aid and ARVs with people on ARVs alone found that the benefits of the food were substantial with respect to improved health, strength, and other measures of well-being.[7] Several prob-

[6]A recognition of the importance of integrating food and nutritional support into HIV/AIDS programming is reflected in policy declarations by several organizations, including the World Health Assembly, UNGASS, and the Africa Forum 2006 (Byron, Gillespie, and Nangami 2006).

[7]Those on food had self-reported health outcomes such as weight gain, recovery of strength, and resumption of labor activities, as well as greater adherence to treatment, fewer side effects, ability to satisfy increased appetites, increased dietary diversity, and increased emotional well-

lems were also identified, one of which was stigma, because the program potentially rendered visible this singled-out group, although stigma was reported to have reduced over time. Many beneficiaries were keeping the food collection a secret from family and friends because of fear of revealing their HIV-positive status and facing discrimination. One problem was the visibility of the food distribution points and the gossip that occurred as a result. Another was the fact that some food packets were labeled with AIDS awareness messages, something that beneficiaries requested be changed (Byron, Gillespie, and Nangami 2006).

These findings have two potentially contradictory implications for targeting. On the one hand, they demonstrate the importance of these food transfers for ART patients. On the other hand, they illustrate the stigma problem and raise the equity question—how can this group alone receive food if their HIV-negative neighbors are also hungry? The answer is that the lives of symptomatic people may depend on these transfers. Given the importance of adequate nutrition for people on ART, it is difficult to argue against programs providing them with food assistance, equity and stigma considerations notwithstanding. Schubert et al. (2007), in arguing for poverty targeting rather than AIDS-specific targeting of cash transfers, suggest a possible exception for people on ART. Although cash assistance for those on ART should also be explored, it may be that food transfers play a better role here, particularly because the money must be spent on food for it to be effective, and food can be fortified with micronutrients, whereas food purchased in the market is less likely to be. This might be akin to an emergency assistance program, in which it is less likely that cash transfers would be used when people were at immediate risk of starvation.[8] Still, in light of equity and stigma concerns, targeting cash and food transfers only to those on ARVs might be difficult to sustain in the long run (despite the fact that cash can be better hidden than food, and family and neighbors are likely to learn about their neighbors' regular new cash infusions). Furthermore, a poverty-targeted program could improve the nutrition of HIV-positive people who are asymptomatic, possibly delaying their need for ARVs.[9]

being. Problems included stigma, costs of transportation to distribution points, seasonal vulnerability to food insecurity, and transitions off the supplement (Byron, Gillespie, and Nangami 2006).

[8] At the other end of the spectrum, food transfers are sometimes used in conjunction with livelihoods activities implemented by NGOs and CBOs where AIDS-affected households may or may not be able to take advantage of them. As noted earlier, these tend to be smaller in scale and found in pockets. These should not be at odds with cash transfer programs, although until cash transfers are operating at a large scale, the interventions should probably be coordinated so that some areas do not have multiple interventions while others have none.

[9] Current research is also looking into whether better nutritional status for asymptomatic HIV-positive individuals may delay the need to start ARVs (Byron, Gillespie, and Nangami 2006, 2).

If well implemented, poverty targeting would reach those on ARVs who need the assistance because not everyone on ARVs is poor. In fact, the very poorest may be less likely to access ARVs, so other targeting means would be needed to reach them. The ideal combination might be a food transfer for the patient and a cash transfer for the family, with the family selected based on the poverty-targeting criteria.

The identification of a family or child as AIDS affected risks not only stigma in the form of shame and social exclusion but also potentially a form of disempowerment, because this public and self-identification reinforces people's victim status and undermines their agency. Although the reality of the illness, poverty, and death of breadwinners and loved ones is arguably disempowering enough, one can see how public stigma and self-identification would compound the problem.

Targeting Approaches in AIDS-Affected Contexts: Experience with Community-Based, Categorical, and Application-Based Methods

Community-Based Targeting in Eastern and Southern Africa

Most of the new cash transfer schemes in eastern and southern Africa have used community-based targeting. Some of these systems have evolved from others used in earlier programs of implementing partners. As previously noted, community-based processes are perceived to have a number of advantages with respect to accuracy, transparency, administration, and local acceptance, and they are also prone to a number of problems. Several variations on community-based targeting systems for cash transfer programs are described and evaluated in this section. Pilot programs in Zambia and Malawi used a very similar design, while Kenya's bears some similarities and some differences. Concern Worldwide's two programs in Malawi use a different community-based process altogether. Several key points are of interest in the descriptions that follow: the structure of the community forums; the system for data generation; the criteria used as proxies for poverty, vulnerability, and "AIDS-affected"; and the nature of checks and balances on community processes.

Zambia's Social Cash Transfer Scheme (SCTS) states the following rationale for use of a community-based method: geographic areas are too large, remote, and sparsely populated to enable a reliable survey method; rural poverty levels are not sufficiently different to be detected in a survey; and finally, Zambia already had a public assistance scheme that used voluntary, community-based processes for beneficiary identification. The targeting process works as follows: The community is briefed about the program at the outset, including the targeting system and criteria, so that people understand the basis of the selection. A volunteer community welfare assistance committee (CWAC) makes a list of all eligible households based on the following criteria: (1) extremely needy (hungry, malnourished, begging); (2) incapacitated (breadwinners are sick or have died; no able-bodied person of working age; a dependency ratio of 3 or higher); (3) no valuable assets (for example, no cattle or functioning television); (4) no regular and substantial source of income (business in town, renting out houses, regular support from relatives) (Zambia, MCDSS/GTZ 2006; World Bank 2007b).[10]

CWAC representatives visit each listed household and fill out an application form with questions about external support, livelihoods, assets, and household problems. This information is verified by the village headman. The CWAC reviews the information and selects the neediest 10 percent, a cap derived from a study indicating that about 10 percent of Zambians are destitute and incapacitated. Those ranked just outside of the 10 percent can enter if others are deleted from or leave the program at some stage. The ranking is presented to the community, which can propose additions or subtractions, and a consensus is reached. In order to avoid the nepotism to which this system could be prone and otherwise check for errors, a system of checks and balances has been instituted: the final list is reviewed by an area welfare committee, district social welfare officer, and district welfare assistance committee official for final approval. Questionable cases are investigated. A reassessment process is conducted every two years, graduating households that have new productive members and allowing other households to be included in their place (Zambia, MCDSS/GTZ 2006; World Bank 2007b). Malawi's Mchinji Pilot Social Cash Transfer Scheme used a process very similar to that used in Zambia and similar targeting criteria (Schubert 2006; Schubert and Huijbregts 2006).

Kenya's pilot Cash Transfer Scheme for OVC in three districts started with a community-based listing process using community-developed criteria based on broad guidelines from UNICEF. These included poverty, the presence of vulnerable children in the household, the chronic illness of caretakers, and other factors, including a lack of able-bodied adults. A detailed questionnaire was filled out for each household, entered into a management information system (MIS), and ranked according to criteria including the presence of orphans, children under age fifteen not attending school, income of less than KES2,000, and receipt of no other support from an organization. A community discussion followed to finalize the selection (Acacia Consultants 2007; UNICEF, Kenya 2007b; Pearson, Alviar, and Hussein n.d.). The new phase of Kenya's scaled-up cash transfer program targets households based on poverty

---

[10] This description reflects both the pre-2006 pilot and the new program under way, which have only a few differences.

or the presence of orphans and other vulnerable children (defined as double or single orphans) living without adults (child-headed households) or with a disabled person. The household also cannot be receiving any other program benefits. Location OVC committees (LOCs) meet with village elders and community leaders to collect information on households that may be eligible based on these criteria. A preliminary form is filled out on a potential beneficiary household and entered into a computerized MIS. Enumerators visit the household and fill out a detailed questionnaire, and this new information is entered into the MIS, which ranks the households. Households are classified as high, medium, or low vulnerability, depending on whether they have one, two, or three of the following characteristics: (1) at least one orphan under age eighteen; (2) a household head under age eighteen; (3) at least one child, parent, or guardian who is chronically ill (with an easily identifiable illness, for example, AIDS). The ranking is reviewed in a public meeting and questionable cases sent for review by the LOC, supported by the District OVC Sub-Committee (Kenya, OVPMHA 2006).

Malawi's Food and Cash Transfers Project (FACT) and Dowa Emergency Cash Transfer (DECT) program used a method different from those already described. A "community triangulation" method divided communities into three groups and asked each to make a list of the neediest households. Criteria were defined by each community, although Concern Worldwide field staff and committees provided some guidance. Although FACT was supposed to respond mainly to the food crisis, some of the criteria steered communities toward people affected by AIDS: households with chronically ill members; households headed by orphans, elderly, or people with disabilities; households involved in Concern's Outpatient Therapeutic Programme; households receiving Concern agricultural input loans; and households facing severe hunger (one meal per day) and not receiving food aid from another source. The three groups' lists were compared in a public forum, and those appearing on all three lists were included, while those appearing on one or two lists were discussed and a consensus reached. This had the advantage of avoiding the nepotism and favoritism that may accompany selection by a powerful individual or elite group, such as a village committee (Devereux, Mvula, and Solomon 2006).

Findings on Community-Based Targeting Processes

Interesting qualitative studies of the community-based targeting processes were carried out for the FACT and DECT programs (Devereux, Mvula, and Solomon 2006; Devereux et al. 2007). The community triangulation method used in the Malawi FACT process was found to be a good system where it was used as planned, but there were many problems in implementation. First, the methodology was not strictly applied in some areas, where Concern staff influenced the choice of criteria. In one area, for example, 75 percent of households were selected because of their caring for orphans or the elderly, a disability, or their health status. This might be considered successful as a method for targeting families affected by AIDS, but this was not the intention of the program, which was aimed at responding to a weather-based food emergency. Second, some areas received the message that Concern livelihoods program participants were to be included so they could repay their loans, and these were not the most needy households. Third, in some places quotas were imposed by headquarters, requiring cuts in the list, which contradicted the principle of inclusion based on self-assessed need. Fourth, the most vulnerable households may not have participated in the selection process because they did not have the time or were out of the village, looking for work, or in the hospital. Fifth, influential elites such as village headmen or their wives managed to find their way into the program. Sixth, poor coordination within the program and across programs meant that some families received double benefits while some received none.

In the program evaluation, Devereux, Mvula, and Solomon (2006) recommend that the community triangulation method be used as intended, emphasizing the importance of using the community's own criteria of vulnerability and need, and that all community members be encouraged to actively participate in the process. They make the controversial but wise recommendation that errors of exclusion be taken as a greater problem than errors of inclusion, with a margin of about 10 percent given for errors of inclusion, allowing the inclusion of some non-needy or politically influential people; they argue that this is a small price to pay in order to ensure that desperate people are not left out. The FACT evaluation also suggests giving the benefits to women rather than men (women sometimes asked Concern staff for this change) to minimize risk of irresponsible spending (although there was little evidence of irresponsible spending by men), to avoid disadvantaging women in polygamous households, and to use female-headed households as a proxy for vulnerability. Although Devereux, Mvula, and Solomon (2006) raise the possibility that this might generate intrahousehold tensions, given that men tend to control cash resources, on balance they recommend this approach. Evidence from CCTs in Mexico and Nicaragua shows that although some tensions arose as a result of designating women as beneficiaries, on balance women and men alike favored giving the benefits to women because they both believed that women make better spending decisions and because the program had come to be seen as a women's and children's program, so giving women the benefits was less threatening to men's identity as the breadwinner (Adato and Mindek 2000; Adato and Roopnaraine 2010b). A study of the Child Support Grant in South Africa, which looked at intrahousehold dynamics and the role of women as the primary caregivers and thus the cash recipients, found that although there were some tensions with male partners over the Child Support Grant, for the most part the receipt of benefits by women was accepted without problems (Hunter and Adato 2007a).

Responding to problems in FACT, Concern dedicated more staff resources to the community triangulation process, improving accuracy but also increasing costs. The DECT baseline survey found that more than 90 percent of 509 beneficiary households were poor and food insecure, using a range of proxies (Brewin 2006, cited in Devereux et al. 2007). Several problems were also identified. First, the community-based wealth ranking identified the neediest within a community but not across communities, so the "middle groups" would be included in some. This had equity implications across communities. Second, because of a rush before the hungry season, some beneficiaries were asked to select others, leading to biases toward family members and debtors. The reduced transparency and inclusiveness of the process led to resentments between families. Third, wealth indicators were sometimes applied that were not appropriate—for example, the type of roofing material used on their dwelling excluded some—but this material may have been acquired long ago and the households may have been destitute since the male household head died. Third, some households were deleted when they did not show up for the targeting or registration process, although they may have been absent because of illness. Fourth, although Concern guidelines specify that each wife in a polygamous family should be registered separately, this often did not occur and wives were left out, receiving inadequate transfers or none.

Oxfam's cash transfer program in Malawi also used a community-based process with committees that had responsibility for targeting decisions but without formal checks and balances, and a number of additional risks were discovered with these methods. First, communities could decide whether to use existing committees or form new ones, and it appears that some committees were cementing inequalities, leading to elite capture and inclusion errors. Second, there was confusion over concepts of vulnerability, and some relatively wealthy households that had taken in orphans or had ill members were using these criteria to justify their inclusion. Some areas were excluding people who did not have national registration cards, whereas the elderly, migrants, or people designated to pick up benefits on behalf of someone else might not have had them. Greater monitoring by Oxfam, along with more clarity and transparency with respect to the resources available and the numbers of people who could be included, would have reduced targeting errors (Harvey and Marongwe 2006).

Assessing targeting systems' effectiveness in reaching AIDS-affected families is difficult because data will normally not indicate whether a household has someone living with AIDS or whether an orphan was orphaned by AIDS.

Schubert et al. (2007) take up this challenge, assessing how well the Malawi Mchinji and Zambia SCTS community-based systems performed in targeting AIDS-affected households. In Malawi, profiles of households in the scheme were compared to those in the national Integrated Household Survey (IHH) for 2004, finding the following shares of households in the program versus those in the IHH, respectively: elderly households—65 versus 12 percent; female-headed households—65 versus 12 percent; households with children—69 versus 56 percent; households with orphans (single and double)—85 versus 12 percent. Using a number of assumptions (because empirical verifications were not available) as to the extent to which the categories described (such as elderly-headed household) are related to AIDS, the analysis estimates that 53 percent of the households have someone who died due to AIDS, and of the 47 percent remaining, 34 percent have absorbed children orphaned by AIDS. This adds another 16 percent to the total of AIDS-affected households, meaning that about 70 percent of the households were AIDS affected, and some additional number were likely to have had members living with AIDS. Another survey of 382 households with a control group similarly concludes that 75 percent of households in the program were AIDS affected. Because extreme poverty is also a criterion, it is assumed that the program also captured the worst off and most vulnerable (Schubert et al. 2007, 21–22).

A similar method was used to assess the targeting performance of the pilot program in Zambia. Data from the program baseline were again compared to a national 2004 Living Conditions Monitoring Survey (LCMS), although it was harder to compare the rural program's households with the LCMS data, which averages rural and urban. The proportion of program households headed by someone age fifty-five or older was 79 percent versus 19 percent in the LCMS. Among these, two-thirds were female headed; of those whose head was under age fifty-five, over half were female-headed; and 63 percent of the female heads were widowed. From there, a calculation using assumptions about the extent to which deaths were due to AIDS and about children orphaned by AIDS led to an estimate that a total of approximately 68 percent of participants were AIDS affected and that an additional number were living with AIDS (Schubert et al. 2007, 13–15). Based on the Zambia and Malawi experiences, Schubert et al. (2007) conclude that cash transfer programs can be most effective in reaching AIDS-affected households if they focus on households that are poor and labor constrained and use targeting criteria with exclusion errors under 20 percent.

Still, the Technical Working Group (TWG) on Social Assistance, which developed the implementation framework for the expanding cash transfer program in Zambia, did not find the evidence on the effectiveness of the targeting system conclusive. Quantitative data found that the dependency ratio criterion was not applied to all households, calling into question its fairness and adequacy. In response, the program proposed to test a universal pension system, improve the training of the committees, standardize the application form but include more questions identifying destitution, and request committees to comment on whether the household assets reported are still functional (MCDSS/TWG 2007a). Furthermore, some have questioned whether community-based targeting on a national scale is the most effective means of reaching the most vulnerable households, defined as female headed, elderly headed, and caring for orphans and other vulnerable children. There are also questions about costs; although proxy means tests are expensive, community-based processes can be as well.

A study comparing different targeting methods in Zambia (Watkins 2008) found that categorical targeting is less expensive than a proxy means test but that additional criteria must be applied to capture the poor. The study found that in two out of three districts, community-based methods (compared with poverty deciles) were effective in identifying the poorest households, whereas in one it was not. The poorly performing district had less easily identifiable ultra poor and more clustering around the mean. The study authors therefore recommended that methods be selected based on local conditions, suggesting these guidelines: for wards with very high poverty prevalence and severity, geographic targeting only; for those with medium to medium-high poverty, community-based targeting if community structures are adequate (otherwise proxy means testing); for those with low poverty and hard-to-identify poor in urban contexts, means testing with household verification if means testing is found to be over 85 percent accurate.

Other proposed improvements to the process included refining the current eligibility criteria and developing an index to provide additional information about the relative position of eligible households to deepen the information on the type and quantity of assets owned, the sources and types of income earned by household members, dependency ratios, and access to public services (World Bank 2007b). Uganda's planned cash transfer program also proposed to combine a community-based process followed by a means test based on census data to determine which families identified by the community process meet the criteria (International Poverty Center 2007).

Means Tests and Categorical Targeting in Southern Africa

South Africa's targeting system for its cash transfers, including the Old Age Pension (OAP), Child Support Grant (CSG), Foster Care Grant (FCG), and others, use an application-based means test. The OAP has been found to be well targeted to poor households and to households caring for children, with three-generation households and skip-generation households (where grandparents are caring for children) accounting for almost three-quarters of pension-receiving households (Case and Deaton 1998, 1341). Although it is means tested, the targeting method is closer in effect to a categorical approach, nearly universal with respect to poor black South Africans (Palacios and Sluchynsky 2006, 20). OAPs in Lesotho and Namibia are also categorical (universal for the elderly). OAPs tend to be well targeted toward elderly with AIDS-affected children because the AIDS epidemic shifts the responsibility of caring for orphaned children onto elderly-headed households. More than 60 percent of orphaned children in Namibia, South Africa, and Zimbabwe are living with their grandparents, as are more than 50 percent in Botswana, Malawi, and Tanzania. In Namibia, the overall percentage of orphans living with their grandparents increased from 44 percent in 1992 to 61 percent in 2000 (UNICEF 2003; Gorman 2004, 18).

Although pension recipients in Namibia are slightly less well off than the general population, most live above the poverty line; however, this is due to the pension, on which most households are highly dependent: 81 percent of household income is pension income (Palacios and Sluchynsky 2006, 24). The Lesotho OAP is still relatively new but thus far has reported errors of inclusion and exclusion due to elderly people's lack of required documentation and areas that are difficult to reach because of poor infrastructure and weather. Nevertheless, for those who receive it, the pension does seem to be benefiting children: data indicate that 50 percent of pensioners in Lesotho spend some of their pension on education and associated costs and 20 percent of their pension on caring for dependent orphans (Croome 2006).

The South African CSG has been found to be well targeted in terms of those who have it; that is, there are few inclusion errors. With respect to exclusion errors, the CSG program did poorly in early years but has improved sharply. One study finds that exclusion errors dropped from 91 percent in 2000 (two years after the program's introduction) to 45 percent in 2004 (Samson, MacQuene, and van Niekerk 2006). In 2007 the Department of Social Development put exclusion errors at just 10 percent (Budlender 2007).[11] Streak (2008) calculates the take-up rate in 2008 at 80 percent, or having 20 percent exclusion errors. A challenge then remains, to learn why this last 10–20 percent is so difficult to reach and how to overcome these obstacles. Two studies have found that the poorest families are those that are the least likely to access the CSG (Rosa, Leatt, and Hall 2005; Goudge et al. 2007). The

[11] Streak (2008) explains that take-up rates for the CSG are hard to estimate due to outdated national household income and expenditure data (from 2005–06) and the difficulty of applying a means test designed for the primary caregiver and spouse to household-level income and expenditure data.

Goudge et al. (2007) study, involving 280 households, found that among households eligible for the CSG, 57 percent of children in the poorest quintile were eligible for the CSG but not receiving it. The percentage not receiving the benefit declined steadily with each better-off quintile, so 39 percent were not receiving it in quintile 4, although this climbed to 48 percent in quintile 5.

The CSG is not rationed in the sense that there are no caps (such as the 10 percent limit in Zambia), although the overall budget restrictions in effect create a cap.[12] From 2000 to 2002 a primary caregiver was eligible for the CSG if she had children under age 7. This gradually increased to include children under age 18 by 2011 for a single caregiver earning R31,200 per year or less or for married caregivers earning R62,400 per year or less. The eligibility criteria have been subject to some criticism: that the poverty thresholds have not kept pace with inflation, resulting in exclusions (Budlender, Rosa, and Hall 2005, 8–9), and that the poverty line used may not be reasonable, especially because such a line is a complicated concept, that is, it does not take into account household size, discriminating against families with many dependents, including families fostering orphans. Finally, the cutoff age has historically excluded coverage of children at a vulnerable age. Earlier data found that for those who applied, only about half of 1 percent of applications were rejected, suggesting that the means test criteria are not prohibitive (Haarman 1998; Rosa, Leatt, and Hall 2005).

Errors of exclusion have had more to do with gaps in take-up among eligible households, initially based on lack of knowledge about the grant, and with requirements related to documents and procedures. The earlier problem has been greatly reduced; now people generally know about the grant. The problems with the requirements remain, although increased uptake figures imply that people have been navigating the process more easily than at earlier stages of the program. The KwaZulu-Natal Income Dynamics Study of 2004 found that the main reason people do not apply for the grant is the difficulty of obtaining documents, including the cost, time, complications, and difficulties in accessing documents needed to obtain other documents (Woolard, Carter, and Agüero 2005; Hunter and Adato 2007b). For example, birth certificates are required to access the CSG, but there are various reasons why births are not registered, exacerbated by an AIDS-related context of extreme poverty, maternal illness and death, and increased mobility of children (Giese and Smith 2007). A review of studies of birth registration in South Africa found

[12] Given the remaining gap in take-up for eligible households, this budget-related "cap" does not currently have that much significance. Where it previously had more effect was with respect to the age cutoff for eligible children.

considerable provincial and local variability, with an inverse correlation between poverty and birth registration (Giese and Smith 2007). Another problem with the South African application method as currently implemented and staffed is that the administration is too burdensome on the welfare offices (Rosa, Leatt, and Hall 2005). As noted earlier, Coady, Grosh, and Hoddinott (2004) found that, globally, targeting performance is less the result of the system type than of its implementation. However, some in South Africa argue that the means test should be eliminated because of the high monetary costs and other burdens it places on administrators and beneficiaries and the fact that these burdens are, at least in substantial part, responsible for undercoverage of the poor (Rosa, Leatt, and Hall 2005).

If we add to these problems the likelihood that many of those not taking up the CSG are AIDS affected, a stronger case could be made for simplifying the application process. Most studies that attempt to surmise the effectiveness of social grants in reaching AIDS-affected households use evidence of the impact of grants on children in high-prevalence regions or the impact of pensions on children (see Chapters 6, 7, and 8 on education, health, and food consumption and nutrition), along with assumptions as to the covariance of AIDS and poverty and of AIDS-affected and fostering households. For example, Case, Hosegood, and Lund's (2005) study in the one region in KwaZulu-Natal found mixed results, based largely on low take-up: only one-third of all age-eligible resident children had the grant accessed on their behalf; among the poorest households, only 50 percent were receiving the grant. Among those with the grant, however, it appears to be well targeted: recipient households were likely to have less educated and less employed parents as well as fewer assets and luxury items. This may reflect a self-targeting process in which better-off households for which the grant would make up a smaller proportion of household income find the time costs of applying and picking up the grant not worth the benefits. Children with deceased fathers were more likely to receive the grant, but the opposite was true for mothers; children living without mothers for all reasons were particularly at risk of not receiving the grant: 41 percent of children living with mothers received the grant versus 29 percent with nonresident mothers, 23 percent with deceased mothers, and 19 percent with mothers of unknown status (Case, Hosegood, and Lund 2005, 472–480). This points to an important targeting challenge: learning how to reach out to children living in households without mothers.

Additional insight into how well the CSG and OAP reach AIDS-affected households is provided by data from 1,428 households in the 2004 KwaZulu-Natal Income Dynamics Survey (KIDS).[13] Using prime-age adult mortality between

[13] We thank Futoshi Yamauchi for assistance with analyzing the KIDS data.

Figure 3.1—Child Support Grant (CSG) targeting of AIDS-affected households (CSG receipt according to prime-age deaths), 2004

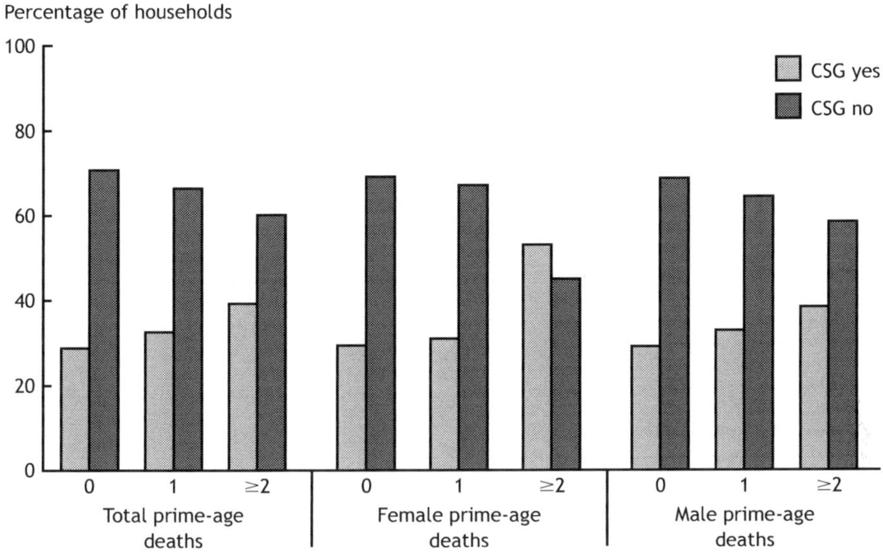

Source: KwaZulu-Natal Income Dynamics Survey data from 2004.

1998 and 2004 as a proxy for AIDS-affected households, we look at cash grant receipts in those households. Figure 3.1 illustrates the trend in CSG receipt by number of household prime-age deaths (note that for two or more deaths, the total numbers are small). As the number of prime-age deaths per household increases, the percentage of households receiving the CSG increases. This effect is slightly larger among households that lose prime-age women than in those that lose prime-age men. This trend suggests that, among those who receive it, the CSG may be fairly well targeted to AIDS-affected households. However, Figure 3.1 also shows that many households, even those with two or more prime-age deaths, do not receive the CSG—more than half in most cases, except among a small group of households with two or more prime-age female deaths. This is consistent with the findings reported earlier from South Africa, suggesting undercoverage of poor eligible households. Although the sample includes some households that do not meet the eligibility requirements for the CSG, because these data come from one of the poorest provinces in the country, we assume that far more of these households should be receiving the grant.

Figure 3.2 shows a similar trend for receipt of the OAP. Again, the trend shows a slight increase in coverage as the number of household prime-age

Figure 3.2—Old Age Pension (OAP) targeting of AIDS-affected households (OAP receipt according to prime-age deaths), 2004

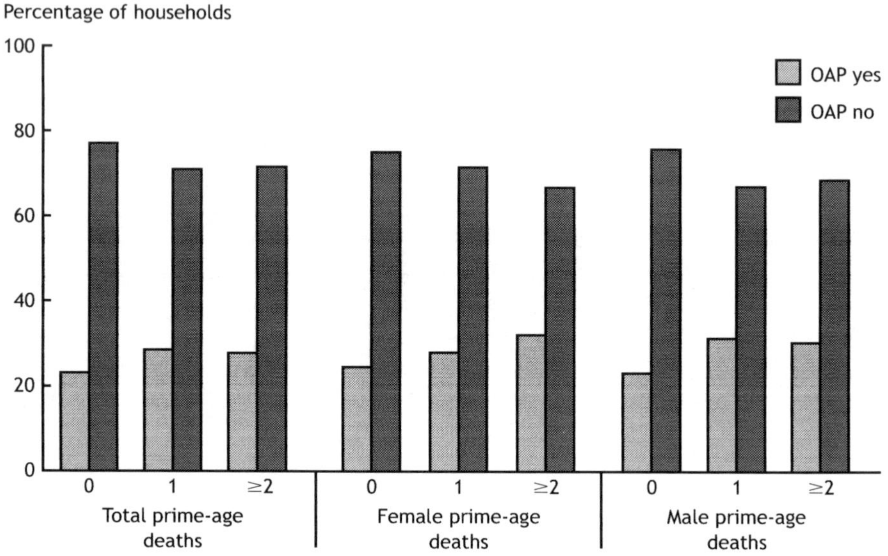

Source: KwaZulu-Natal Income Dynamics Survey data from 2004.

deaths increases, although the trend is weaker and only consistently upward for prime-age female deaths. As in the case of the CSG, the percentage of households *not* receiving the OAP is always greater than the percentage receiving it. The meaning of this is less certain, because we do not calculate how many of these households do not have elderly members.

We also tried another proxy for AIDS-affected households, the presence of fostered orphans, and found that only 30 percent of households fostering orphans were receiving the CSG. Despite the small overall sample size of 207 fostering households, this suggests that the CSG is not yet reaching this important category of AIDS-affected households. We do not know whether this finding to any extent represents better-off households (those not eligible for or choosing not to access the CSG) disproportionately fostering orphans.

Booysen's (2004a) study in Free State Province in South Africa is able to directly assess the targeting of AIDS-affected households because this sample is of households identified as experiencing morbidity or mortality due to AIDS. For 296 of these households, the OAP is accessed by more than 80 percent (in two periods by as much as 90 percent) but the CSG by just between 15 and 35 percent of households over a 19-month period. The FCGs and Disability Grants reached fewer households. These figures are at best only representative of the two communities, but they do suggest that the OAP is an effective means of reaching AIDS-affected households. Because it is likely that most of these households would be CSG eligible, these communities appear to suffer from the same uptake problems as found elsewhere (Booysen 2004a).

The South African grants that could arguably be most directly suited for AIDS-affected households are the Disability Grant and the FCG, although they were not intended for this. The Disability Grant can be obtained by adults who are HIV positive when their CD4 count falls below 200. The take-up rate was about 36 percent in 2000, but although higher take-up would both reduce poverty (Samson et al. 2004) and help families with a very ill member, its potential reach for AIDS-affected families is very limited. The FCG is a means-tested grant for children determined to be "in need of care" (Meintjes et al. 2003) regardless of whether their biological parents are alive (devised as part of the child protection system), but orphans fall into this eligibility category. This grant provides a much higher payment (about three times higher) than the CSG and is much more complicated to obtain and monitor, involving court orders and referrals to social workers. It has increasingly been used to support families fostering children orphaned through AIDS, although take-up by eligible households is far more limited than that of the CSG. Among households that have accessed the grant, it appears to be well targeted toward AIDS-affected families. Schubert et al. (2007) estimate that among FCG recipients, about 50 percent are AIDS affected. The FCG has been given considerable attention in social assistance policy with respect to children affected by HIV/AIDS. The national Minister of Social Development, in a 2002 address to the national Department of Education's HIV/AIDS conference, states that the Department of Social Development (DSD) was encouraging relatives to care for orphaned children under the FCG and reaffirmed this in a 2004 document, stating that a DSD priority was the increased registration of orphans for the FCG (South Africa, Department of Social Development 2004).

The larger grant provides much better support for households, and many have advocated for an aggressive expansion in response to the orphan crisis. A strong case has also been made, however, as to why it is an inappropriate response (Meintjes et al. 2003). Aside from issues of prohibitive application burdens on beneficiaries (indicated by the low take-up) as well as administrators and social workers (much greater than those of the CSG), it is argued that the FCG is fundamentally inequitable. The concern is that many children living with biological parents are just as impoverished and at risk, especially because many are living with ill parents, as children living with other relatives and that there is no basis for giving the latter a grant that is so much larger (the FCG) than the grant given to the former (the CSG). The funds could instead go to increasing the CSG or expanding it to children up to age eighteen. The FCG perhaps best illustrates the equity dilemma and the constraints of political economy: although it is one of the few grants large enough to provide adequately for the needs of orphans and their fostering families, many (although not all) advocates for child welfare do not see it as a viable option.

Conclusion

This chapter reviewed the literature on two interrelated issues: alternative methods for targeting cash transfers and whom to target in the context of communities hard hit by HIV and AIDS. The evidence points clearly to the recommendation that cash transfers be targeted to reach poor households, not specifically AIDS-affected households. The primary reason is equity, because non-AIDS-affected households and individuals may be equally in need of support. There is no clear correlation between poverty and AIDS in the sense of exposure; that is, poorer people are not necessarily at higher risk than wealthier people. However, we know that poor families are less able to cope and that for them HIV and AIDS are far more likely to mean a downward spiral of poverty. The implication of this fact is that although AIDS-affected families are not the only ones who need support, they certainly are among them and very likely have the greatest need because they are the most vulnerable to becoming destitute as income earners are lost through illness and death, medical expenses grow, and food is needed to make their ART more effective. These conditions point to poverty targeting. In a country like South Africa, where the grant is not rationed, poverty criteria alone are sufficient to reach AIDS-affected households (although only those with children, which is problematic). In countries like Malawi and Zambia, where the grants are rationed to 10 percent of a given community, reaching AIDS-affected households means overlaying poverty criteria with proxy indicators for those affected by AIDS: specifically, those that are labor constrained or have illnesses and high dependency ratios. A community-based approach allows for additional locally appropriate, or at least nationally appropriate, criteria to be assigned.

The evidence on and conditions under which orphans are or are not better off than nonorphans is exceedingly complex, with so much variation related to poverty, household structure, gender, and country specificities that one set of recommendations cannot be made as to how to reach them. Instead, poverty targeting again emerges as the best solution: orphans in poor households will be reached, and those in better-off households who can afford to take them in will not. What is clear is that many poor households have taken in orphans, which has stressed their coping abilities, and these households need support. Cash transfers targeted to poor households with high dependency ratios, such as the programs in Zambia, Malawi, and Kenya, will reach these orphans. Cash transfers received by households for each child in those households, as in South Africa, will also accommodate orphans who are now members. Stigma is another reason that targeting households because they are AIDS affected or children because they are orphans is not recommended.

The other category of AIDS-affected people that offers a great moral dilemma in terms of targeting is that of people who are HIV positive or have AIDS. We know that food is necessary for ART to be effective and that good nutrition can slow disease progression. Stigma complicates any targeting process, but a disability grant for people with AIDS is a viable option (currently South Africa has this, but the stage of disease progression at which they receive the grant is too far along for this program to serve as an effective protective system). Given the particular nutritional requirements of people living with AIDS and the importance of ensuring adequate food consumption for ART patients, a food transfer is probably a better approach than a cash transfer for people at a certain stage of illness. However, cash is needed for transportation and other basic necessities. Research is needed on the efficacy of food versus cash in this context, but the best policy approach is likely to be a food transfer for the patient and a cash transfer for the household if it has been captured by the poverty criteria.

Another issue on which there is little evidence is the relative benefit of the household or child support grant versus an OAP if the objective is household well-being and protection of children's human capital. The evidence shows that both of these approaches are effective, but there is little comparative evidence (though some work is under way in Zambia). We know that children are reached with pension income, but there are also those who are not because the funds are not spent on them, there are no elderly people in the household, or the elderly member is no longer there. A CSG is thus a more certain route, although this debate has a number of considerations and there is no consensus. This issue is taken up again in Chapter 6.

Finally, there is the question of which methods to use to target benefits. To some extent the criteria for making such decisions are the same as those outlined in reviews such as that by Coady, Grosh, and Hoddinott (2004). These lessons are reviewed in this chapter. What stands out in the countries with high levels of HIV prevalence that are the focus of this review is that the high cost and administratively complex national proxy means test methods used in Latin America are unlikely to be adopted. For a country with the administrative capacity of South Africa, an application-based proxy means test has proved to be viable. In Zambia, Malawi, and Kenya, community-based methods have the advantage of being administratively and technically feasible, politically and socially acceptable, and adaptable to local circumstances. Evidence to date indicates that they are fairly effective in reaching AIDS-affected families and in identifying the poor, except where there are fewer extreme poor to distinguish and there is clustering around the poverty line. These methods have some disadvantages with respect to scalability: the transaction costs are high, as is the need for capacity building. They will miss people in need due to politics and human error, although they are arguably less prone to the latter than is a proxy means test. They need institutional checks and balances, accuracy assessments, and supplementation with proxy means tests where these would have the greatest efficiencies. Additional lessons and recommendations on targeting are reported in the conclusions in Chapter 10.

CHAPTER 4

To Condition or Not to Condition? Key Considerations and Policy Options

Among the most significant debates currently occurring over cash transfers surrounds the issue of conditionality. The large cash transfer programs in Latin America have been conditional, that is, have required beneficiaries' participation in a specific set of education, health, and nutritional services as a condition of receiving cash. The programs in southern and East Africa, evolving against the backdrop of the AIDS crisis, have been unconditional; no obligations are tied to receipt. Debates over conditionality raise many issues that are discussed in this chapter. The main questions of relevance in considering conditional versus unconditional cash transfers for AIDS-affected families are (1) does conditionality add value over and above an unconditional transfer, that is, does it increase human capital impacts, and (2) is conditionality feasible in Sub-Saharan Africa, and, if there are constraints on implementation, will conditionality interfere with getting cash into the hands of families who urgently need it? There is little research to date that directly compares conditional cash transfers (CCTs) and unconditional cash transfers (UCTs) in a given setting, and the debate over conditionality is sometimes passionate and ideological, without enough evidence in support of either position, although there is some evidence supporting both. Discussed next are five broad sets of issues to take into account when considering whether and under what circumstances to condition as well as the evidence available to date, a discussion of key concerns, and some conclusions.

Appropriate Design

As CCT programs migrate across the globe and settle on new continents they can be used to achieve different objectives than those that were primary in Latin America. However, in practice, they look very much alike in most places. This is largely because the earlier programs were widely considered very successful, for example, those in Brazil, Mexico, and Nicaragua, and other countries have hoped to replicate their results. Furthermore, many of the early program adopters in Latin America had similar human capital deficits, reasons for these deficits, and objectives, and many countries around the world indeed share similar problems, for example, discrimination against girls in schooling decisions. However, different countries have different levels of achievement and different failings with respect to human capital and other objectives, as well as different factors contributing to poverty. As seen in Chapter 6, the reason that CCT programs in several countries had very low impacts on primary school enrollment was that enrollment levels were already very high before the program. Primary school enrollment does not need to be a condition of a CCT as often as it is. There are often regional variations, in which, for example, primary enrollment is high nationally but very low in some parts of the country, as is the case in Turkey, which had a national CCT for primary (as well as secondary) school. Variations may also occur within countries across groups defined by gender, ethnicity, age, or other variables. CCTs can be designed to respond to these differences.

Relevant design differences can also respond to the nature of shocks; HIV and AIDS are key examples of shocks in Sub-Saharan Africa. In Lesotho and Tanzania, CCT studies have been planned to condition on testing negative for sexually transmitted diseases (STDs) (Özler and de Walque 2009). In India, a small program conditions benefits on delaying marriage to age eighteen and completing school (Chaudhury 2007). In Malawi, a study found that incentives in the form of cash transfers and school fees reduced early marriage, teenage pregnancy, and self-reported sexual activity among adolescent girls (Baird et al. 2009). In South Africa, a study is under way to determine the effectiveness of a CCT in promoting schooling and reducing risky sexual behavior and HIV/AIDS risk among young girls (Pettifor and MacPhail 2009). There is growing interest in developing conditional programs with early childhood development services (World Bank 2006a, 36). Conditioning cash in some form has been used to create incentives for behavior change in the area of sexual and reproductive health in Bangladesh, India, and the United States, and small studies have experimented with incentives for participation in HIV/STD prevention counseling and steps related to treatment goals (Kamb et al. 1998; Petry, Martin, and Finocche 2001, cited in Medlin and de Walque 2008; Mauldon 2003). More recently, a small program examined the impact of monetary incentives and costs on obtaining HIV test results (Thornton 2008). Given some successes in this area, it is a concept worth pursuing. However, these are areas that must always be approached very carefully. Depending on the outcomes pursued and the indicators needed to determine achievement of the desired outcomes, particular complications with respect to feasibility and ethics may be introduced where HIV prevention is the objective (Medlin and de Walque 2008).

There are two broad questions to ask in considering and designing a CCT. First, what are the priority problems that the program should target? For example, is there an urgent need to provide basic subsistence to ensure survival or protect against destitution? This may be the case among families the hardest hit by AIDS. If so, an unconditional transfer, of cash or food, is the most appropriate response. Or is the main objective to increase investment in children's health or education? For girls, boys, or both, and at which ages? Are there particular micronutrient deficiencies to target?

Second, what is the *reason* for low levels of participation in health services or school enrollment or for nutritional deficiencies? Is it people's lack of knowledge about prenatal healthcare or girls' education or an undervaluing of these? Is it lack of access to nearby facilities? Or is it an issue of cost: the cost of transportation to the clinic, the cost of school fees, or the opportunity cost of child labor? Is child labor even a problem in the region? In Turkey, Adato et al. (2007) found that although cost was a major constraint to children's schooling and thus a cash transfer responded to the problem, in some regions, other concerns were as important to schooling decisions or more so: inadequate supply of nearby schools, inadequate transportation, unsafe schools, lack of perceived value of education (as opposed to the value of work for boys or the value of marriage for girls), and other gender issues revolving around sexuality and threats to family reputation and honor. With respect to conditioning in the context of AIDS, other questions should be asked: Does HIV and AIDS affect families' behavior in particular ways so that the conditions may not work or may deny benefits to those who most need them? Are children in households with ill parents affected in particular ways? Is this related to care responsibilities, stigma, or emotional or psychological problems? What are the main influences on adolescent behavior and choices? Do fostering families discriminate against orphans? Conditioning is a concept used to create incentives for change; the object of that change and ways to achieve it will vary widely from one context or another. Conditions, if used at all, should be developed flexibly and creatively to achieve carefully thought-through objectives.

Does Conditionality Matter in Terms of Human Capital Impacts?

Once the nature of the problems to be tackled, their underlying causes, and program objectives are defined, the next issue to face is whether conditionality is necessary to achieve these objectives. What difference does it make? There is no reason to expect that UCTs would necessarily be less effective than CCTs with respect to short-term poverty reduction. There is more reason to believe that they might be less effective in increasing school enrollment and attendance and the use of health services, because with UCTs such participation would be optional rather than mandatory and because supply-side interventions—such as building schools or contracting NGOs to deliver health services—sometimes accompany CCTs. However, a UCT could also provide the cash needed for school fees or transportation or to compensate for lost child labor, increasing school attendance without the conditionality. Although we know that cash transfers can have an impact on human capital (see Chapters 6, 7, and 8), we do not know the relative importance of the different mechanisms through which either CCTs or UCTs work. Even rigorous CCT evaluations have presented results as a "black box," studying the combined effects of all components on a given outcome without assessing which components are responsible for which outcomes (Burtless 1995; Heckman and Smith 1995, cited in de Brauw and Hoddinott 2008). Conditionality is one of those components; we know little about whether, to what extent, and under what conditions conditionality would be responsible for increasing a particular outcome.

Evidence is beginning to emerge, however, and new research is being designed to answer this question. Simulating the impact on school enrollment of the CCT Bolsa Escola in Brazil and that of a UCT, Bourguignon, Ferreira, and Leite (2003) conclude that the main enrollment impact is due to the conditionality: among ten- through fifteen-year-olds not in school, about 60 percent enroll in response to the program, whereas a UCT has no effect. Using a model for Mexico's CCT PROGRESA, Todd and Wolpin (2003, cited in de Janvry and Sadoulet 2006) attribute 80 percent of the program's impact on school enrollment to the conditionality and 20 percent to the income effect. Using data from Mexico, de Janvry et al. (2006, cited in de Janvry and Sadoulet 2006) also reach a similar conclusion on conditionality, finding that one dollar of CCT income is about eight times more effective in inducing enrollment than a dollar of UCT income at the mean income of the poor.

Two other studies take advantage of "accidental experiments" to assess conditionality. Data reflecting widespread implementation errors, such that transfers were not conditioned or people thought they were not, were used to construct a group of beneficiaries receiving "unconditional" transfers to compare with a group of beneficiaries receiving "conditional" transfers. The first study, by de Brauw and Hoddinott (2008), takes advantage of the fact that in Mexico's PROGRESA, some beneficiaries did not receive the forms needed to monitor school attendance. If the form was not received, attendance could not be monitored. In order to control for the fact that some households without the form might still have thought that attendance was required, this group was further divided into those who listed (on the evaluation survey) school attendance as a condition and those who did not. A number of statistical techniques were used to ensure that the results were not due to unobserved differences between the "conditioned" and "unconditioned" groups at the household or the community level. The analysis found statistically significant impacts of conditionality: for all age groups that had completed grades 3–8, the "unconditioned" group's enrollment rate was 5.4 percent lower than that of the "conditioned" group. This varied substantially at the grade level, however: the greatest impact was for children who had completed grade 6 and were about to make the transition from primary to lower secondary school, when many children are most likely to drop out. For this grade cohort, children in the "unconditioned" group (those who did not receive the enrollment form) were 18–20 percent less likely to enroll in school, whether or not the parents knew of the conditionality. For other grade levels, the differences were smaller and not always statistically significant or the unconditioned groups were slightly more likely to enroll. Adding all parental, household, and community controls had little effect on the overall outcome, although there was some evidence suggesting that the impact of conditionality was greater when the household head was not literate. In the smaller sample of households that did not receive the enrollment forms and did not know the conditions, the overall enrollment rate was 9.1 percent lower, or 7 percent with all controls applied. These outcomes of conditionality are quite large compared with other educational outcomes in the PROGRESA study (although the results are not directly comparable): for example, the enrollment impact of being in PROGRESA (as compared to not being in the program) for children who completed grade 6 was only 8.3 percent (Schultz 2004), compared to the 18–20 percent increase in the conditionality impact analysis.

The second study, of the program Bono de Desarrollo Humano (BDH) in Ecuador (Schady and Araujo 2006), provides evidence that conditionality is important in increasing enrollment effects, although this evidence could be interpreted in different ways. The results of the impact evaluation found that the effect of the program on school enrollment was an increase of between 9.8 and 12.8 percent. BDH was different from most CCTs in that school enrollment was not enforced; however, program officials and television ads stressed the importance of enrollment, so many households believed it was a requirement. The study thus tested a "conditionality impact" by splitting the beneficiary households into those that stated that there was an enrollment requirement and those that did not, also using statistical techniques to control for other (observable) differences between the households (although not unobservables). It found that the program's effect on enrollment for "conditioned" households was 7.3–13.0 percent, while the effect on enrollment for "unconditioned" households was only 1.4–2.1 percent. Significant program effects were found only for those who believed that there was an enrollment requirement.

Whether such results would be found in African contexts is unknown. There are some reasons to believe that they would not, or would not be as strong, with some evidence from Malawi (discussed later). However, the magnitude of the impacts found in Asia and Latin America and the importance of strengthening human capital make the issue worth exploring carefully. Research comparing UCTs with CCTs was planned in Kenya, Uganda, and Zambia (Kenya, OVPMHA 2006; Uganda, MGLSD 2007), though it did not end up achieving this as anticipated.[1] A study by Baird, McIntosh, and Özler (2010) in Malawi used an experimental design to isolate the impact of conditionality, comparing a CCT with a UCT for adolescent girls (discussed earlier in relation to the HIV risk reduction objective). The study randomly assigned communities to treatment or control status, and then the treatment group was further randomly divided into three groups: adolescent girls receiving a conditional transfer, girls receiving an unconditional transfer, and girls receiving no transfer. The conditionality was school attendance on 80 percent of the number of days school was in session for the previous month. The authors found that the UCT had a strong effect on schooling rates and that conditionality had limited added impact. The impact on school attendance, defined as attending school regularly at least one term, was identical (4 percent) for the CCT and the UCT. Looking at attendance defined as regular attendance during all three terms, the CCT had a higher impact than the UCT (6.6 percent versus 4.7 percent, respectively); however, the difference is not statistically significant. One possible explanation for this is that some beneficiaries with different treatment statuses came into contact (for example, in school and at monthly cash transfer meeting) with one another. Although the study found little evidence of spillover effects, the unconditional arm of the intervention could be considered a "light social marketing/information campaign that 'promotes' schooling" (Baird, McIntosh, and Ozler, 2010, 36).

The study also randomly assigned a transfer size (from US$5 to $15 per month) to estimate the elasticity of schooling outcomes with respect to transfer size and found that the effect on school enrollment is very small and does not vary by treatment status and that increasing the total transfer size is not more effective when the transfer is conditional.[2] Therefore, the authors conclude that small UCTs can have approximately the same impact as larger CCTs

[1] Zambia had planned to test a "hard" conditionality and a "soft" conditionality, one not enforced, but due to administrative costs it planned instead to apply only a soft conditionality of school attendance and issue an under-five health card (Zambia, MCDSS/TWG 2007b). There is some question as to the extent to which hard conditions, where adopted, will be applied in other country programs, a point to look out for in assessing results.

[2] All dollar amounts in the monograph are U.S. dollars.

(Baird, McIntosh, and Özler, 2010, 19). This is the first evidence on conditionality in Africa and the first study designed to empirically test conditions versus no conditions. Albeit limited to one study, it does suggest that conditions may not be necessary to achieve education impacts in some contexts.

Choice, Autonomy, and Power

One of the conditionality debates revolves around the social implications of state-imposed behavioral change. Whether a CCT involves state imposition can itself be debated, because people can opt out of the program. In this sense CCTs can be seen as a form of self-targeting, in the same way that public works are; in the latter, people choose whether to work, weighing the costs versus the benefits. The state is not forcing behavior change but rather changing the "price" of decisions; with CCTs they are compensating parents for the loss of child labor so that the price of schooling becomes cheaper. A price subsidy could be seen in the same way—as not forcing people to buy a certain item but changing the price to influence choices. If a policy decision is to be made between an unconditional and a conditional cash transfer, a factor to be considered is that there is comparatively more imposition in the case of the conditional transfer.

In the conditionality debate, the imposition of conditionality can be seen as both a problem and a strength, depending on one's perspective. The problem lies in the loss of autonomy implied by the imposition. Schubert and Slater (2006, 576) argue that a conditionality cost-benefit analysis should take into account "dimensions of human dignity, self-esteem and autonomy. . . . Imposing conditions on people may smack of top-down attitudes of 'we know better' and 'the poor cannot be trusted'" to make good decisions. Although CCTs do have this flavor of paternalism, parents are not really making an autonomous "decision" when they take their children out of school because they cannot afford fees and supplies or because the children are needed to work in the fields. In this sense, by decreasing the "cost" of a schooling decision, a CCT can be seen to increase parents' real choices about whether to educate their children. On the other hand, a UCT would give them even greater choice. In laying out the pros and cons of conditionality, Samson raises the concern that conditions "deprive the poor of freedom to choose appropriate services—and to freely make decisions to improve household welfare" (Samson 2006). The fact that people choose to make use of services even without conditions is an indication that they do not necessarily need the state to require them (although the extent to which they will make these decisions with an unconditional rather than a conditional transfer is not known). More controversially, reversing the autonomy argument, conditionality has also been advocated as a means of promoting citizenship, involving families as active agents in their own integrated development process (Oportunidades 2003, 58).[3]

There is also a concern that CCTs are used to impose consumption of items preferred by the program implementer and curtail "undesirable spending" (Schubert and Slater 2006, 572). CCT programs do usually involve communicating to beneficiaries, normally during orientations, that cash should be spent on children and spent by the woman, and spending on food purchases is encouraged. However, beneficiaries are not required to spend the money in any particular way; that is, this is not a conditionality. In Nicaragua, some of the community *promotoras*, the beneficiaries elected by the others to serve as their liaison with the program, were checking shop receipts, creating the impression that spending on food was a requirement. But this was not a practice that the program promoted or even approved of (Adato and Roopnaraine 2004). Oportunidades in Mexico actually sees the fact that beneficiaries decide how to spend the money according to their own priorities as part of the program's promotion of families as autonomous agents (Oportunidades 2003).[4]

A risk is that conditionality is prone to misinterpretations, as in the Nicaragua case above; to rumor, because people talk among themselves in trying to figure out how not to lose benefits; and to perverse incentives. Another example from Nicaragua is a case in which people believed that an initial condition—requiring children to gain weight—was still in place, even though it had been dropped. In response, some mothers were stuffing their children with food and water on the growth-monitoring days (Adato and Roopnaraine 2004). Another case of a possible perverse incentive was in the nutrition CCT in Brazil, Bolsa Alimentação, in which an early evaluation found that child height for age had decreased by a small amount among participating households. A hypothesis based on anecdotal information (no research was conducted to investigate this) was that parents were withholding food from children because of a mistaken belief that growth improvements would lead

---

[3] Oportunidades' policy strategy states that it "considers of highest importance the strengthening of 'co-responsibility' of families through concrete actions to themselves to improve and elevate their level of well-being. . . . The participation of families allows them to take on a role as active subjects in their own development. For them co-responsibility implies the challenge of acting as autonomous agents, capable of setting goals that conform to their aspirations and to work to realize them" (Oportunidades 2003, 58, translated from the Spanish).

[4] Oportunidades' strategic planning document states: "To promote this co-responsibility, the benefits are given in a manner that respects social specificities of families, expanding their options and opportunities within a framework of taking decisions that are informed and responsible. Families best know their most pressing needs and decide how to spend their benefits. The program strengthens their knowledge about actions that contribute to improving their conditions through information provided through the health and nutrition workshops (Oportunidades 2003, 58, translated from the Spanish).

to their being dropped from the program. This had been the case with a previous program providing milk powder for children, although it was not the case with the CCT (Morris et al. 2004). In Mexico and Nicaragua, a fair amount of stress was generated by fears over losing the benefit, although this had more to do with a lack of understanding of the targeting system than with the conditionality (Adato 2000; Adato and Roopnaraine 2010a). All of these examples point to the need for conditions to be carefully designed and monitored to catch unanticipated consequences. They also point to the importance of effective and continuous communications with beneficiaries. In the CCT in Turkey, weakness in communications reduced program impacts (Adato et al. 2007; Ahmed et al. 2007).

From an economics perspective, state influence on people's decisions can potentially be a strength for the broader society. If society places a value on certain outcomes, for example, a literate, educated female population or children who are vaccinated against contagious diseases, it may decide that the social benefits to imposing certain requirements outweigh the social costs to households of imposing a conditionality. People sometimes make investment decisions that are not optimal from a societal standpoint. A common example in the context of CCTs would be a case in which parents choose not to continue their daughters' education. An example in the context of families affected by AIDS is one in which families fostering orphans may choose not to invest in the fostered children's health or education. These spillover effects at the societal level are referred to by economists as externalities and can be positive or negative. Where society perceives a net benefit from altering household decisions, a CCT that changes the incentives to influence those decisions is seen as a good thing.

There are a number of reasons that parents make decisions that are perceived by others as suboptimal. In the case of education, they may not perceive sufficient value in education because of the structure of the local economy and their position within it. There may be no jobs to employ graduates, or parents and children may not be aware of job opportunities resulting from technological change or migration. Strengthening the economy and creating jobs could thus serve as a better incentive for educating children than a CCT. The need for the economy to be able to absorb new school graduates created by CCTs has been recognized as a major challenge in Mexico and Turkey.[5] There are also social bases for parents' schooling decisions. In parts of Turkey, some parents were reluctant to invest in their daughters' education where the benefits would be reaped by their in-laws when the girls married; others

[5] This point was made with respect to Mexico by Santiago Levy in a seminar at the Brookings Institution in 2007. The findings for Turkey are from Adato et al. (2007).

saw too much education as counterproductive to marriage (Adato et al. 2007). In these cases, people's choices may be the best ones for them, given local economic or sociocultural realities. There are also reasons that poverty, culture, and historical processes of social exclusion and discrimination may prevent people from participating in activities regardless of the benefits. In these cases, it can be the very people most in need of cash transfers who are excluded.

The example of parents' decisions not to educate girls or fostered children speaks to another issue in this debate, that of power relations within households. Households are not a homogenous entity with one will, which would exhibit one unified expression of autonomy. Rather, they are fraught with unequal power relations in which the will of more powerful members is imposed on the less powerful; a common example is seen in decisions about educating girls. For some families in Van Province in Turkey, the conditionality provided state legitimation for choices that challenged powerful biases against girls' schooling, allowing women to make the case to their husbands that they had to send their daughters to school (Adato et al. 2007). As in other cases of policies that enforce women's rights or protect them from violence through legislation or education campaigns, the state can be a force for positive (though perhaps not in everyone's eyes) social change, providing women with new options.

Finally, with respect to issues of power and choice, there are other gender dimensions of CCTs. These relate to the central role that CCTs give women with respect to receiving program benefits as well as carrying out program responsibilities. The benefits provide women with new sources of power through cash, and the responsibilities they incur provide them with new knowledge and opportunities to engage in the public sphere. These responsibilities also involve an added time burden. Molyneux (2006) is concerned that CCTs depend on normatively ascribed women's responsibilities, retraditionalizing women's roles and leaving men out of any shared responsibility for meeting program goals related to family care, thus leaving the social relations of reproduction unchallenged. Discussions of a broad range of gender issues related to CCTs is found in Adato, Feldman, and Karelina (2009) and in Adato and Roopnaraine (2010b).

Political Economy

An argument in support of conditionality is that it is important for maintaining political support for CCTs. This has two main dimensions. One relates to social attitudes toward the poor. Where poverty is seen as related to a lack of effort or responsibility (as Handa and Davis [2006] explain is the case in Latin America), setting reciprocal obligations makes programs more palatable to policymakers and taxpayers and can increase budget size and sustainability (de Janvry and Sadoulet 2006).[6] Schubert and Slater (2006) counter that sociocultural, ethnic, and political attitudes toward the poor may be different in Africa and that this must be determined before assuming that conditioning benefits is necessary. The other dimension of a political economy perspective has to do with political interests, where politicians and policymakers may be evaluated by performance indicators such as changes in school enrollment or use of health clinics. CCTs provide a clear and measurable means of improving, monitoring, and measuring these impacts. Conditionality has also increased the credibility of programs where historically the public has been suspicious of antipoverty efforts that were deemed ineffectual (Adato and Hoddinott 2007).

Service Availability and Quality, Costs, and Administrative Constraints

Probably the most important issues in considering conditionality are the availability of services on which to condition and the administrative capacity to implement the system. The principal objection raised to conditionality for African cash transfer programs is that there will not be a sufficient quantity and quality of schools and clinics within a reasonable distance or with adequate transportation and with reliable and sufficient staffing, skills, and supplies. Schubert and Mwiinga (2005), citing findings by Care International in Chipata in Eastern Province, Zambia, report that primary schools were turning away applicants because they had no space for them. They estimated an excess demand of about 20 percent beyond capacity. Were a CCT introduced under these conditions, many could not meet a schooling condition. Leatt and Budlender (2006, 4) explain how in South Africa, eligibility for the CSG originally required proof of child immunizations—a condition dropped when it became clear that it discriminated against those without access to health services—and required participation in development programs—dropped because they did not exist. One of the main problems with the grant was slow take-up; once these requirements were dropped, take-up increased rapidly. On the other hand, demand-side interventions have made a difference in many countries, as seen in the many evaluations of CCT programs, as well as the CCT versus UCT comparisons cited earlier. Probably demand plus supply interventions will be the most effective. In Bangladesh, for example, a study com-

[6]As de Janvry and Sadoulet (2006) argue, this support will come only when a program involves a condition that the public sees as not met without the condition; for example, it cannot be a primary school condition if attendance is already 95 percent. This seems contradictory, however, in that if families have achieved such a high attendance rate, they might seem particularly "deserving."

pared a supply-side grants-to-schools intervention with one that combined these grants with an educational allowance for students. It found that the supply-side intervention alone had no significant impact but that the combined intervention had a large impact on school enrollment (Ahmed 2006; see Chapter 6 for more details).

The idea of conditioning on a nonexistent service is unlikely, so the supply-side concern is sometimes overstated. Where it becomes problematic is with respect to capacity, distance, transportation, supplies, and quality, where "access" becomes more subjective. The other problem concerns geographic targeting: if only regions with service access become part of the CCT, people who are already most disadvantaged, those living in the poorest, least served areas, who are also most likely to need the cash transfer, will not receive the program. Program designs can adapt in other ways to supply constraints, however. For example, in the pilot CCT that was proposed in Uganda, the conditionality does not apply to the elderly, the disabled, others with mobility problems, or those long distances from schools or clinics (Uganda, MGLSD 2007).

There is, however, another side of the supply argument. Precisely because CCTs require adequate services, they can serve as a strong impetus for increasing the quantity and quality of services, putting pressure on governments and their respective departments to increase supply. CCTs are often joint undertakings by ministries of social development or welfare, education, and health, requiring intersectoral collaboration; in fact, the ability to achieve this is another prerequisite for a CCT. Farrington and Slater (2006) argue that conditionality may not promote increased supply because health and education services remain largely in the public domain, which is less responsive to demand. Although this may often be true, ministries of health and education are participating in CCTs in many countries. In Nicaragua, the Red de Protección Social "forced" important supply-side improvements (Maluccio, Murphy, and Regalia 2006). Honduras's CCT program, Programa de Asignación Familiar (PRAF), consisted of two "packages," a demand-side package of conditional transfers to families and a second package called "supply-side incentives" consisting of cash transfers to healthcare provision units—conditioned on their undertaking quality improvements—and to the schools. Teachers also participated in a continuous training program to improve their teaching of math and Spanish (IFPRI 2003b). Nicaragua's supply-side component was successful; Honduras's was not, which was, in part, responsible for the low impacts of the latter country's CCT program. In Nicaragua, where the government health services could not meet new demand, NGOs were contracted to supply health services and monitor participation. Because of the large presence of NGOs in the health sector in Africa already, they are likely to play a large role in a CCT program. To what extent African governments will step up to the supply-side task, either themselves or through contracting NGOs, is another open question.

Another major consideration is that of capacity to administer the conditionality. In the African context, Schubert and Slater (2006) point to limited administrative skills, low salaries, lack of guidance, lack of supervision, little experience with results-oriented management, a need for behavior change, and weak ministries, particularly in social welfare. They argue that transfer schemes should therefore be kept as uncomplicated as possible. These problems will apply to unconditional transfers as well, but monitoring and enforcing conditions do introduce significant additional burdens. In South Africa, Leatt and Budlender (2006) cite too few school inspectors and no database to verify attendance. These are serious concerns to confront if considering a CCT. Lack of current capacity does not mean that building capacity is impossible, however. Many much poorer countries (for example, Bangladesh and Nicaragua) monitor attendance (via teachers), and presumably this is a goal that South Africa should set apart from the question of CCTs. Whether teachers will report absences and deprive families of resources in the context of communities suffering extreme poverty and illness, with so many vulnerable children, is another question, which can be answered only empirically.

Finally, an important dimension of capacity is that of the cost of conditionality, for service delivery as well as for setting, monitoring, and enforcing conditions, which are data- and management-intensive processes. Any analysis of the benefits versus the costs of conditionality should bear in mind that neither the economic benefits nor the costs are easy to quantify (although the costs are easier to quantify than the benefits), much less the social benefits and costs. In the case of PROGRESA in Mexico, conditionality represented approximately 18 percent of program costs, on average, between 1997 and 2000. In Honduras's PRAF, conditionality costs averaged about 9 percent over three years, and in Nicaragua the cost averaged about 3 percent over two years (Caldés, Coady, and Maluccio 2006). Funds otherwise used to implement conditionality could instead be used to distribute more benefits (Campbell et al. 2007), although this brings us back to the overall cost-benefit analysis.

Whether it is supply-side components or administrative capacity for delivery or monitoring conditions, each must be adapted to local circumstances. For many reasons—from selecting objectives that make sense to designing a feasible program—CCT programs should not be blueprints of each other but rather should be adapted to local circumstances so that they are relevant to the problem at hand and can work. Where families are affected by AIDS, incentives could be structured to meet appropriate priority objectives.

Poorer countries with less capacity could adopt simpler designs, with fewer conditions or "soft conditions" that are encouraged but not enforced. Beneficiaries can sign a paper or consent by oral agreement to meet conditions, with no sanction carried out if they do not. Exemptions can be made for people who cannot meet the conditions. Another approach is to link cash transfer programs to complementary but not required activities, for example, service delivery, receipt of information, or training (discussed further in Chapters 6–9).

Conclusion

This chapter reviews the key issues that policymakers must consider in determining whether to condition cash transfers. Although most of these debates have thus far played out in the Latin American context and others in which HIV/AIDS does not figure into their resolution, each issue has relevance for Sub-Saharan African countries. The primary issues are (1) designing conditions appropriately and contextually to specific priority objectives, including affecting the prevention and mitigation of HIV and AIDS; (2) whether there is likely to be added value from conditioning; if not, the additional burden of administering the conditionality, coupled with the risks of reducing access to urgently needed cash if program administration is slowed or if families cannot or do not comply with conditions; (3) power dynamics, that is, the power relationships altered by CCTs; (4) political economy considerations, that is, whether conditionality, requiring something in return for the money, makes the programs more acceptable to the middle class and treasury officials; and, perhaps of highest relevance in the near term, (5) the potential of Sub-Saharan African countries to cope with CCT demands for administrative capacity, service availability, and costs.

The first issue with respect to design is where the greatest challenges arise in the context of HIV and AIDS. Rather than simply conditioning on school attendance or clinic visits, as in the traditional CCT design, a number of experiments are under way to try to achieve HIV prevention objectives. With respect to human capital impacts, the information is simply not yet there to allow us to make a determination on the added value of conditionality; this calls for carefully run small pilot programs to determine whether conditionality contributes impact beyond the cash. Furthermore, although conditionality in the African programs has thus far not been required to gain the political support needed for pilot programs and limited scaling up, the difficulties some countries have faced (for example, Uganda and Zambia) in winning high-level support for national programs suggests that conditionality may someday be introduced. In South Africa, despite the fact that the unconditional CSG has been in operation for over 10 years and conditionality has been highly controversial and even legally questioned, a schooling conditionality was introduced.

The power issues are likely to play out both ways, and on balance conditional programs probably give more power to people than they take away, including women when benefits are given to them or when girls' schooling enrollment is increased. It is the last point, related to capacity and service supply constraints, that argues the most strongly against CCTs in Sub-Saharan Africa, particularly when meeting the basic subsistence needs of AIDS-affected families is the primary objective. NGOs provide many health services in Africa, and these can be scaled up, as they have been in Latin American countries, which have also faced significant supply constraints; however, coverage and quality are still certain to be lacking. For this reason, we conclude that UCTs are the more appropriate intervention to scale up to deal with the current AIDS crisis. These programs should be accompanied by pilot programs that test conditionality to meet specific priority objectives and research that evaluates the added value of conditions.

CHAPTER 5

Poverty Impacts of Cash Transfer Programs

Cash transfer programs are increasingly used as a component of poverty reduction strategies. The degree to which these programs affect poverty on a broad level varies by country and program and is affected by the poverty rate in each country, the size of the target population, and the size of the transfer, among other factors. Poverty reduction can be evaluated using three different measures, known as the Foster, Greer, and Thorbecke class of poverty measures (Foster, Greer, and Thorbecke 1984). The poverty headcount measure represents the share of the population that is poor, that is, the proportion of the population for which income or consumption falls below the poverty line. The poverty gap measure describes the depth of poverty in a given population. Defined as the mean distance separating the poor from the poverty line (with the nonpoor having a mean distance of zero), the poverty gap corresponds to the amount of resources that would be needed to pull the poor up to the poverty line. The severity of poverty measure, or the squared poverty gap, takes inequality of the poor into account by weighing the extreme poor, who fall far below the poverty line, more heavily than the less poor, who may hover just below the poverty line (Coudel, Hentschel, and Wodon 2002, 405–407).

These measures are best used in combination because they provide different kinds of information about poverty. Using the headcount measure, a policy that benefits those just below the poverty line appears as effective as a policy that brings the extreme poor closer to the poverty line. Adding the poverty gap and severity of poverty measures to a poverty analysis captures the effect of a poverty intervention on all poor households, no matter where they fall below the poverty line, thereby providing a more complete picture of potential program impacts.

For each of these measures, a poverty line or the minimum income or expenditure necessary to keep a household out of poverty must be defined. Poverty lines vary according to different assumptions and methodologies. For example, adjustments of consumption based on age or gender or on assumptions of economies of scale can affect a household-level poverty line. Poverty lines can be constructed based on income or expenditure measures. Expenditure is generally preferred because, compared to income, it is a more direct measure of consumption. When households experience economic hardship, they are likely to smooth their consumption by borrowing or using household savings. Therefore, expenditure rather than income is likely to be a more dependable indicator of household welfare. And in many developing countries, income is much harder to capture because many people work in the informal sector and because self-reported income is frequently inaccurate (Samson et al. 2004, 22).

Impacts of Unconditional Cash Transfer Programs on Poverty

Estimates of the poverty impacts of UCTs (Table 5.1) come primarily from South Africa and mostly from the OAP. Case and Deaton (1998) estimated that the national poverty headcount (using a poverty line of $1 per day) would have been 5 percentage points higher without the OAP (40 percent without the pension compared to 35 percent with the pension), and this result was independent of the choice of poverty line (Case and Deaton 1998, 1342). Comparing total household income to income minus pension income, Barrientos (2004) found that the pension resulted in impacts of slightly smaller magnitude on headcount poverty (2 percentage points, from 43 to 41 percent) and a 10.4 percent reduction in the average poverty gap (Barrientos 2004,

Table 5.1—Summary of impacts of unconditional cash transfers on poverty

Country, program	Headcount poverty	Poverty gap	Poverty severity
South Africa, all grants	-7.2 percent	-22 percent	-75 percent (HIV-affected households)
South Africa, OAP	-5 percentage points -2.8 percentage points (-2.3 percentage points indigence headcount) -48 percent (HIV-affected households)	-81 percent (-20 percent indigence poverty gap) 61 percent (HIV-affected households)	
South Africa, CSG	-8 percent (HIV-affected households)	-15 percent (HIV-affected households)	-20 percent (HIV-affected households)
South Africa, FCG	-6 percent (HIV-affected households)	-20 percent (HIV-affected households)	-33 percent (HIV-affected households)
Mozambique, GAPVU	-6 percentage points	-27 percent	-44 percent
Uganda (projected)	No impact	-15 percent	

Sources: Datt et al. (1997); Case and Deaton (1998); Barrientos (2003); Booysen (2004b); Samson et al. (2004).

Notes: CSG = Child Support Grant; FCG = Foster Care Grant; GAPVU = Gabinete de Apoio à População Vulnerável; OAP = Old Age Pension. Blank cells indicate that results were not evaluated.

17). Jensen (2003) found a much larger poverty impact of the OAP in the Venda region: a reduction of 26 percentage points in the poverty rate among elderly households, taking into account the crowding out associated with pension receipt (Jensen 2003, 110).

Booysen (2004b) estimated the impact of four social grants on HIV-affected households, both urban and rural, in Free State Province using a purposive sample of 351 HIV-affected households. Each household included at least one person known to be HIV positive or known to have died from AIDS in the past 6 months (Booysen 2004b, 5). The CSG reduced the incidence of poverty among HIV-affected households by 8 percent, the poverty gap by 15 percent, and the severity of poverty by 20 percent. The FCG (three times as large as the CSG) had an even larger impact on poverty reduction among HIV-affected households, reducing the headcount poverty by 6 percent, the poverty gap by 20 percent, and the severity of poverty by 33 percent. The OAP (more than four times as large as the CSG) reduced headcount poverty by 48 percent, the poverty gap by 61 percent, and the severity of poverty by 75 percent (Booysen 2004b, 16). Although the sampling design and sample size mean that this household impact study cannot be generalized across South Africa, the results suggest that social grants have had an important impact on HIV-affected households.

With an average transfer of $1.14 per person per month, representing 12.7 percent of mean gross consumption expenditure, the Gabinete de Apoio à População Vulnerável (GAPVU) cash transfer program in Mozambique was estimated to have contributed to a reduction in headcount poverty of 6 percentage points and, more significantly, to reductions in the poverty gap and poverty severity of 27 percent and 44 percent, respectively.[1] Cash benefits were fairly constant across income deciles but represented a much larger share of income for poorer deciles, which helped to reduce the poverty gap and the severity of poverty (Datt et al. 1997, 46–47, 51). This study had no control group, so the results do not establish causality.

Simulated Impacts of Unconditional Cash Transfer Programs on Poverty

Although there is growing documentation of the poverty reduction impacts of CCT programs in Latin America (discussed later), in Africa empirical evidence remains limited. Given this lacuna, several authors have conducted simulations of the poverty impacts of social transfers in Sub-Saharan Africa using different transfer sizes, targeting mechanisms, and poverty measures to predict the range of impacts that can be expected.

[1] The transfer was Mt 10,353, converted to dollars at the May–August 1995 exchange rate of US$1 = Mt 9,045 (IMF 1996, cited in Datt et al. 1997, 45).

Samson et al. (2004) analyzed the role of three of South Africa's six social grants—the State OAP, the CSG, and the Disability Grant—in reducing poverty at the national level. The study used a microsimulation model developed by the Economic Policy Research Institute (EPRI) to assess the three grants, both in their current form and under different scenarios with variations in take-up and transfer size.

Samson et al. (2004) used an absolute poverty line that was created based on the cost of basic needs method, employing data from South Africa's Household Subsistence Level (HSL) survey on the cost, in urban areas, of food, housing, transport, clothing, and necessary household items. Notably, education costs were excluded, even though school expenses were among the basic needs of many South African families. The HSL accounts for variation in consumption requirements by age and gender and for regional food price variation (Samson et al. 2004, 18). Using these data, EPRI constructed an absolute poverty line specific to each province in South Africa using several poverty lines, including scaled (adjusted for economies of scale and adult equivalency) and unscaled poverty lines (Samson et al. 2004, 24–25, 31).[2]

To estimate the impact of existing social grants on poverty, Samson et al. (2004) simulated a scenario of no social assistance by calculating the income of all grant-receiving households exclusive of grants and estimating the resulting headcount and poverty gap measures based on income with and without grants. The results showed that at the national level, social grants would reduce headcount poverty by 7.2 percent and the average poverty gap by more than 22 percent.[3] This masks considerable variation across provinces, from the highest rate of household poverty headcount reduction in Western Cape at 21.9 percent to the lowest rate in the Free State at 3.9 percent. Nationally, social grants would reduce the poverty gap by 14.6 percentage points based on mean income and 13.6 percentage points based on median income and the rand poverty gap by 29 percent, or about $12.8 billion. This amount represents what it would take to eliminate poverty in South Africa.

Overall, Samson's (2004) results illustrate that South Africa's social grants have contributed to poverty reduction but the impacts vary depending on the

---

[2] The convention in literature on poverty lines in South Africa has been to give children under age eighteen the weight of half an adult equivalent and to account for economies of scale with an exponential scale of 0.9. However, these numbers are not based on empirical studies for South African household economies (Samson et al. 2004, 23). The poverty lines are HSL poverty lines based on expenditure data from the HSL survey (R311 per person); Committee of Inquiry poverty lines based on the terms of reference of the Taylor Committee of Inquiry (R394 per adult equivalent) (variations: scaled and unscaled; based on both income and expenditure); the destitution poverty line, the lowest 20 percent of households in the income distribution (scaled) (R180 per person per month); and the relative poverty line, the lowest 40 percent of households (based on expenditure and scaled).

[3] These numbers vary by poverty line used.

Table 5.2—Summary of impacts of South African social grants, assuming full take-up (percent change)

Program	Poverty headcount	Poverty gap
Old Age Pension	-1.5 to -4.5	-3.8 to -6.2
Child Support Grant (to age eighteen)	-12.4 to -35.6	-29.9 to -58.7
All social security grants	-15.2 to -45.4	-33.5 to -58.6

Source: Samson et al. (2004).
Notes: Range reflects different poverty lines. Poverty headcount is measured for individuals, and poverty gap is the aggregate national poverty gap.

choice of poverty line and the methodology for quantifying impact. Similarly, there is notable variation in the potential poverty impacts of the various types of grants (Table 5.2). With respect to expanding take-up, the OAP with full take-up would have small impacts on all poverty measures because the level of coverage is already quite high and most of the elderly who would be eligible are less poor. However, extension of the CSG is likely to have significant poverty reduction impact, particularly if the age for eligibility is raised from the current level of age fourteen to age eighteen and the transfer value is adjusted to the current-day value.

Gassmann and Behrendt (2006) simulate the impact of several types of social transfers in Tanzania including an old-age and disability pension, a universal child transfer, and a targeted transfer for vulnerable households using data from nationally representative household budget surveys. Their microsimulations are based on household consumption measured by expenditures and use a food poverty line and a basic poverty line, both calculated per adult equivalent.[4] The study assesses the impact of several types of transfers. The basic old-age and disability pension entitles all individuals age sixty or older, regardless of income or other social assistance benefits, to a transfer representing 70 percent of the food poverty line per person. In Tanzania this represents about $10 PPP, considered sufficient to lift the elderly out of poverty in each country.[5] The universal child benefit covers all school-age children (ages seven through fourteen) and orphans under age seven and provides 35 percent of the food poverty line per eligible child, representing just under $5 PPP. The targeted cash transfer provides cash equivalent to the value of

[4]The food poverty line is based on the cost of a food basket covering specified daily calorie requirements (2,200 kilocalories per adult equivalent). The basic poverty line is adjusted to account for the need for nonfood goods and services (Gassmann and Behrendt 2006).
[5]PPP: purchasing power parity.

the OAP to vulnerable households, defined as those without an able-bodied household member (households with members who are under age twenty or over age fifty-nine or are sick, injured, or disabled) (Gassmann and Behrendt 2006, 19).

Table 5.3 shows the range of poverty impacts of an OAP and a targeted transfer in Tanzania. The results show that noncontributory OAPs reduce poverty not only among the elderly who are direct beneficiaries but also for households with children and without able-bodied members. The poverty gap is reduced by about 1 percentage point, representing an 18 percent reduction in Tanzania.

The targeted cash transfer demonstrates a powerful impact on the headcount poverty of the target group (households without an able-bodied member) (Table 5.4). Although the transfer would not have a large impact on overall headcount poverty, it would reduce the poverty gap very significantly for the target group.

Looking beyond this country example, a set of simulations by Kakwani and Subbarao (2005) and Kakwani, Soares, and Son (2005) examines the poverty impacts of cash transfers and social pensions in 15 countries in Sub-Saharan Africa. The countries were chosen based on data availability but also because they are broadly representative of the whole of Sub-Saharan Africa, with rep-

Table 5.3—Poverty impacts of old-age pensions and targeted transfers in Tanzania

Impacts	Old-age pension	Targeted transfer
Headcount poverty		
Overall	-2 percentage points; -9 percent	-1.4 percentage points; -6 percent
Children (birth through age fourteen)	Girls: -1.7 percentage points; -7 percent Boys: -1.7 percentage points; -7 percent	Girls: -1.8 percentage points; -7 percent Boys: -1.5 percentage points; -6 percent
Households with children (birth through age fourteen)	-1.9 percentage points; -8 percent	-1.5 percentage points; -6 percent
Households without an able-bodied member	-2.5 percentage points; -13 percent	-8.4 percentage points; -43 percent
Poverty gap		
Overall		-15 percent
Households with children (birth through age fourteen)		
Households without an able-bodied member		-4.9 percentage points; -93 percent

Source: Gassmann and Behrendt (2006).
Note: Blank cells indicate that results were not evaluated.

Table 5.4—Percent change in poverty from a transfer of 30 percent of the average poverty line

Country	Headcount ratio	Poverty gap ratio	Severity of poverty
Kenya	15.9	33.7	45.4
Malawi	10.3	24.5	35.0
Mozambique	8.6	25.9	37.6
Uganda	18.2	33.3	43.8
Zambia	8.1	20.6	30.4

Source: Kakwani, Soares, and Son (2005).
Note: Transfer to all children ages five through sixteen.

resentation from East and West Africa and areas of high and low HIV/AIDS prevalence (Kakwani, Soares, and Son 2005, 16, 2). Both studies use unit-record household datasets from the 15 countries, which have been standardized (all use a systematic set of variables) by the World Bank for the purpose of comparing welfare across countries (Kakwani, Soares, and Son 2006, 555).

The first simulation is an ex ante assessment of the impact of a cash transfer on national poverty using several cash transfer scenarios.[6] First, the authors designate a transfer budget based on a specific share of the country's gross domestic product (GDP). The authors select 0.5 percent because they assume that African countries would need larger programs than those provided by existing CCTs in richer Latin America, which represent between 0.1 and 0.2 percent of gross national income (Kakwani, Soares, and Son 2005, 18). Under the 0.5 percent of GDP budget allocation are three scenarios: universal targeting (a transfer for every child age five through sixteen), poverty and geographic targeting (a transfer for poor children and children in rural areas), and progressive targeting (a transfer whose value rises by 5 percent after a common base transfer, according to the child's age). Finally, the authors simulate a transfer not as a percentage of GDP but instead as a proportion of the national poverty line (20, 30, or 40 percent). The simulations assume that transfers provided to children are pooled within families and allocated such that each family member enjoys the same level of welfare (Kakwani, Soares, and Son 2005, 17, 33).

A transfer representing 0.5 percent of GDP to all school-age children brings about little impact on the headcount ratio but much greater impacts on the

[6] Estimates use the national poverty line for each country, which the authors have adjusted for equivalence and household economies of scale. For years in which no poverty line was available, the authors used the consumer price index to adjust the poverty lines to correspond to the survey years (Kakwani, Soares, and Son 2005, 16; Kakwani, Soares, and Son 2006, 555).

poverty gap and the severity of poverty. Although 0.5 percent of GDP is insufficient to bring about significant poverty reduction (particularly when measured by headcount) in the short term, the impact would likely be higher if the transfers were made over a longer time period if accompanied by positive economic growth. Additional results show that the impact on poverty is higher when transfers are made to rural children rather than all children and that there is little difference in impact between a progressive transfer and a fixed-value transfer across age groups (Kakwani, Soares, and Son 2005, 35, 38).

A transfer proportional to the poverty line has a much greater impact than one equivalent to 0.5 percent of GDP. Table 5.4 shows the poverty impacts of a transfer given to all children ages five through sixteen representing 30 percent of the average poverty line in countries in southern and eastern Africa (the focus of this monograph). Here even headcount poverty is affected.

A transfer equivalent to 30 percent of the poverty line is slightly larger than the value of Kenya's cash transfer and smaller than those provided in Malawi and Zambia. The transfer given by Kenya's Cash Transfers for OVC Programme (providing about $20 per OVC per month) is, on average, equivalent to 12 percent of the poverty line and 24 percent of the ultra poverty line (Kenya, OVPMHA 2006; UNICEF, Kenya 2007a).[7] In Zambia, the SCTS transfer ($10 per household per month, plus an additional $2.50 if the household has children) represents 55 percent of the 2003 national basic poverty line (calculation based on Demombynes 2005; Zambia, MCDSS/GTZ 2007, 8).[8] In Malawi, the average transfer of $12 per month represents more than 100 percent of the 2005 national poverty line (calculation based on Malawi, Ministry of Economic Planning and Development / World Bank 2005, 4; Schubert and Huijbregts 2006).[9]

The second study, by Kakwani and Subbarao (2005), focuses on the poverty impact of social pensions in the same 15 African countries. The methodology is similar to that of the study described earlier in that scenarios are defined in terms of a fixed budget (0.5 percent of GDP in local currency) and a fixed benefit level (equal to 35 and 70 percent of the national poverty threshold expenditure level).[10] Impacts on the headcount and the poverty gap are measured under several targeting alternatives: perfect targeting, univer-

[7] These figures refer to the rural poverty line of 2,228 ksh and assume an average family size of 5.5 people. Ultra poverty is half the poverty line (UNICEF, Kenya 2007a).

[8] According to Demombynes (2005), the national poverty line in 2003 was MK73,394.

[9] The national poverty line is MK16,165/person per year and the ultra poverty line is MK10,029/person per year. The average transfer per year is MK20,400, or $144 (Schubert and Huijbregts 2006; Malawi, Ministry of Economic Planning and Development / World Bank 2005, 4).

[10] The authors choose the second value due to the significant poverty gap that characterizes some vulnerable groups, such as the elderly with children (Kakwani and Subbarao 2005, 19).

sal targeting, and targeting of different household types (all elderly regardless of income, elderly living with children but no prime-age adults, poor elderly, and households headed by elderly) (Kakwani and Subbarao 2005, 6, 17).[11]

The simulations suggest that targeting a social pension of 0.5 percent of GDP to elderly-headed households, elderly living with children, and poor elderly would bring about greater poverty reduction (both headcount and poverty gap) gains than would a universal elderly pension. Overall, targeting a pension to the poor elderly over age sixty-five (rather than to all elderly) would produce the best results in all of the 15 countries (Kakwani and Subbarao 2005, 20, 23).

Kakwani and Subbarao (2005) summarize the expected impact on the poverty headcount in each of the 15 countries if a social pension of 35 percent of the average poverty line were transferred to poor elderly: headcount poverty would fall by just under 1 percent, to 2.3 percent. If 70 percent of the average poverty line were transferred, headcount poverty would fall by 1.5–4.6 percent.

According to calculations by the Ministry of Gender, Labour, and Social Development (MGLSD) in Uganda, the currently proposed basic household transfer of $10 provided to all poor households would be insufficient to lift these households up to the poverty line, so it would have no effect on the poverty headcount. However, this transfer was predicted to reduce the poverty gap by 15 percent (from 8.7 to 7.4 percent). Adding supplementary transfers of $1.14 for each child from birth through age seventeen, to each elderly person over age sixty, and to each person with a disability in the household (up to a limit of five supplementary transfers per household) would bring about a 20 percent reduction in the national poverty gap (driving the poverty gap down to 6.8 percent) (MGLSD 2007, 22–23).[12]

Conclusion

Although evidence of the poverty impacts of social transfers in Africa remains somewhat limited, program evaluations and simulations have shown that such transfers can have a significant impact on poverty reduction to the benefit of HIV-affected households. The impacts vary depending on the poverty measure used. Even when programs do not change headcount poverty substantially, they often reduce the poverty gap and the severity of poverty significantly

---

[11] Perfect targeting is defined as "filling the poverty gap," that is, bringing everyone up to the poverty line (Kakwani and Subbarao 2005).

[12] The basic household transfer is Sh 18,000. The supplementary transfer is Sh 2,000 (Uganda, MGLSD 2007, 22).

for the target group. Simulations have shown that noncontributory OAPs reduce poverty, not only among the elderly who are direct beneficiaries but also for households with children and without able-bodied members. Targeting a pension to the *poor* elderly over age sixty-five (rather than to all elderly) produced the strongest results. However, there are trade-offs between OAPs and child grants, as considered in Chapter 3.

CHAPTER 6

Cash Transfers and Education

Interest in the impact of cash transfers on education derives from the body of evidence demonstrating the role that children's educational status plays in explaining the intergenerational transmission of or escape from poverty (see Chapter 2). Cash transfers have the potential to increase children's education by several means. First, the cash can be spent on school fees, uniforms, supplies, and other school-related expenses. Second, the transfers can compensate for lost income from child labor, so that parents are more likely to enroll children and they will miss fewer school days. Third, cash can contribute to food budgets so that children are better fed and can concentrate and perform better in school. These effects can potentially be realized through CCTs and UCTs.

Cash transfers may have particular advantages for girls in the context of HIV and AIDS. Girls are at risk of being withdrawn from school because they are often the ones who bear the burden of care for children and ill adults in HIV-affected households (Subbarao, Mattimore, and Plangemann 2001, 4; Soul City and CDC 2007, as cited in van Dijk 2007). Staying in school may have benefits for girls in addition to education. In Malawi and South Africa, trials are under way to examine the impact of randomized CCT interventions that provide cash transfers conditioned on school attendance. In both countries, girls are targeted because the incidence and prevalence of HIV are higher among young adult females than among males of the same age. In South Africa, young women are infected at three to four times the rate of young men. By the time a woman reaches age twenty-one, she has a one in three chance of being infected. In a recent national survey in South Africa, among young women with one lifetime partner, the only modifiable factor found to be associated with HIV infection was high school completion: young women who had not completed high school were almost four times more likely to be HIV infected than those who had (Pettifor et al. 2008).

Furthermore, two recent reviews of HIV and education indicate a protective association between higher education and HIV infection, particularly as epidemics mature (Hargreaves et al. 2008; Jukes, Simmons, and Bundy 2008). One study in Kenya (Duflo et al. 2006) suggests a possible causal relationship between schooling and HIV risk factors: an intervention paying for school uniforms was found to reduce dropout rates, teen marriage, and childbearing. In the Malawi CCT study, an average transfer of $10 per month, along with payment of secondary school fees, was found to significantly reduce early marriage, teenage pregnancy, and self-reported sexual behavior. For young women who were out of school at baseline, the probability of getting pregnant declined by more than 30 percent. Furthermore, the incidence of the onset of sexual activity was 38 percent lower among all program beneficiaries compared to the control group, whose members did not receive the transfers (Baird et al. 2009). The transfers also had an impact on sexual activity and risk behaviors: the reduction in onset of sexual activity was 5.5 percentage points among girls out of school at baseline and 2.5 percentage points among girls in school at baseline, representing a reduction of 46.6 percent and 31.1 percent, respectively. Although there was no impact on condom use, girls who were in school at baseline were significantly less likely to have sexual intercourse on a weekly basis and to have an older sexual partner. Although these changes in sexual behavior do not necessarily result in a decline in HIV incidence among program beneficiaries, the findings are promising, because the impacts of this program—improved school attendance and increases in a girl's age at first marriage and pregnancy—are known to improve outcomes for the next generation. Further rounds of data collection are expected to test the program's impacts on HIV incidence (Baird et al. 2009).

The South Africa study will examine the impacts of the CCT on a wide range of economic and social outcomes. This study will also compare the CCT to a community mobilization approach for HIV prevention among young adults, as well as to a combined CCT-community mobilization arm. Findings in Malawi on the role of conditionality—in short, that it makes less of a difference than the income effect—are discussed later in this chapter. What is important here is the possibility that if cash transfers can succeed in keeping girls in school, because of either the financial assistance or the conditionality or both, this approach to social protection can potentially serve a preventive function vis-à-vis HIV, as well as a mitigating function.

Impacts of Unconditional Cash Transfers on Education

Table 6.1 summarizes the results of studies on the impacts of UCTs in South Africa, Zambia, and Malawi. In South Africa, some evidence of the effect of a UCT on enrollment comes from a study of the CSG in the Umkhanyakude District of KwaZulu-Natal Province (Case, Hosegood, and Lund 2005), a district that is very poor and hard hit by illness and deaths due to AIDS. The study used data from a survey of more than 11,000 African households, just

Table 6.1—Impacts of unconditional cash transfers on education

Country, program	Enrollment	Attendance
Ethiopia, Productive Safety Net Programme		+12 percentage points (boys ages six through ten) No impact (girls)
Malawi, Mchinji Cash Transfer	+12 percentage points enrollment rate +5 percentage points newly enrolled -3 percentage points dropout rate	-1.3 days absent in previous month
South Africa, Child Support Grant	+8.1 percentage points (age six)[a] +1.8 percentage points (age seven)[a]	+25 percent[b]
South Africa, Old Age Pension		+20 to +25 percent[b] +3 percent (boys); +7 percent (girls)[c]
Zambia, Social Cash Transfer Scheme[d]	+10.4 percentage points (ages five through six) +3 percentage points (ages seven through eighteen) +8 percentage points (ages fourteen through fifteen) -2 percentage points (ages sixteen through eighteen)	

Sources: Samson et al. (2004); Case, Hosegood, and Lund (2005); Zambia, MCDSS/GTZ (2006); Miller, Tsoka, and Reichert (2008).
Note: Blank cells indicate that results were not evaluated.
[a]KwaZulu-Natal, Umkhanyakude District.
[b]National Income and Expenditure Survey 2000 and Labour Force Survey September 2000.
[c]National October Household Survey data.
[d]Kalomo District.

under a third of which received the CSG. Children for whom households received the CSG were compared to their older siblings who did not receive the grant because it was not available when they were age six or younger (about one-third of the children in CSG households had a sibling that could be compared). Although not a strict control group, the older siblings offer a reasonable counterfactual: what was likely to have happened to the younger siblings in the absence of the CSG. This approach at least removes the possibility that enrollment is a result of characteristics of parents. The level of primary school enrollment was already high in the study area (as in the rest of South Africa), although slightly lower among six- and seven-year-olds (85 and 95 percent, respectively), so there was some room for improvement, especially among six-year-olds. Controlling for many variables, Case, Hosegood, and Lund

(2005, 479) found that receipt of the CSG in 2002 was associated with an increase of 8.1 percentage points in enrollment among six-year-olds and an increase of 1.8 points for seven-year-olds. Because CSG households were poorer than the average, these enrollment increases are particularly meaningful. Although it is not possible to know why the CSG had this impact for six-year-olds, the authors suggest that it could have been by improving their health and nutrition and thus their school readiness.

More evidence from South Africa comes from Samson et al. (2004), who used national-level data from the 2000 Income and Expenditure Survey and the September 2000 Labour Force Survey, building a model of income and other variables with which to evaluate the impact of the CSG and the OAP on children's school attendance. The attendance rate in the full sample averages 94 percent. The model establishes that household receipt of an OAP is associated with a 20–25 percent reduction in the school nonattendance gap, and receipt of a CSG associated with a 25 percent reduction in the nonattendance gap (receipt of a Disability Grant has no impact). Significantly, the OAP results are strongly affected by the gender of the recipient: receipt by a female is associated with about a one-third reduction in the nonattendance gap, but receipt by a male has no significant impact. The most significant of other socioeconomic variables positively affecting attendance is the number of years of education of the household head; one year of education is equivalent to twice the impact of the OAP. This suggests that cash grants can have very long-term impacts. If they succeed in increasing schooling now, the results will be even better for the next generation. Household income is also significantly and positively correlated with attendance, but interestingly cash grant income has a greater impact than non-grant income. Samson et al. (2004, 62–63) hypothesize that grant recipients have different spending patterns, prioritizing school attendance more than non-grant recipients. Poverty has a significant negative impact on attendance. Attendance is also more likely in female-headed households and where there are resident elderly members (controlling for pension receipt). These results hold across provinces and the rural-urban divide.

Some similar results are found in national-level October Household Survey data, also analyzed by Samson et al. (2004), with respect to the importance of the poverty level and education of the household head. Controlling for demographic, geographic, and other variables and using several models with different specifications, pension receipt has significant positive effects on school attendance in poor households. Disaggregating gender differences for households in the poorest quartile (measured by expenditure), receipt of an OAP increases the likelihood of boys' full-time school attendance by 3 percent and girls' attendance by 7 percent. A R500 increase in the OAP given to a household of five increases boys' school attendance by 2 percent and girls' school attendance by 5 percent. Household size has no bearing on the effects on boys, but it has a significant negative impact on girls, consistent with the findings from many countries that under conditions of limited resources, girls' education is likely to suffer first, and thus cash transfers can have a greater impact on girls than on boys (see also the CCT results given later).

Other evidence of the impacts of UCTs on education comes from an evaluation of the SCTS started in 2004 in two agricultural blocks of the Kalomo District in Zambia. The evaluation used a survey of approximately 300 households (considered representative of the 1,000 households in the SCTS), focus groups, and key informant interviews. The survey and focus groups were conducted at baseline and one year later. The study did not have a control group, so the results are not definitive because the influence of environmental factors, institutions, and economic conditions could not be determined; in particular, a severe drought probably had a significant effect (Zambia, MCDSS/GTZ 2006, 9–12). For almost all age groups, children in households in the SCTS at baseline had lower enrollment rates than the provincial average. Between baseline and program evaluation, school enrollment for children ages seven through eighteen increased by 3 percentage points, from 76.1 to 79.3 percent. This occurred for almost all age groups, except those ages sixteen through eighteen, suggesting that the grant was least able to affect schooling choices for this age group (this was also the one age group that had a baseline average almost 9 points higher than the provincial average). The largest increase, however, was for fourteen- to fifteen-year-olds (8 percentage points), as well as five- to six-year-olds (10.4 percentage points) (Zambia, MCDSS/GTZ 2006, 36). Like Case, Hosegood, and Lund (2005) in the South Africa study, the Kalomo study authors hypothesize that children were starting school earlier and staying in primary school longer due to improved nutrition as well as their ability to pay school fees.

The study also found significant gender differences. For girls, enrollment stayed the same or went down slightly for almost all age groups, whereas for boys it went up substantially for almost all age groups. For seven- through thirteen-year-olds, enrollment went down by 1 percentage point for girls and up by 7.1 points for boys. For ages fourteen through eighteen, it was unchanged for girls but went up by 7.7 points for boys. The exception to the gender pattern was the enrollment of five- through six-year-olds, which showed a huge increase for both (10.9 points for girls and 9.5 for boys), and the sixteen through eighteen age group. Some households appear to have decided to send some and not other children to school, with the percentage of households not sending at least one child (age seven through eighteen) dropping from 41.4 percent to 33.8 percent (Zambia, MCDSS/GTZ 2006,

36–37). With a very small cash grant, parents may feel able to let one or more children go to school while keeping the others at home (see the reasons for absenteeism discussed later).

The authors attribute the lack of a greater impact on the already high enrollment rates to the small amount of the grant. However, there was substantial room for improvement in enrollment rates, and this also does not explain the gender differences. The study sample at baseline had substantially higher enrollment rates for older girls ages fifteen through eighteen but not for the younger ones. The difference could also be due to parents' choices to prioritize boys' education over girls' under conditions of scarce resources. The notion of conditioning a cash transfer to respond to gender biases—with grants higher for girls than boys and higher for secondary school attendance than primary—might be effective in this context. The conclusion that the grant (about $10 per month for households with children) was too small to have the desired impact for all children is an important operational lesson. This is felt most at the secondary level, where school is not free and often involves boarding costs, although primary education also involves costs for transportation and for school-related associations and activities.

The evaluation also measured the program's impact on absenteeism, finding that longer periods of absenteeism (10 days or more) increased, whereas shorter periods (1–9 days) decreased, for both boys and girls. Substantially more cases of absenteeism involved the short periods, so the authors hypothesize that the program could have contributed to mitigating effects of the drought (this could not be tested due to the presence of neither a control group nor information on district averages of absenteeism). Rises in absenteeism are seen as possibly resulting from the major drought; increased food insecurity could have led to more illnesses and the need for children to miss school in order to work. The main reasons given for absenteeism included illness, unpaid fees, and the need for children in the household. These reasons support the conclusion that the amount of the cash transfer was not sufficient to overcome these problems (Zambia, MCDSS/GTZ 2006, 38).

Results from the evaluation of the scaling-up Mchinji Cash Transfer program, which began in 2007, showed some impact on school enrollment and attendance for children ages six through eighteen over the approximately one-year period between the baseline and final follow-up survey. From March to September 2007, the study looked at school enrollment and retention among 721 children under eleven years old and 459 children from eleven to fourteen years old. The program appears to have served a protective function, keeping some children from leaving school. For intervention households receiving the transfers, there was an increase of less than 1 percentage point in school enrollment; however, among children in households not receiving the transfers (the comparison group), the enrollment figure dropped by 4 percentage points for the under-eleven-year-olds and about 2 percentage points for eleven- to fourteen-year-olds (Miller et al. 2007).[1] From March 2007 to March/April 2008, the percentage of children newly enrolled in school was more than twice as high in intervention households (8.3 percent) as in comparison households (3.4 percent). Over this same period, a total of 96 percent of children from intervention households were enrolled in school compared to 84 percent of children in comparison households, representing a difference in enrollment of 12 percentage points (Miller, Tsoka, and Reichert 2008, 29).

Although absences were roughly equal at baseline, after a year, children from households receiving the Mchinji cash transfer were absent 1.3 days fewer (the previous month) than children from comparison households. Dropout rates were higher in the comparison group (5 percent) than among intervention children (2 percent). The transfer may also have had an effect on school performance: 14 percent of intervention household heads reported that their children had excellent school performance compared to 10 percent of comparison household heads; however, the study could not confirm these findings with school officials due to inadequate data from local schools (Miller, Tsoka, and Reichert 2008, 29–31).

The 2006 evaluation of the Ethiopian Productive Safety Net Programme (PSNP) did not measure changes in rates of school enrollment or attendance but rather asked whether households enrolled more children and kept children in school longer in the present year versus the previous (pre-program) year. Thirty-nine percent of households reported that they had enrolled more children, with 32.6 percent attributing this to the PSNP. Almost 50 percent of households said that they had kept children in school longer rather than withdrawing them when cash or food was short, with 43 percent attributing this to the program (Devereux et al. 2006, 36). A more recent and larger evaluation of the PSNP found that households receiving at least half the transfer amount they should have received over a one-year period showed a large increase in the school attendance of boys ages six through sixteen, of 12 percentage points, increasing boys' average attendance rate to 51 percent relative to 39 percent in the control group.[2] However, there was almost no impact on girls'

[1] The group against which the intervention group was measured is referred to as a comparison group rather than a control group because the intervention and comparison households were not demographically identical at baseline; children appear to have been prioritized in the intervention areas, whereas elderly households appear to have been prioritized in the comparison areas. However, the authors of the study point out that the households were the same in terms of monthly expenditures, food insecurity, and asset ownership (Miller, Tsoka, and Reichert 2008, viii).

[2] Half the transfer amount was equivalent to 90 birr per person (at a wage of 6 birr per day, equivalent to 15 days' work per person). Households were intended to receive up to 5 days' work per month for each household member, but actual employment, as well as payments, were less than that planned.

school attendance. In fact, the study found some evidence suggesting that the time spent on domestic chores fell for boys while rising for girls (Gilligan, Hoddinott, and Taffesse 2007, 56–58). These gender differences found in Ethiopia and elsewhere highlight the importance of attention to reaching girls in program design (this could include, but is not limited to, CCTs).

The remaining findings on the impact of UCTs on education come from assessments of how the cash transfer was spent or the general distribution of expenditures, looking at the proportion spent on education expenses (Figure 6.1). Although not an indication of the impact of grants on education, it does suggest that the grant helps parents to afford education. Some studies are specific with respect to the percentage of the grant or the overall income spent on education, while others report on whether or not some grant income was spent on education. Where proportions are included, the amount spent on education is usually seen to have been quite small, with food and food-related expenses by far the largest use of the grant. Given that the poorest people normally spend a greater proportion of their income on food, this is to be expected and is not out of line with the main program objectives. Furthermore, expenditures on school expenses do not capture the contributions

Figure 6.1—Unconditional cash transfer spending on education

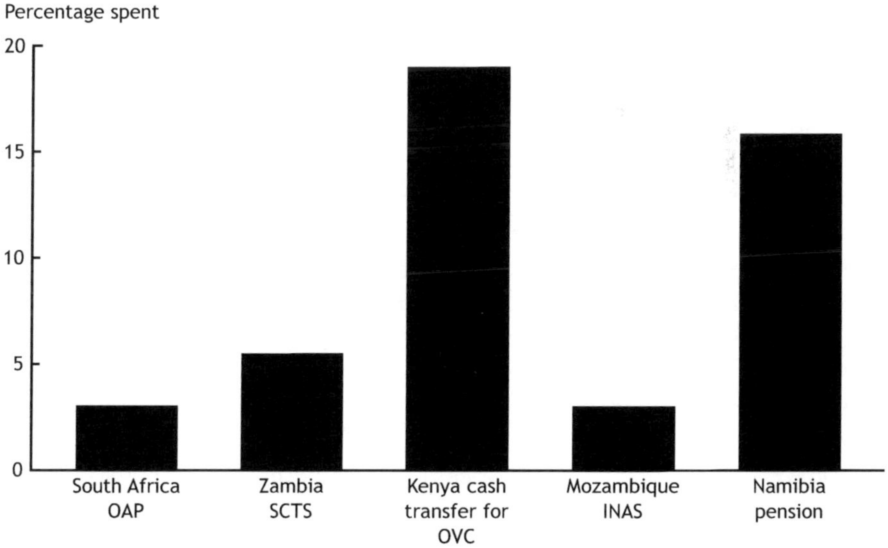

Sources: Devereux (2002); Moller and Ferreira (2003); Zambia, MCDSS/GTZ (2006); Acacia Consultants (2007).

Notes: In the case of Zambia's Social Cash Transfer Scheme (SCTS), the figure represents the proportion of overall spending by beneficiaries on health. INAS = National Institute of Social Welfare.

to education from having healthier and better-nourished students. Nevertheless, expenditures contribute to the educational impacts of cash transfers.

Education spending was one issue examined in a study of social grants by Booysen (2004b) in two communities in South Africa's Free State Province in 2001–02. This study compared HIV- and AIDS-affected households (defined as experiencing morbidity or mortality with at least one person known to be HIV positive or to have died in the past six months) with nonaffected households. An earlier study by Booysen et al. (2004) found that AIDS-affected households spent less on education than nonaffected households, probably due to expenditures on healthcare and funerals, the need to take children out of school to help the household cope with illness and death, or the inability to pay for school fees. Comparing employment with grant income, Booysen (2004b, 22–23) found that employment income led to greater expenditures on food, education, and healthcare. Grant income resulted in a higher rate of increase in food expenditures compared to employment income. However, social grants did not increase expenditures on education; in fact, receipt of the CSG was associated with a reduction in education spending.[3] There are a few possible explanations for these results. One is that people prefer to use the additional income from grants to increase their food intake. Another is that the CSG is used for the entire family, not for specific child-based expenditures. Booysen clarifies that given the small sample size and purposive sampling, the findings cannot be generalized to other parts of South Africa. Still, at least where these spending patterns hold, Booysen asks whether reaching school-age children more directly might require grants administered by the education system, for example, via a system paying for school fees.

In Malawi, recipients reported spending some of the cash transfer from the DECT program on school uniforms, pens, books, and other education costs, but this amount was very small: between January and March 2007, an average of only 3 percent of the transfer was spent on education (Devereux et al. 2007, 38, 72). In the FACT program in Malawi, education and health expenditures are reported together, so we cannot disaggregate education spending; however, the average for both between January and March 2007 was 9.7 percent of total expenditures. It appears that more of this was spent on health costs than on education, because the study reports that the second major item of spending after food and groceries was healthcare and devotes some discussion to what the health expenditures were on, whereas no mention was made of education spending (Devereux, Mvula, and Solomon 2006, 29–30).

The Zambian SCTS study did not capture spending of the transfer specifically but rather looked at the breakdown of overall consumption at baseline

---

[3] Spending on education was also positively associated with more educated and with younger household heads, and with urban households.

and evaluation (a better measure, because the cash is fungible). Expenditures on education increased by a small amount during the evaluation period: from 3.9 to 5.5 percent of overall expenditures (Zambia, MCDSS/GTZ 2006, 49). Education spending varied widely across locations, however: in two of the three blocks, almost no one reported spending on education, whereas in the third block, entirely rural, the percentage of households spending some amount on education rose from 15.2 to 29.7 percent, which may reflect the required contribution from parents to the schools in rural areas (Zambia, MCDSS/GTZ 2006, 37, 49).

In the pre-pilot cash transfer program in Kenya, 67 percent of households reported spending some of the grant on school fees. Breaking down the use of the grant across expenditure categories, 19 percent of the grant was spent on school expenses (Acacia Consultants 2007). Caretakers' claims that they spent some of the grant on school expenses were backed up by children, "who more often than not, proudly showed off new school uniforms. Many of the children who had been out-of-school said that they were now attending classes again" (CRIN 2005, 4).

OAPs also appear to be affecting children's education via spending allocations. In Lesotho, 50 percent of pensioners spend some of their pension on education and associated costs (Croome 2006). In Namibia, 15.5 percent of the pension income diverted to grandchildren is spent on education-related expenses, including school funds (for building upkeep), uniforms, hostel fees, books, and exam fees (Devereux 2001, 43, 49). In the north, due to higher income levels and the higher value placed on education, the percentage of pension income going to education is 28.6 percent. There is no evidence of gender discrimination in pension income benefits (Devereux 2001, 48). Moller and Ferreira (2003) report that in South Africa, only 3 percent of the OAP was spent on educational expenses. However, a report by HelpAge International (2002, cited by Schubert et al. 2007) finds that between 30 and 40 percent (for men and women, respectively) of South African older people's expenditures were on school expenses. Although one study measures pension spending and the other overall expenditures, the discrepancy appears large and the reason is not clear.

A less positive assessment of the impact of UCTs on schooling is found in the simulations undertaken for 15 African countries by Kakwani, Soares, and Son (2005). The first study is an ex ante assessment of the impact of a cash transfer on national poverty and school attendance. It examines the determinants of school attendance based on households' demand for education to determine the impact of the different transfer scenarios on school attendance. The analysis indicates that a transfer worth 0.5 percent of GDP does not bring about significant increases in school attendance rates. Even if the transfer is targeted only to the poor, the boost in attendance is negligible (ranging from 0.04 percent in Malawi to 0.42 percent in Côte d'Ivoire). If 30 percent of the poverty line is transferred to all school-age children, impacts range from negative in Nigeria to just shy of 3 percent in Burundi and Zambia (Kakwani, Soares, and Son 2005).

A second study in the same 15 African countries offers a more positive outlook with respect to OAPs. Kakwani and Subbarao (2005) examine whether children living in elderly-headed households or with elderly alone suffer a disadvantage in education compared to children not living with elderly. They find that for boys, moving from a non-elderly-headed household to an elderly-headed household increases the probability of school attendance, particularly in urban areas. For girls, the relationship varies by country: in Burkina Faso, Burundi, Côte d'Ivoire, Ghana, and Guinea, the probability of girls' attending school falls when they shift to elderly-headed households. In Cameroon, Nigeria, Uganda, and Zambia, the opposite is true. The authors conclude that a social pension targeted to poor elderly-headed households *could* contribute to reducing female disadvantage in schooling (Kakwani and Subbarao 2005, 26–27).

Impacts of Conditional Cash Transfers on Education

Cash transfers conditioned on education are the oldest form of CCT, seen as early as 1995 at a regional level in Brazil, and the most commonly implemented. Table 6.2 summarizes some key impacts of CCTs on education in 11 countries. The education component of CCTs normally requires school enrollment, resulting in a school attendance rate of around 85 percent. With respect to these conditionalities, education CCTs tend to have less variation than the health and nutrition components, which have more varied requirements with respect to service participation, age of family members targeted, and adult education. The main variations with respect to education CCT design are, first, whether they are conditioned on primary school only, secondary school only, or both; second, whether they offer a different transfer size for girls and for boys; third, whether they include an in-kind transfer of school supplies; and fourth, whether they include a small transfer intended for the teacher or for school improvements. Other variations may include voluntary forms of participation for parents, such as in parent-teacher associations. For CCTs with primary and secondary school conditions, the transfer is higher for secondary school because the opportunity cost of children's schooling is normally higher for older children and because parents are more likely to send their children to primary school, giving less priority to higher levels of education. Children who themselves decide to drop out are also more likely to make this decision at the secondary level. It is most often at the point of transition from primary to secondary school that children are likely to be taken out or decide to leave school. These risks tend to be more pronounced for girls than for boys (except for the opportunity cost of schooling, which in many contexts tends to be higher for boys than for girls), so CCTs often provide a larger transfer for girls than for boys, at both primary and secondary levels.

CCTs have had dramatic impacts on education outcomes for children. The magnitude varies considerably, often based on the level of education indicators at baseline; that is, if pre-program enrollment levels are very high, the CCT's impacts tend to be lower. The type of impact also varies, including, among others, enrollment, attendance, grade progression, return of school dropouts, and school achievement. The impacts reported are from evaluations conducted in Honduras, Mexico, Nicaragua, and Ecuador using randomized designs, and from evaluations in Bangladesh, Brazil, Cambodia, Colombia, Pakistan, and Turkey using quasi-experimental methods.[4] A number of African countries are piloting or have proposed to pilot CCTs, including Kenya, South Africa, Uganda, and Zambia, with others under discussion. As noted in Chapter 5, some of the evaluations involve comparisons of CCTs and UCTs.

Mexico

Schooling impacts for Mexico's PROGRESA are based on a panel survey carried out in 1998-99 by IFPRI. PROGRESA was found to have brought about a minimal change in primary school enrollment of only about 1.45 percentage points for girls and 1.07 percentage points for boys.[5] This was because the level of primary school enrollment started out very high, between about 90 and 96 percent at baseline. At the secondary school level, where enrollment started out low—at 67 percent for girls and 73 percent for boys—impacts were much higher: 9.3 percentage points for girls (a proportional increase of 14 percent) and 5.8 points for boys (an 8 percent increase). The largest impact was on girls enrolling in grade 7, the transition year when they most often drop out: 14.8 percentage points (Schultz 2001, 2004). For all children ages eleven to fourteen, the program was especially effective in reducing the dropout rate, encouraging the transition to secondary school. It also encouraged school reentry, although this lasted only about a year and children tended to drop out

[4] The evaluations in Honduras, Mexico, and Nicaragua, by IFPRI, used a "difference-in-difference" methodology whereby control and treatment groups are compared at baseline and at some point in time (often at several points in a repeated panel) after program implementation. Because there are likely to be some observable or unobservable differences between the two groups at baseline and because changes are likely to occur in both groups that are not attributable to the program, the difference-in-difference methodology subtracts these differences in the control groups from that in the treatment group to obtain a measure of the impact of the program. Note that these evaluations used the fact that the program could only be rolled out gradually to identify control groups—localities that were not yet in the program.

[5] The enrollment impact figures reported are from a smaller "unpooled" sample that includes only households interviewed in every round of the panel survey.

Table 6.2—Impacts of conditional cash transfers on education

Country, program	School enrollment				School attendance	
	Primary		Secondary			
	Girls	Boys	Girls	Boys	Primary	Secondary
Mexico, PROGRESA	+1.45 percentage points	+1.07 percentage points	+9.3 percentage points	+5.8 percentage points	*	*
Mexico, Oportunidades			+24 percent (rural) +4 percent (urban)			
Nicaragua, RPS	+12.8 percentage points		n.a.	n.a.	+17 percent girls +23 percent boys	n.a.
Brazil, Bolsa Escola					+3 percentage points (ages ten through fifteen; not reported by level of school)	
Honduras, PRAF	*				+4.5 percentage points	
Colombia, Familias en Acción	+2.5 percentage points (rural) +1.5 percentage points (urban ages eight through thirteen)	+17.2 percent (rural) +13.9 percent (urban)				

Ecuador, Bono de Desarrollo Humano	+10 percentage points	n.a.	n.a.	+12 percentage points for (girls ages eleven through eighteen)	*	n.a.
Bangladesh, FSSAP	n.a.					
Bangladesh, ROSC	+8.9 percentage points (ages six through fourteen) +10.6 percentage points (ages six through eight) (grant + allowance) * (grant-only)					
Pakistan			+9 percentage points	n.a.		
Turkey	*		+10.7 percentage points	+22.8 percentage points (rural)	+1.3 percentage points (girls)	+5.4 percentage points (girls) * (boys)
Cambodia	n.a.	n.a.	+22-33 percentage points	n.a.	n.a.	+43 percentage points (girls) * (boys)
Jamaica, PATH					+3	

Sources: Schultz (2001); IFPRI (2003b); Khandker, Pitt, and Fuwa (2003); Attanasio and Gomez (2004); Ahmed (2006); Attanasio et al. (2006); Filmer and Schady (2006); Ahmed et al. (2007); Levy and Ohls (2007); Schady and Fiszbein (2007).

Notes: FSSAP = Female Secondary School Assistance Project; PATH = Programme for Advancement through Health and Education; PRAF = Programa de Asignación Familiar; PROGRESA = Programa de Educación, Salud y Alimentación; ROSC = Reaching Out of School Children Programme; RPS = Red de Protección Social; n.a. = not applicable. * indicates that no significant impacts were found. Blank cells indicate that results were not evaluated.

again. For children ages six through ten, the program was associated with less grade repetition and better grade progression (Behrman, Sengupta, and Todd 2001). The program was also associated with a reduction in child labor. For boys ages eight to seventeen, there was a reduction in the probability of working of about 10–14 percent, even higher for ages twelve to fifteen. Girls ages eight to seventeen also had about a 15 percent reduction in the probability of working. The program had no impact for boys or girls ages sixteen to seventeen, however (Parker and Skoufias 2000). PROGRESA had very little impact on school attendance, on achievement as measured by cognitive achievement test scores, and on bringing children back to school who had dropped out (it brought them back initially, but they tended to drop out again after a year) (Behrman, Sengupta, and Todd 2000, 2001).

PROGRESA turned into Oportunidades in 2001, and a subsequent evaluation found a 24 percent increase in secondary school enrollment in rural areas and 4 percent in urban areas. The effects were again stronger for girls than for boys, and almost twice as great for girls in urban areas. The program is credited with increasing the number of girls enrolled in rural secondary school from 83 to every hundred boys enrolled to 96 per hundred boys (Parker 2004).

Nicaragua

Nicaragua's Red de Protección Social (RPS) provided a cash transfer conditioned on primary school (not secondary school) enrollment and attendance. The IFPRI evaluation was of a pilot program in two rural "departments" that started in 2000 and expanded in 2002.[6] Primary school enrollment was low at baseline, 72 percent. The enrollment impacts were huge: for program participants, enrollment increased by about 20 percentage points by 2002. However, the rate for the control groups also rose by 7.6 percentage points, so that the net program impact was 12.8 percentage points. This control group increase was greater than the national rural average and appears to have been the net effect of several factors possibly "contaminating" the controls, including (1) increases in school feeding in the area, (2) possible crowding out at the school level, (3) improvements in supply as a result of the program, and (4) likely changes in expectations in the control group, where some hoped that school attendance might hasten their incorporation into the program. The impacts were greatest for the extreme poor, at 25 percentage points versus 14 points for the poor and 6 percent for the nonpoor (although there were few nonpoor in the sample). There was no significant difference between the impacts on girls and on boys, an outcome expected more at the primary than at the secondary level (Maluccio and Flores 2005).

[6] In 2004, some 21,619 families were enrolled in the program, but the program has since been cancelled.

Nicaragua's RPS also had very high impacts on school attendance rates, at 20 percentage points on average, and as high as 33 percentage points for the extreme poor, 23 points for the poor, and 12 points for the nonpoor. There was a relatively small gender difference, with the program increasing the attendance of girls 17 percent and that of boys 23 percent. Although the program was implemented in areas where schools were generally available, supply-side interventions were also undertaken to accommodate the large enrollment changes: these included increasing the number of sessions per day and the number of teachers. The schooling outcomes are thus interpreted to be a combined effect of the demand and the supply interventions (Maluccio and Flores 2005).

Another program impact was the school continuation rate, measured as grade advancement for two consecutive years, which was 7.3 percentage points on average. An unanticipated impact was a large impact on students making a transition to the fifth and sixth grades, because fifth-grade enrollment and higher was not a program requirement. This could have been a result of confusion as to this requirement, an income effect, or a result of changing attitudes toward education. More evidence on the sustainability question was provided by a follow-up survey two years after households were rotated out of the program. An enrollment drop of 12.5 percentage points indicates that, for many, the cash incentive was driving the impact more than a change in attitude toward education. However, enrollment remained 8 percentage points higher than at baseline, suggesting that for this substantial group the program had some sustainable impact. The program impact on child labor was a decrease of 4.6 percentage points in 2001 and a decrease of 5.6 points in 2002, although child labor decreased significantly among both groups in 2001 due to an economic downturn (Maluccio and Flores 2005). RPS was also found to have protected human capital during the shock of the coffee crisis of that period, with program impacts on enrollment and child labor greater in coffee-growing regions than in non-coffee-growing areas (Maluccio 2005).

Latin America and the Caribbean: Brazil, Colombia, Ecuador, Honduras, and Jamaica

In Brazil's Bolsa Escola, the average program impact on attendance was 3 percentage points among boys ages ten through fifteen, which was not small given that the attendance rate of the comparison group was around 92 percent (Cardoso and Souza 2003). The program was associated with a reduction of 7.8 percentage points in dropout rates (an improvement in complete-year attendance) and a gain of 6.2 percentage points in grade promotion (de Janvry, Finan, and Sadoulet 2006).

Colombia's Familias en Acción had an enrollment impact on eight- through thirteen-year-olds of 1.5 and 2.5 percentage points in urban and rural areas, respectively, probably explained by the high enrollment starting point. Secondary school enrollment impacts were higher: 13.9 percentage points in urban areas and 17.2 points in rural areas. Attendance increased by between 4.6 and 10.1 percentage points among children ages twelve through seventeen in rural areas and by between 3.5 and 5.3 percentage points in urban areas (Attanasio and Gomez 2004).

Ecuador's Bono de Desarrollo program increased primary school enrollment by 9.8–12.8 percentage points and reduced child labor by 15.4–20.7 points. The effect on sixth graders was an increase of 17.8 percentage points (Schady and Araujo 2006). The program did not include a secondary school transfer. The evaluation found no impact on achievement test scores (Ponce 2006).

The evaluation of Honduras's PRAF showed a huge increase of 17 percentage points in the probability that children ages five through twelve who were out of school in 2000 would enroll in or return to school in 2001, but this dropped to zero when comparing average rates using a double-difference approach. It may be a result of high levels of enrollment at baseline or of the fact that the control group also sent children to school, hoping to receive the cash transfer. However, the program did show robust impacts on attendance rates of approximately 4.4–4.5 percentage points and reduced dropout rates, from 7.0 to 2.4 percent (IFPRI 2003b).

Jamaica's Programme for Advancement through Health and Education (PATH) focused on school attendance because enrollment was already very high in Jamaica, with an attendance increase of about 3 percent. No significant difference was found in grade advancement or grades (Levy and Ohls 2007).

Asia: Cambodia, Bangladesh, Pakistan, and Turkey

The highest impact of any CCT program was in Cambodia, where pre-program secondary school enrollment for girls was very low. Cambodia's Scholarships for Girls Programme was found to have increased enrollment by 22–33 percentage points and increased attendance by 43 percentage points (Filmer and Schady 2006).

Bangladesh has experimented with three programs: the Bangladesh Primary Education Stipend Program, the Bangladesh Female Secondary School Assistance Project (FSSAP), and the Bangladesh Reaching Out of School Children Programme (ROSC). At the baseline for evaluations of the first two programs, girls' attendance rates were very low, 65 percent and 42 percent, respectively (Ahmed 2004). For FSSAP, the results come from a model, because no control group was available. School-level data indicate that, on average, an additional year of stipend program duration increases the female student secondary enrollment of an incoming cohort by as much as 8 percent. Household-level data, considered a better measure, suggest that an additional year of program duration increases the school enrollment rate of girls ages eleven through eighteen by 12 percentage points, and has no discernible effect on boys' enrollment (Khandker, Pitt, and Fuwa 2003, 24–25).

Implemented in 2005, ROSC was designed to bring out-of-school children to school with (1) a cash educational allowance for students and (2) grants to schools where these children enrolled. In 60 percent of the project area, both educational allowances and grants to schools were provided. In the remaining 40 percent of the area, only grants to schools were provided, but the amount of the grant was almost double the amount received by grant-plus-allowance schools. In grant-only areas, ROSC did not seem to bring about any significant net change in enrollment in primary school. In grant-plus-allowance areas, however, ROSC induced an average net increase in primary school enrollment of 8.9 percentage points for children ages six through fourteen and 10.6 percentage points for children ages six through eight, implying the importance of the demand-side stimulus over the supply-side stimulus alone. The actual increase in program areas was 21 percent, but the control areas also saw increased enrollment of 12.1 percent during the project period, resulting in the 8.9 percent program-related impact (Ahmed 2006).

A CCT program in Pakistan also had an impact on girls' secondary school opportunities. The Female Secondary School Stipend program in Punjab increased enrollment by 9 percentage points (Schady and Fiszbein 2007).

The CCT program in Turkey had a strong objective of increasing education, particularly for girls. It had little impact on primary school enrollment because of the high enrollment rate at baseline but had large effects for secondary school girls, increasing their enrollment by 10.7 percentage points. In rural areas, there was an increase of 16.7 percentage points in the probability of enrollment in secondary school; for boys this impact was 22.8 percentage points. The program increased primary school attendance for girls by 1.3 percentage points, and secondary school attendance for girls by 5.4 percentage points. The program appears to have improved test scores for primary school children, but, given the small impact on school attendance, the authors propose that the effect may have been through helping beneficiary households to make better use of the schooling inputs and increasing the attention given to schooling within the family. The program had no effect on the rate of progression from primary school to secondary school (Ahmed et al. 2007). Adato et al. (2007) used ethnographic research that helped to explain the education results, including the reasons that girls' schooling rates did not increase more than they did, particularly in socially conservative parts of southeastern Turkey. Women's primary roles as wife and mother and concerns over honor and reputation, compounded by the long distances that would need to be traveled to reach secondary schools and other issues, often overpowered the cash incentive, pointing to the importance of a contextual understanding of the constraints to increasing demand for education if CCTs are to be effective (Adato et al. 2007).

Complementary Activities in Education and New Program Designs in the Context of AIDS

Cash transfers can support AIDS-affected families by helping them to keep their children in school when families face financial constraints that might force children to leave school. Children may also leave voluntarily. For certain age groups, leaving school may not only affect their future economic prospects but also pose a risk to their health. As noted earlier, recent studies have found that girls enrolled in school are less likely to engage in risky sexual behavior than those who are not enrolled. Also as noted earlier, two new studies, in Malawi (Baird, McIntosh, and Özler, 2009) and South Africa (Pettifor and MacPhail 2009), are investigating how effective monetary incentives can be in promoting schooling and reducing HIV risk. In the South African study, cash transfers combined with a community-based mobilization approach around prevention is being compared with each intervention alone to determine what kinds of synergies exist between these approaches (Pettifor and MacPhail 2009). Opportunities for education programs for children and adults can be provided in association with cash transfers, even when participation in services is not obligatory but rather voluntary. The existence of a cash transfer program can be used creatively to encourage participation in activities that strengthen the human capital of children and adults. Some examples follow.

Early Childhood Development

One of the opportunities under exploration is for early childhood development (ECD) services. Many aspects of the HIV/AIDS epidemic can jeopardize early childhood development. Young children depend on caregivers, who may be overworked and demoralized—and possibly ill themselves—and therefore less attentive to children and less able to meet their needs. As discussed earlier, young children suffer from the trauma of facing the illness and death of parents and other family members, social instability as they are moved across families, abandonment, and other stresses. These conditions can compromise children's physical and psychological development (Richter, Foster, and Sherr 2006, 8). An ECD component of a cash transfer program could boost the effect of the transfer on child development and promote better learning and other outcomes as children reach school age (Kakwani, Soares, and Son 2006). The World Bank explored options for conditioning ECD services in a session on this topic at the Third International Conference on Conditional Cash Transfers in 2006 (World Bank 2006a).

In South Africa, the Human Sciences Research Council was designing a demonstration project to test alternative approaches to ECD, such as home- versus center-based care and alternative job hierarchies in provision and supervision that are suitable to low-skilled service providers (Altman 2007). Although the project is not currently linked to a cash transfer, ideas had been discussed for creating synergies with the CSG.[7] In Malawi, the Ministry of Education, along with UNICEF, is supporting expanded ECD services. Guides for ECD caregivers were distributed to community-based childcare centers, and initial efforts have been made to incorporate ECD into the country's primary curriculum (UNICEF 2007a). In Malawi's SCTS, there are plans for CBOs to follow up with especially vulnerable beneficiaries and, along with extension workers and child protection workers, ensure that these children can access ECD services (UNICEF 2007b).

School-Based Interventions

Other plans envision the extension of linkages (hard or soft conditionalities or unconditional linkages) between cash transfer programs and schools through school-based interventions such as after-school programs, care and support programs, and AIDS education.[8] In South Africa, the KwaZulu-Natal Department of Education and the Media in Education Trust (MiET) has recently piloted a program based on MiET's concept of "schools as centres of care and support," including a package of training for school management, staff, and support teams to identify vulnerable children, refer them to support agencies, and assist them in gaining access to resources such as food, grants, and psychosocial support. Training is also provided to peer educators on HIV and AIDS, including coping, access to treatment, and other information.[9] In Cambodia, World Education's in-school Information, Education, and Communication (IEC) and Life Skills Training for HIV/AIDS combines a life skills approach with peer education for in-school youth. Another part of the strategy creates health clubs for in-school youth where members engage in HIV education and outreach activities, community mobilization, and IEC development and dissemination.[10]

If cash transfers succeed in increasing children's presence in school, their benefits multiply by increasing children's exposure to these additional services. In turn, contacts with children and parents through schools could serve as a means of promoting awareness of and access to cash transfers.

---

[7] Personal communication with Miriam Altman, March 2007.

[8] Exploring the potential of these linkages was a proposal that emerged from a meeting of international organizations in late 2007 (UNICEF 2008).

[9] See www.miet.co.za/content.aspx?ContentId=12.

[10] See www.worlded.org/WEIInternet/projects/ListProjects.cfm?Select.

Conclusion

Several key lessons emerge from the findings on the impacts of UCTs and CCTs on education. First, we know that both types of transfers have significant positive impacts on school enrollment and attendance, though with a number of caveats noted further later. The fact that we find these impacts with and without conditionalities raises questions about the added value of conditionality, also discussed further later. The fact that CCTs have not demonstrated an impact on indicators of school achievement raises a critical issue: the importance of supply-side constraints. School quality deficiencies are suspected as contributing to the lack of achievement impacts in Mexico (see Behrman, Parker, and Todd 2009). The significance of supply-side constraints will only be magnified in Sub-Saharan Africa, limiting the potential of cash transfers, conditional or unconditional, to protect the education of children in AIDS-affected families. As discussed in Chapter 4, the insufficient quantity and quality of schools also calls into question the feasibility of schooling-based conditions.

There are still other questions about the need for conditions in Sub-Saharan Africa. Research in several Latin American countries has demonstrated the added value of conditionalities in education. But this has not been demonstrated in Sub-Saharan Africa. In fact, the only results from Africa thus far comparing CCTs with UCTs, conducted in Malawi among AIDS-affected communities (and with the aim of HIV risk reduction), found no additional benefit from conditionality (with some caveats). This suggests that the cash transfer there increases school attendance because people have more money, not because they fear losing their transfer if their children do not attend school (Baird, McIntosh, and Özler 2009).

Most cash transfer programs to date in southern and East Africa have been unconditional. This chapter reviewed the evidence on the impacts of these programs thus far, finding that although evidence is just emerging from a few countries, that which exists shows positive impacts. However, there are strong gender differences in the data in several countries, highlighting the fact that putting cash in the hands of households will not reduce gender discrimination in education and may, in fact, increase the gender disparities if new resources lead to gains in boys' schooling only. Gender disparities may be exacerbated in households where AIDS has undermined income sources; where fewer children can continue schooling and parents must choose between them, they may choose the boys, as was seen in the Zambia data. Furthermore, gender disparities are likely to be even greater in households where family members are ill or have died, where girls are required to stay at home to provide care for adults or children. Conditioning transfers is one way to confront these disparities, offering higher transfers for girls' school attendance than for boys', which is a feature of many CCT programs designed to counteract discrimination against girls in education. Another option would be to offer a supplemental transfer—above the amount of the standard transfer—to families that have all of their girls enrolled. But again, these designs would work only if other contextual aspects were right for conditioning transfers. There are also age differences in cash transfer impacts—with impacts tending to be higher at the youngest ages. This may reflect lower baseline enrollment at these younger ages, improved school readiness because of better diets, or an initial enthusiasm to send children to school that diminishes in subsequent years. Higher impacts at older ages also sometimes reflect lower baseline rates, as in the Latin American programs.

Another interesting choice is between OAPs and household or child support grants. Modeling of data from 15 African countries indicated that OAPs had a significant effect on girls' schooling, whereas a UCT did not; however, whether real-world conditions would bear this out is untested, and evidence is needed to compare these two types of interventions in a given country's context (a study in Zambia will provide this in the future). Thus far, evidence from these different types of grants alone show the impacts on children's education of both, again with important gender dynamics and caveats. The proportion of OAPs spent on children's education in Lesotho and Namibia also suggests that these pensions may be an effective means of improving enrollment and attendance rates. Given that many parents have died from AIDS and their children are left living with grandparents ("skip-generation households") and that children who have parents still live with grandparents for a variety of reasons, an OAP can be an effective way to reach children. In some countries, OAPs may also be more politically acceptable because the elderly are seen as a group more in need or deserving of government grants than families with adults who could, in theory, be working. However, there are also reasons that OAPs are likely to miss families and children in need. There are many children in families who do not have pensioners or whose pensioners may not be able or willing to spend their income on children's education. There is also the risk that when the pensioner dies, the income will be cut off and the child will no longer be able to afford school. Ideally, a country with a good social protection system would have both types of grants, as in the case of South Africa. But where this is not yet viable and a major objective of a cash transfer is to keep children in school, a CSG given to each child is the more direct route for targeting. Still, there remain differences of opinion on this issue, and there is insufficient evidence to allow us to make definitive statements in a given country context.

CHAPTER 7

Cash Transfers and Health

Cash transfers can affect families' health in several ways: by covering costs directly associated with accessing healthcare (including transportation expenses, medical fees, and the opportunity costs of time), by increasing food consumption (both the quantity and the quality of nutrients), and by incentivizing participation in preventive healthcare and health education when transfers are conditional. Also, other investments associated with income gains, such as improved hygiene and sanitation, can stimulate better health. All of these pathways are beneficial for HIV- and AIDS-affected communities, including households that suffer from increased healthcare costs and face increasing nutritional needs, as well as households that could benefit from behavior change to prevent infection.

Impacts of Unconditional Cash Transfers on Health

Access to Health Services and Service Use

Evaluation results from Concern Worldwide's DECT project in Malawi found that the transfer contributed to better access to healthcare during the five months of the program. The DECT transfer provided purchasing power for expenses such as transportation, hospital bills, and medicines, which enabled beneficiaries to access healthcare services more easily. In qualitative interviews, program participants reported improved access to healthcare, leading to overall improvements in their health status and general well-being. This benefit is particularly noteworthy because it occurred during the time of year when disease prevalence is highest in rural Malawi. These improvements were important for groups with the weakest resistance to disease, such as malnourished individuals and those affected by HIV and AIDS (Devereux et al. 2007, 40). A factor that may have facilitated this outcome is the fact that Concern Worldwide community liaison staff delivered health-related messages as part of sensitization campaigns on DECT paydays. Messages promoted using the transfer to feed the family and invest in farming and also conveyed information about HIV prevention. Concern staff also targeted chiefs and elders separately in an effort to reach more men with sensitive messages about HIV and AIDS (Devereux et al. 2007, 9–10).

Evaluation results from the scaling-up Mchinji Cash Transfer program illustrated important improvements in healthcare access for both adults and children. At baseline in March 2007, the share of households reporting inadequate healthcare for adults was about equal between intervention and comparison households at roughly 80 percent. By June 2007, about three months after the start of the program, fewer than 20 percent of the intervention households claimed inadequate healthcare compared to more than 60 percent of the comparison households (Miller et al. 2007). Members of intervention households—both adults and children—were also more likely than those in comparison households to obtain care when they were ill: 84 percent of beneficiary adults received care when sick compared to 10 percent of nonbeneficiary adults, and 80 percent of beneficiary children received care compared to 8 percent of nonbeneficiary children. Of all children, 80 percent of those in intervention households were reported to receive "just enough" or "more than enough" healthcare when ill, compared to only 20 percent of children in comparison households (Miller, Tsoka, and Reichert 2008, 23, 25). As of September 2007, of all children who did not receive care during their last illness due to lack of money, 75 percent were from comparison households and only 14 percent were from intervention households. Among the intervention children, there was an increase in the use of private hospitals and medicines such as antibiotics and painkillers, as well as decreased use of herbs for treatment (Miller, Tsoka, and the Mchinji Evaluation Team 2007).

In South Africa, a study of barriers to healthcare use and illness-related impoverishment involving 280 households across two communities (Goudge et al. 2007, 2009) found that cash transfers accelerated access to healthcare beyond the effect of the income transfer. The study found that grant recipients seeking treatment at health facilities were far more likely to be granted the fee exemptions for which they are eligible (based on their poverty status) than were those eligible for the exemptions but not receiving grants: 100 percent of CSG recipients and 82 percent of pension and disability grant recipients received the exemptions. Of those neither receiving grants nor earning income, only 55 percent received the exemptions. Those receiving grants were assumed to be eligible and thus not required to show proof of income, while those not receiving grants had to document their eligibility (Goudge et al. 2007). Qualitative research also found that cash transfers protected against illness-related risks by making healthcare and transportation to clinics and hospitals more affordable, by enabling automatic qualification for fee exemptions, and by strengthening social networks that could be called upon if needed (Goudge et al. 2009).

Health Outcomes

Although there is limited evidence documenting the impact of UCTs on health outcomes—mostly because quantitative impact evaluations of UCT programs measuring these have not yet been completed—evidence from several countries shows the protective effect of these cash transfers on health (Table 7.1).

Much of the important evidence on health impacts comes from studies of impacts of the OAP in South Africa. These are important findings because so many households affected by AIDS have pensioners, either in three-generation households or in skip-generation households (those in which grandparents are caring for children in the absence of parents). More than 60 percent of the

Table 7.1—Impacts of unconditional cash transfers on health

Country, program	Use of transfer for health	Health outcomes
Ethiopia	29 percent of households spent some of the transfer on health	
Kenya	6 percent of transfer spent on health	
Lesotho	8 percent of pension spent on health	
Malawi, DECT	5 percent of transfer spent on health	Reported improvement in health status (qualitative assessment)
Malawi, Mchinji Cash Transfer	75 percent of households spent some of the transfer on health	Reduced illness in past month: -21 percentage points (adults) -13 percentage points (children) Improvements in child health: +67 percentage points improved health -56 percentage points no change -11 percentage points worse health
Namibia	13.8 percent of pension spent on pensioner health	
South Africa, OAP	3 percent of pension (rural black households)	Improved health for all household members when income is pooled
South Africa, OAP and CSG	Grant made healthcare affordable and ensured automatic hospital fee waivers	
Zambia, SCTS	1.2 percent of transfer spent on health[a]	Reduced incidence of illness: -12 percentage points (children birth to age five and adults ages nineteen through sixty-four) -14.3 percentage points (elderly)

Sources: Case (2001); Devereux (2001); Moller and Ferreira (2003); Croome (2006); Devereux et al. (2006, 2007); Zambia, MCDSS/GTZ (2006); Acacia Consultants (2007); Goudge et al. (2007); Miller, Tsoka, and Reichert (2008).

Notes: CSG = Child Support Grant; DECT = Dowa Emergency Cash Transfer; OAP = Old Age Pension; SCTS = Social Cash Transfer Scheme. Blank cells indicate that results were not evaluated.

[a]This figure represents the proportion of overall spending by beneficiaries on health.

orphaned children in Namibia, South Africa, and Zimbabwe live with their grandparents, as do more than 50 percent in Botswana, Malawi, and Tanzania. The responsibility of elderly caring for orphaned children is increasing as the AIDS epidemic advances. For example, in Namibia between 1992 and 2000, the overall percentage of orphans living with their grandparents increased from 44 to 61 percent (UNICEF 2003; Gorman 2004, 18). Children and adults in a household are likely to benefit if the pensioner is healthier and therefore better able to provide care and to improve living standards in the household (for example, through food and healthcare expenditures for all, being able to afford piped water, and so forth).

In South Africa, Case (2001) compared the self-reported health status of adults living with pensioners with that of adults living without pensioners. She finds that pension income (at R520 per month) had a positive impact on the health of *all* adults in households that pooled their income but only on the health of pensioners in households that did not pool their income. This is consistent with the expectation that in non-income-pooling households pensioners would use a larger share of their pension for personal use, including health needs. Indeed, in income-pooling households, every adult in the household experienced an improvement in health status of 0.5 points on a five-point scale, while in non-income-pooling households pensioners benefited by a full point. The number of non-pension-receiving household members was not associated with health status in income-pooling or non-income-pooling households (Case 2001, 7–10).

Case also explored the mechanisms by which pension income improved health status. In response to open-ended questions, some beneficiaries reported using the pension to purchase more food, and some said they upgraded household facilities through the purchase of paraffin stoves, phones, or improved kitchens, some of which can have consequences for health (Case 2001, 12). Having a pensioner in the household was positively and significantly correlated with the presence of a flush toilet in the home and negatively correlated with an off-site household water source, and the likelihood of having a toilet increased significantly as the duration of pension receipt increased (Case 2001, 14–15). Samson et al. (2004) report a similar finding about piped water: the amount of the OAP and receipt of a Disability Grant were significantly associated with a higher probability that the household had access to piped water (Samson et al. 2004, 85), an amenity that can affect the health of adults and children in the household.

According to the 2006 evaluation of the SCTS in Zambia, the incidence of illness among SCTS beneficiaries declined between the baseline and the follow-up evaluation. At baseline, 43 percent of beneficiaries reported having some illness, and by the evaluation one year later, only 35 percent reported an illness.[1] The most significant impact (a change of 14.2 percentage points) occurred among the elderly (older than age sixty-five), who experienced the highest rate of morbidity at baseline (82 percent). Children under age five and adults of productive age (nineteen through sixty-four) also experienced a reduction of 12 percentage points in the incidence of illness. The evaluators speculate that this was probably due to improved nutrition and hygiene (Zambia, MCDSS/GTZ 2006, 43).

The 2008 evaluation results from Malawi's Mchinji Cash Transfer indicate that there were improvements in the health status of both children and adults. After the program had been in place for one year, the number of adults who reported being ill in the previous month had fallen by 21 percentage points among intervention households (from 80 to 59 percent) compared to 8 percentage points for comparison households (from 81 to 73 percent) (Miller, Tsoka, and Reichert 2008, 23). Similar gains were noted among children. The number of children under age eighteen who were sick in the month before the survey was 13 percentage points lower among intervention households than in comparison households (42 versus 55 percent). The evaluation results also showed a difference in the percentage of change in child illness. In intervention households, 23.4 percent fewer children experienced illness in the previous month versus only 12.5 percent fewer children in comparison households. Intervention households were also more likely than comparison households to report that their children had excellent health (31 versus 13 percent) and less likely to report that their children had poor or fair health (13 versus 33 percent). Among intervention households, 81 percent reported that their children's health had improved from March 2007 to March/April 2008 compared to 15 percent among comparison households. At the same time, 3 percent of intervention households said their children's health had worsened compared to 14 percent of comparison households (Miller, Tsoka, and Reichert 2008, 26).

Spending on Health

In the absence of impact data on access to health services, health service use, or health outcomes, some evaluations have used documented changes in household spending on health as indicators of likely health impacts. The results should be interpreted cautiously, however, because high or increased health spending after receiving a transfer can have very different meanings. Although increased spending could indicate improved access to services, it

[1] Illnesses included measles, malaria, tuberculosis, AIDS, asthma, bronchitis, diarrhea, vomiting, anemia, abdominal pains, skin infections, pneumonia, a cough, eye and ear infections, high blood pressure, chest pain, toothaches, mouth infections, and backaches (MCDSS/GTZ 2006, 43).

could also signify increased need for healthcare services. At the same time, low or decreased spending could indicate limited access to healthcare services or a reduced need.

Health expenditures among Zambia's SCTS beneficiaries fell from baseline to evaluation, perhaps indicating that spending priorities had changed or that there was less need for health-related spending because illness prevalence had decreased (Zambia, MCDSS/GTZ 2006, 49). At evaluation, beneficiaries spent an average of 1.2 percent of the transfer on health but 13.2 percent on hygiene products, which could have made some contribution to improving their health (Zambia, MCDSS/GTZ 2006). Similarly, health spending in South Africa fell slightly in the presence of social grants, by just under 1 percentage point for the OAP and just under 0.025 percentage point for the CSG (Samson et al. 2004, 76). Again, this may be because social grants promote better nutrition and education outcomes, which can lead to better health outcomes, making medical spending less necessary.

Croome (2006) found that elderly pensioners in Lesotho spent more on health (hospital or clinic visits and medicine) after they received the transfer compared to before and that, overall, beneficiaries used an average of 8 percent of their pension income on health (Croome 2006). The Namibian social pension provided N$160 per month to the elderly over age sixty, an amount estimated to be sufficient to feed three adults, on average (Devereux 2001, 43). Of the total pension, 13.8 percent was dedicated to pensioner health expenses. Only 28 percent of total pension income was spent on pensioners themselves, with the remainder going to the household or relatives. Grandchildren were the largest group of secondary beneficiaries, receiving more than half of the remaining pension income (55 percent), followed by adult children (25 percent) and spouses (9 percent) (Devereux 2001).

According to the 2006 evaluation of Ethiopia's PSNP, 29 percent of beneficiaries spent some of their cash benefits on health (Devereux et al. 2006, 34). Of these beneficiaries, the poorest were almost twice as likely to use PSNP cash to pay for healthcare (56 percent in the two poorest quintiles versus 23 percent in the two richest quintiles) (Devereux et al. 2006, 35).

Three quarters of all households receiving the Mchinji Cash Transfer in Malawi spent some of the transfer on healthcare (Miller, Tsoka, and Reichert 2008, 40). According to data from September 2007, the average expenditure represented 12.3 percent of the monthly transfer (Miller et al. 2007).

A 2007 evaluation of Kenya's Cash Transfer for OVC found that 37 percent of beneficiaries spent part of their transfer on medical fees, with the average expenditure on health equivalent to 6 percent of the cash transfer. The report also noted that HIV-positive children received ARV treatment, which they had not been able to afford before the cash transfer program, and that some adult beneficiaries, 30-50 percent of whom were HIV-positive or had developed AIDS, used the transfer to purchase ARVs (Acacia Consultants 2007, 16, 24).

Impacts of Conditional Cash Transfers on Health

As in the case of education, many CCT evaluations assess the impact of programs on beneficiaries' use of preventive health services. Although the countries with CCT evaluations have very low HIV prevalence rates, it is nonetheless valuable to investigate program impacts on health—and trends in the types of impacts—achieved by these programs to get a sense of the range of possible impacts associated with different types of programs. Among the documented health-related impacts of CCTs, there is more evidence of changes in the use of services (that is, health checkups and growth monitoring) and less evidence of changes in health outcomes, such as illness prevalence. Table 7.2 and Figure 7.1 summarize health-associated impacts of CCTs in five countries.

Use of Preventive Health Services

The Honduras PRAF evaluation compared three types of CCT interventions: the demand-only intervention involved cash transfers contingent on attendance at health centers, growth monitoring, and school; the supply-only intervention involved the improvement of health and education services; and the demand plus supply intervention involved a conditional transfer along with service improvement. Beneficiary groups receiving each of these interventions were compared to a control group that did not receive any intervention. The impact evaluation showed that the type of intervention affected changes in health service use. For example, the percentage of children under age three who visited healthcare provision units increased by 21 percentage points under the demand-side intervention (a 45 percent relative increase) and 15 percentage points under the demand plus supply intervention. This effect did not vary by child age. The supply-only intervention had no impact on healthcare visits.

PRAF impacts on beneficiary participation in child growth monitoring and prenatal visits followed the same pattern according to type of intervention. The percentage of children under age three attending growth monitoring as reported by mothers increased by 22 percentage points under the demand-side intervention and 17 percentage points under the demand plus supply intervention. Again, the impact was consistent across all ages. Although attendance remained stable under the supply-only intervention, this represented an improvement over the control group, whose attendance decreased. Administrative data (from Tarjetas del Niño, or Child Cards) showed a smaller impact than did interviews with mothers, but the relative changes remained the

Table 7.2—Impacts of conditional cash transfers on health

Country, program	Attendance at growth monitoring	Attendance at health checkups or visits	Illness prevalence
Honduras, PRAF	+17 to +22 percentage points (birth through age three)[a]	+15 to +21 percentage points (birth through age three)	* (diarrhea)
Mexico, PROGRESA	+30-60 percent (birth through age two)[b]	+18.2 percent (clinics in PROGRESA areas)	-12 percent (birth through age five) (-4.7 percentage points)
Nicaragua, RPS	+13.1 percentage points	+16.3 percentage points	
Colombia, Familias en Acción	+16 percentage points (birth through age two, urban)	+23 percentage points (birth through age two)	
	+21 percentage points (birth through age two, rural)	+33 percentage points (ages two through four)	-11 percentage points in diarrhea incidence (birth through age four, rural)
	+48 percentage points (ages two through four, rural)		
Jamaica, PATH	n.a.	+38 percent (birth through age six; no impact on elderly)	*

Sources: Gertler (2000); Gertler and Boyce (2001); IFPRI (2003b); Attanasio and Gomez (2004); Attanasio et al. (2005); Maluccio and Flores (2005); Skoufias (2005); Hernandez-Prado and Hernandez-Avila (2006); Levy and Ohls (2007).

Notes: PATH = Programme for Advancement through Health and Education; PRAF = Programa de Asignación Familiar; PROGRESA = Programa de Educación, Salud y Alimentación; RPS = Red de Protección Social; n.a. = not applicable. * indicates no impact. Blank cells indicate that results were not evaluated.

[a]The group exposed to demand-side incentives exhibited a 21.7-percentage-point increase in growth monitoring attendance and the group exposed to both demand- and supply-side incentives experienced a 17.4-percentage-point increase (IFPRI 2003b, 36).

[b]The difference in the numbers reflects two models. One controls for per capita income (Gertler 2000).

Figure 7.1—Conditional cash transfer impacts on health service usage, by program beneficiaries

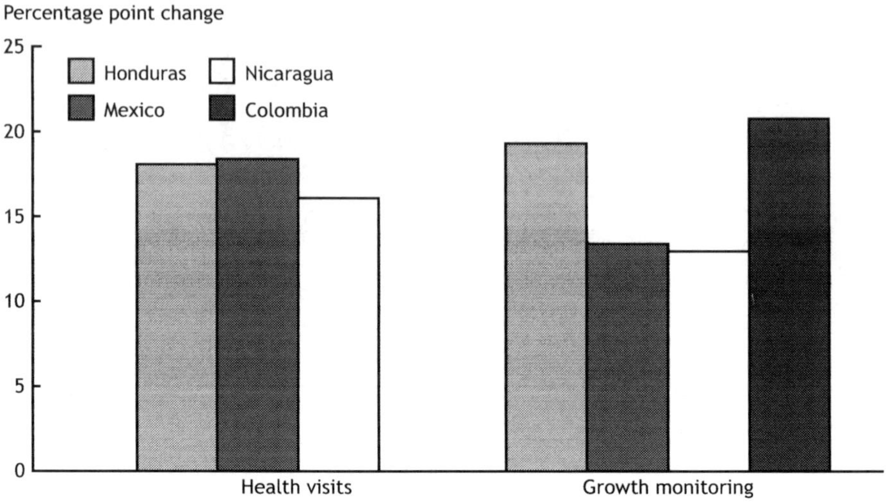

Sources: Gertler (2000); Gertler and Boyce (2001); IFPRI (2003b); Attanasio et al. (2005); Maluccio and Flores (2005).

Notes: The mean of the range of estimates is plotted for Honduras. For Mexico, the figure represents the impact on growth monitoring visits 15 months after baseline. No information on health visits separate from growth monitoring is available for Colombia.

same: the demand-only intervention brought about an increase of 16 percentage points in growth control visits; the demand plus supply intervention, an increase of 13 percentage points; and the supply-only intervention, an increase of 8.3 percentage points. The percentage of pregnant women having attended five or more antenatal care sessions increased by 19.5 percentage points under the demand-only intervention, 18 percentage points under the demand plus supply intervention, and 14 percentage points under the supply-only intervention (albeit these results were slightly less statistically significant) (IFPRI 2003b, 36–45).

The fact that the supply-only interventions showed small and statistically insignificant impacts on service usage and that the combination of demand and supply added little significant additional impact above and beyond the impact of the demand-only intervention was attributed to the low degree of supply-side implementation (IFPRI 2003b, 70). This is unfortunate, because results from better implementation would have shed light on an important debate about conditionality, that is, whether improving supply is sufficient to bring about human capital improvements without the need for conditionality. It did, however, provide evidence on another issue in the conditionality debate, that is, the implementation difficulties that can be encountered as a poor country attempts to improve the supply of services. Nicaragua provides a contrary example, however, because it was able to successfully improve supply.

In Nicaragua, RPS resulted in an increase in the percentage of children under age three making well-child visits, with an average increase of 16.3 percentage points in 2001 and 8.4 percentage points in 2002. The reduction in impact measured in the second year was due to more visits among the control group in 2002 (10.5 percentage points) and only a slight decline in intervention areas. There was also a 13.1 percentage point double-difference estimate of the percentage of children taken to healthcare providers and weighed. From 2000 to 2002 the control group increased their visits to healthcare providers by 15.2 percentage points, whereas beneficiary households increased their visits by 28.3 percentage points, nearly double the increase in the control group. Several hypotheses exist to explain the increase in control group usage of health services. It could have been because other providers established new healthcare services in the area; because RPS drew beneficiary families away from public clinics, reducing the waiting time and making these health centers more inviting to control households; or because control households increased their use of services in anticipation of the CCT (Maluccio and Flores 2005, 24, 44).

Impacts on both visits to health centers and growth monitoring were larger among poorer RPS households. Extremely poor households experienced an increase of 29.9 percentage points in the weighing of children from birth to age three in the previous six months compared to poor households, which experienced an increase of 23.5 percentage points. Effects for children ages three to five were even greater than those for children from birth to age three (Maluccio and Flores 2005, 45–46).

In Colombia, Familias en Acción brought about significant increases in preventive healthcare visits. Attendance of growth monitoring and development checkups, in which children are weighed and mothers receive child nutrition advice, increased by 22.8 percentage points for children under twenty-four months of age and by 33.2 percentage points for children ages twenty-four through forty-eight months (Attanasio et al. 2005, 10).

In Jamaica, PATH increased the average number of preventive healthcare visits for children from birth through age six by approximately 38 percent (or 0.28 visits every six months) but had no impact on child immunization rates or on healthcare use by the elderly (age sixty or older) (Levy and Ohls 2007). This difference may have been because compliance with health conditions was not enforced for the elderly but was frequently enforced for children, creating incentives for children's visits to health centers. The limited impact of PATH on immunization may have been because the immunization rates of both beneficiaries and nonbeneficiaries were high at the outset. Forty-six percent of the families that took their children to health checkups more regularly said they did so because of the PATH requirement, and the majority reported "change in health circumstances" (Levy and Ohls 2007, 76, 80).

Mexico's PROGRESA required beneficiaries to visit public clinics for preventive health visits. Depending on the regression specification used, PROGRESA beneficiaries averaged 2.09–11.49 more visits per day to clinics in PROGRESA areas compared to those in non-PROGRESA areas.[2] The lower estimate represents about 18 percent more visits—by both beneficiaries and nonbeneficiaries—to clinics in PROGRESA areas compared to control areas. If all the increase were attributed to PROGRESA beneficiaries, visits would have increased by roughly 60 percent among this group. Because beneficiaries represent roughly 20 percent of the total number of families in PROGRESA service areas, the impact estimates suggest that beneficiary visits increased twice as much as visits by non-PROGRESA families (Gertler 2000, 10; Gertler and Boyce 2001, 11).

Disaggregating the visits to public and private clinics indicates that the use of public clinics increased by 53 percent overall. There was no reduction in the use of private health providers, suggesting that increases in the use of public clinics was not a result of substitution of public care for private care (Gertler 2000, 12).

PROGRESA increased the number of growth monitoring visits by beneficiary children from birth to age two by 30–60 percent and those of children ages three to five by 25–45 percent, based on different regression models (Gertler 2000, 13).[3] Additionally, PROGRESA resulted in an 8 percent increase in initial prenatal visits during the first trimester of pregnancy. This focus on earlier prenatal care reduced the number of initial visits in the second and third trimesters of pregnancy, a behavior change that is recognized to improve the health of pregnant women and their infants (Skoufias 2005, 56).

Figure 7.1 summarizes the results on health service usage.

Health Outcomes

Only the CCTs in Colombia and Mexico show evidence of impacts on health outcomes. Other program evaluations either did not measure this (those in

---

[2] The smaller figure comes from a regression using a dummy to indicate whether the facility was located in a PROGRESA service area; the larger figure emerges from a regression using the number of families in the service area receiving PROGRESA benefits (Gertler and Boyce 2001, 10).

[3] One model adds per capita income to try to separate the transfer income effect from the impact of the nutrition and preventive care (Gertler 2000).

Brazil and Nicaragua) or demonstrate no impact (Honduras and Jamaica). In Honduras, it was hoped that PRAF would reduce the prevalence of diarrhea because required growth monitoring, conducted via the strategy of the country's national community-based nutrition program, Atención Integral a la Niñez Comunitaria (AIN-C), also provided counseling to help mothers modify hygiene and eating behaviors related to diarrhea risk. Diarrhea prevalence was very high before the project started, but instead of decreasing, the percentage of children experiencing episodes of diarrhea increased from 2000 to 2002 in all intervention groups. The most significant increase was among the supply-only group, again explained at least in part by the low levels of supply-side implementation (IFPRI 2003b, 71, 84). In Jamaica, the lack of impact could have been because changes in health outcomes take longer than beneficiaries had been exposed to the program or because the measure of health status was fairly crude (because it was not a primary outcome indicator of the PATH evaluation) (Levy and Ohls 2007, 82).[4]

Mexico's PROGRESA significantly lowered illness rates among children from birth to age five, as reported by mothers, but only for children who had been receiving benefits for at least 12 months (Gertler and Boyce 2001, 13). PROGRESA children from birth to age five had a 12 percent lower incidence of illness than did non-PROGRESA children (Gertler 2000, 14). This estimate should be considered a lower bound of the impact of PROGRESA, because mothers' definitions of illness may have changed due to health and nutrition messages conveyed in the regular lectures (also a condition of the program) and because the increased frequency of well-child preventive health visits may have made mothers more likely to report illness than before (Gertler and Boyce 2001, 13).

Adult PROGRESA beneficiaries also benefited from improved health outcomes. Even though adults were required to make only one preventive health visit per year, 70 percent of the monetary transfer, on average, was used to increase the quantity and quality of household food consumption, perhaps contributing to improved health status (Gertler and Boyce 2001, 13). Adult PROGRESA beneficiaries (ages eighteen through fifty) experienced 17 percent fewer days incapacitated by illness, 22 percent fewer days in bed due to illness, and 19 percent fewer days of difficulty with daily activities. Beneficiaries over age fifty also benefited from fewer days incapacitated or "in bed" and fewer days of difficulty in daily activities than did nonbeneficiaries of the same age (Gertler 2000, 15; Gertler and Boyce 2001, 16).

[4] The PATH survey asked: "Relative to last year, is [NAME]'s current health: much better, better, about the same, worse, or much worse?" (Levy and Ohls 2007, 82).

Oportunidades (the follow-up to PROGRESA) was associated with an 11 percent reduction in maternal mortality and a 2 percent reduction in infant mortality. The effect of Oportunidades on maternal mortality was stronger in municipalities characterized by high marginality, and the effect on infant mortality was stronger in municipalities characterized by very high marginality. The protective effect of the program manifested itself immediately after program implementation, and there was no evidence that the effect changed over time (Hernández et al. 2004).

In Colombia, Familias en Acción resulted in a reduction of nearly 11 percentage points in diarrhea incidence in the previous 15 days among children from birth through age four living in rural areas. There was no statistically significant impact on diarrhea incidence among children living in urban areas or for respiratory disease incidence in either rural or urban areas. These results may be due to the educational lectures provided, focusing on nutrition and hygiene, which trained mothers to better recognize symptoms of diarrhea (Attanasio and Gomez 2004, 145; Attanasio et al. 2005, 10).

Complementary Activities for Health and New Program Designs in the Context of AIDS

Like education services, health services and related activities can be linked with cash transfer programs, whether or not they involve conditions. People's contact with health facilities, for example, where young children are brought in for immunizations or people seek treatment for illnesses, can be used as an opportunity to promote access to cash transfers. Health facility visits and HBC could be used to identify people who are eligible for a transfer program but not receiving benefits, to provide information and support with respect to transfer eligibility and the application process, and to facilitate access to the documents needed to access cash transfers, such as birth certificates (see also Chapter 9).

Given the importance of behavioral change for preventing the transmission of HIV, education and sensibilization activities could be extremely important complements to cash transfer programs in HIV-affected areas. There is also research examining new forms of linking cash to health interventions that are particularly relevant in the context of HIV and AIDS. Some examples follow.

Voluntary Testing and Counseling

Voluntary testing and counseling (VTC) for HIV/AIDS is considered an effective HIV prevention and control strategy. In Sub-Saharan Africa, where most new infections occur through heterosexual transmission, this is a particularly promising approach. A study by Bakari et al. (2000) in Zambia looked at appropriate formats and venues for VTC using a community survey of attitudes toward VTC (comparing those seeking and declining HIV testing), pre- and post-counseling surveys of HIV knowledge, and a pilot study of same-day VTC in urban antenatal care clinics. The results indicate that 98 percent of participants supported the promotion of VTC in the community. The majority thought that community workers were most effective in promoting this, and 83.8 percent preferred same-day testing. Counseling accompanying VTC was found to improve knowledge by reducing incorrect understanding of transmission by at least one-half. Even with strong community support for VTC, however, there are often important logistical constraints to testing, such as the costs faced by potential beneficiaries (for example, transportation costs, testing fees, and the opportunity cost of time), hours of operation (for example, convenient times available for both men and women), availability of child-care on site, and the regularity of couples testing (giving couples an opportunity to consult beforehand) (Bakari et al. 2000).

Several studies look at the relationship between cash incentives and HIV testing and provide examples of how experimental cash transfer programs (conditional or unconditional) have been adapted to respond to health priorities. A study in Malawi provided monetary incentives to people to pick up their HIV test results, taking into account distance to results centers, and found that even a small incentive doubled the percentage of participants who learned their results. In addition, sexually active individuals who learned their results and tested positive were three times more likely to purchase condoms two months later, though only two additional condoms. There was no impact on condom purchase among those who tested negative (Thornton 2008). In Tanzania, cash transfers are provided to young adults conditional on periodic negative tests for curable STDs. Their purpose is to evaluate the impact of combining a CCT with counseling on STD incidence and economic impacts. Treatment is offered, and participants may rejoin the program after being cured. Significantly, there is no conditioning on HIV and HSV-2 because these are not curable. In Lesotho, another pilot program uses a similar design but provides lottery tickets for larger prizes instead of a cash transfer (Özler and de Walque 2009).

Antiretroviral Therapy

The use of ARVs can be an effective way to inhibit viral replication and reduce viral load, and it can also improve individuals' nutritional status. Highly active antiretroviral therapy has been shown to positively affect child growth among children with advanced disease and poor nutritional status prior to taking ARVs, and also to promote sustained weight gain, increase body mass index (BMI), and reduce anemia among adults (Silva et al. 1998; Schwenk et al. 1999; Semba, Shah, and Vlahov 2001, cited in Gillespie and Kadiyala 2005, 56; Verweel et al. 2002). Kenya's Cash Transfer for OVC plans to provide referrals to programs that provide ARVs for beneficiaries who voluntarily declare that they are HIV positive or living with AIDS (Kenya, OVPMHA 2006, 9).

Of course the provision of ARVs does not guarantee their benefits; compliance with the drug regimen is critical. It may be possible to use cash transfer programs as a means of strengthening communications systems and counseling around drug regimen adherence, for example, by using lay providers and expert patients (van Damme and Kegels 2006). In Uganda, a study by Weidle et al. (2006) found that adherence interventions, including individual and group counseling, personal adherence plans, and weekly home delivery of ART, improved adherence. Cash transfers can also improve adherence through enabling the purchase of food, reducing the side effects of the drugs.

Home-Based Care

The World Health Organization defines home-based care as any type of care given to sick people within their homes, such as physical, psychosocial, palliative, and spiritual interventions (WHO 2002). A study by ActionAid in Zambia showed that 90 percent of HIV-affected individuals prefer to be cared for in their own homes (Voluntary Service Overseas 2006). HBC can include physical palliative care, such as treating illnesses and managing pain; nutritional counseling and support; support for ARV adherence and mitigating side effects; and psychosocial support for people living with AIDS (PLWA) and their families (Slater 2004). In Zambia, community nurses provide examinations and care plans, home visits and consultations, prescription and provision of drugs free of charge, general nursing care, training for family members about how to care for patients, patient assessment and referral, pre- and post-test counseling, counseling for family members and children, provision of information and awareness raising, and training for community volunteers. Community HBC volunteers, in turn, identify patients with chronic illness and provide information, basic nursing care (including drug provision), and practical household support (for example, help with household activities, farming, and funeral arrangements). They also counsel individuals before and after HIV tests as well as family members of people with HIV, often incorporating spiritual and emotional support (Nsutebu et al. 2001). Zimbabwe's Red Cross HBC program has been operational since 1992 and benefits an estimated 40,000 patients (McCord 2005). As noted earlier, there are various ways in which HBC programs could build mutually supportive links with cash transfer programs. In Malawi's SCTS, CBOs, extension workers, and child protection workers are tasked with providing access to HBC for cash transfer beneficiaries (UNICEF 2007b).

Despite the promise of HBC, there are several important constraints to its expansion. First, many programs rely on volunteers who may themselves face challenges associated with HIV/AIDS, including taking care of ill family members or being sick themselves. Given the likelihood of conflicting demands on HBC volunteers' time, some programs have introduced incentives to increase motivation. A cash transfer offers this potential, in effect creating a work-based transfer program. In fact, public works programs paying people in cash or food to work in HBC have been considered in several countries. For example, the Ndola Catholic Diocese HBC program in Zambia allows HBC volunteers to purchase food at a reduced rate, and the Red Cross HBC program in Zimbabwe pays HBC workers low wages as part of the public works program (Voluntary Service Overseas 2006).

South Africa's Department of Health, as well as its Expanded Public Works Programme, are also scaling up home- and community-based care involving training and payments to volunteers, providing forms of social protection for caregivers and care recipients. More information is provided on these initiatives in Chapter 9.

Conclusion

Several key points emerge from these findings on cash transfers and health. CCTs have demonstrated positive impacts on the use of health services, particularly child growth monitoring. However, evidence of their impact on health outcomes appears to be mixed. As in the case of education, the supply and quality of services available bear some part of the responsibility for this (for more information on the issue of supply quality, see Morris 2010 and a review by Adato and Hoddinott 2010). The constraint on impacts imposed by the quantity and quality of supply of health services will be even more significant in the case of countries and families affected by HIV and AIDS. This is because, first, the supply challenges are simply much greater in these countries independent of, but particularly in the context of, the HIV and AIDS crisis. Second, the need for good-quality health services in more locations is even more critical for AIDS-affected families. Hence a cash transfer's ability to affect healthcare when services are lacking or of poor quality will be limited. Nevertheless, we know that both UCTs and CCTs have had some positive impacts on health indicators.

Although these evaluations provide useful information about the impacts of cash transfers on health, there is still a critical gap in the information available to enable us to identify the pathway by which these transfers improve health behaviors and outcomes. This gap applies to CCTs as well as UCTs. In the case of CCTs, the impact could be a result of the cash itself (income effect), price changes effected by conditionalities (price effect), or both. Alternatively, the impact could derive from the fact that transfers are made to women, who have been found to spend a larger share of income they control on children when compared to men. Or the social marketing accompanying cash transfers, even in the absence of conditions, could affect the use of cash. Furthermore, CCTs often require monthly participation in health training workshops. These could certainly affect health behaviors, and qualitative evidence suggests that they do but that strong sociocultural influences also limit the effectiveness of CCTs (Adato, Roopnaraine, and Becker 2011).

Unfortunately, data that would allow us to tease out the relative effects of these different pathways are not available, so we cannot draw conclusions about the value of health conditionalities or about the relative value of different components of program designs. Unlike in the case of education, there are not yet any findings on healthcare outcomes using accidental experiments comparing transfers believed to be unconditional with those thought to be conditional (see Chapter 4). We can conclude, however, that UCTs have resulted in improved access to healthcare services in several countries (Malawi and South Africa) and improved health status (self-reported illness and health status) in several others (Malawi, South Africa, and Zambia). Whether these impacts could have been larger if accompanied by a health conditionality is unclear. Whether conditionalities in their current form are even relevant, given the main healthcare priorities of AIDS-affected families (for example, going to the clinic for ART), is another open question. Withholding cash from people at advanced stages of AIDS because they did not go to the clinic seems unethical, but one could design a program whereby beneficiaries would receive cash when they picked up their drugs (as is currently often the case with food) as a conditionality. However, the main objective of CCTs has been to protect the health of pregnant women and children, and AIDS-affected families need this type of protection every bit as much. Several evaluations under way (for example, in Kenya and Uganda) that compare a conditional and unconditional program may shed light on this question; however, further studies focusing specifically on healthcare uptake as well as effects on health service provision would be valuable.

In the absence of additional evidence, and given the positive results of several UCT programs in Africa in countries with a high HIV prevalence, UCTs appear to be a promising start to improving health outcomes among AIDS-affected communities. Apart from some of the indicators reported earlier, the access these programs provide to food is likely to contribute to health impacts. However, further examination of conditionality in contexts of high HIV prevalence could suggest implications for program design. Relevant design issues for consideration include the optimal value of transfers, the types of conditions that could be appropriate to achieve various health objectives, the types of services that must be available, and under what circumstances conditions should be enforced or waived. Finally, the role of social marketing, training, and communications campaigns to bring about behavioral change is particularly significant in the context of AIDS, as are other complementary interventions that can be implemented in conjunction with or parallel to cash transfers.

CHAPTER 8

Cash Transfers, Food Consumption, and Nutrition

Children in AIDS-affected families face multiple sources of risk that threaten to undermine their food security and nutritional status. As discussed in Chapter 2, malnutrition at early ages, particularly under two years of age but also continuing through early childhood, has long-term impacts on children's school enrollment and performance, their cognitive development, and their productivity and earnings later in life. Adequate food consumption and nutrition are of particular importance to HIV-positive individuals due to the impact that food insecurity and malnutrition can have on the risk of infection and disease progression and, concurrently, the effect that the disease can have on nutritional status (Haddad and Gillespie 2001). HIV and AIDS contribute to food insecurity and malnutrition in a variety of ways: by undermining livelihoods, decreasing food intake, and increasing malabsorption, metabolic alterations, and energy requirements. At the same time, food insecurity and malnutrition can heighten susceptibility to HIV exposure, infection, and disease progression by increasing transactional sex, migration, susceptibility to tuberculosis, and mother-to-child transmission (Gillespie 2008). Furthermore, many countries with high HIV prevalence also have high underlying levels of food insecurity and malnutrition. For these reasons, we focus on the potential of cash transfers to affect nutritional status, reviewing the evidence to date. This includes evidence on the impacts of cash transfers on food expenditures, the quantity and quality of food consumed, and changes in measures of child nutritional status. The measures of malnutrition reported are stunting, underweight, and wasting.[1] Although few evaluations specify impacts on HIV-affected households, we draw conclusions on implications for these groups at the end of this section.

[1] Stunting (height for age more than 2 standard deviations below the international reference level) reflects past as well as current nutrition and illness and is considered the best measure of long-term undernutrition. Wasting (weight for height more than 2 standard deviations below the international reference level) indicates significant recent or current weight loss. Underweight (weight for age more than 2 standard deviations below the international reference level) can reflect either stunting or wasting (World Bank 2006b).

Impacts of Unconditional Cash Transfers on Food Consumption and Nutrition

Food Expenditure and Food Consumption

Given the important implications of food consumption on HIV risk and disease progression, program impacts on food expenditure and consumption can be particularly important for poor families affected by HIV and AIDS. There is considerable evidence that UCT programs have increased food expenditure and food consumption. In most programs, beneficiaries use the majority of the transfer to purchase food. Figure 8.1 illustrates the relative shares of transfer spending, with the highest amount of spending on food, followed by spending on other goods (including clothing and shoes, blankets, transportation, and household spending, for example, on water and electricity, hygiene, and livestock).

According to Samson et al. (2004), in South Africa the number of male OAP pensioners in a household was significantly associated with a larger share of

Figure 8.1—Use of cash transfers, by type of spending and program

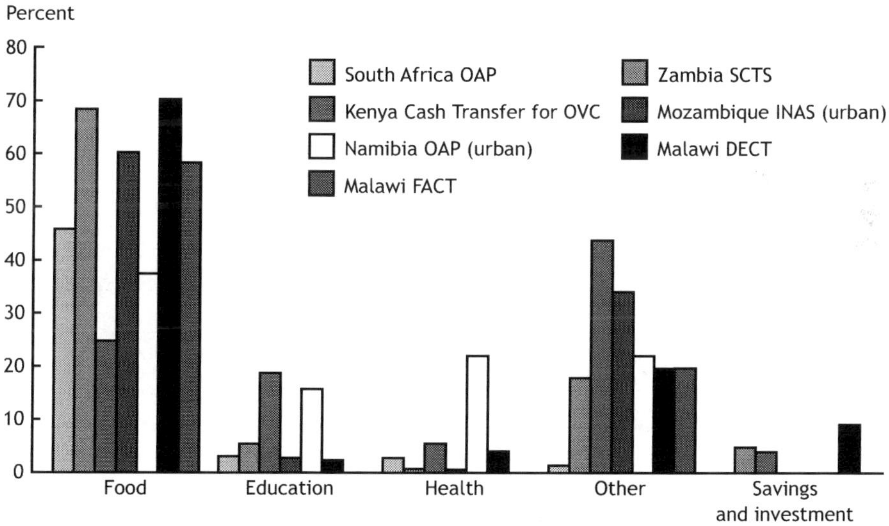

Sources: Devereux (2002); Moller and Ferreira (2003); Devereux, Mvula, and Solomon (2006); Zambia, MCDSS/GTZ (2006); Acacia Consultants (2007); Devereux et al. (2007).

Notes: DECT = Dowa Emergency Cash Transfer; FACT = Food and Cash Transfers Project; INAS = National Institute of Social Welfare; OAP = Old Age Pension; OVC = Orphan and Vulnerable Children; SCTS = Social Cash Transfer Scheme. In the case of Zambia's SCTS, the figure represents the proportion of overall spending by beneficiaries on health. In the case of Malawi's DECT, these spending numbers refer to three months of the five-month program period, January–March 2007.

the household expenditure dedicated to food, although this had no impact on reducing hunger. On the other hand, the number of female pensioners in the household was associated with a lower prevalence of hunger but had no impact on the share of the household expenditure on food. These results are consistent with the theory of the nonunitary household in which increases in household expenditures do not automatically translate into improved household consumption for all household members. Male pensioners may have spent pension money on food for themselves instead of other household members, while female pensioners may have allocated more of the pension to young children and other household members (Samson et al. 2004, 82). In Namibia, 27 percent of pension income was dedicated to food for the family and 10.6 percent to food for the pensioner (Devereux 2001).

A 2006 evaluation of Ethiopia's PSNP found that 80 percent of beneficiaries used some cash to purchase staple foods, and 11 percent used some of the transfer for other foods (Devereux et al. 2006, 34). The 2007 PSNP evaluation found no significant effect of PSNP transfers on per capita food consumption, although other measures of food security improved (Gilligan, Hoddinott, and Taffessee 2007, 39, 42).

On average, beneficiaries of Kenya's Cash Transfer for OVC spent at least half of the transfer on expenditures related to program objectives (food, health, and education) (Acacia Consultants 2007, 16). Eighty-six percent of households reported spending some of the transfer on food, mostly purchasing maize, as well as tea, sugar, beans, rice, and fruit. The relatively smaller share of the transfer spent on food (25 percent) than in other programs (Figure 8.1) may have occurred because the transfer was given in a six-month lump sum, making it difficult to spend all the money on immediate consumables (Acacia Consultants 2007, 15).

Bazo (1998) noted that in Maputo, Mozambique's GAPVU cash transfer had no effect on food consumption because the transfer was too small. If the entire monthly subsidy ($3–$6 per month) had been used to purchase food (which, in general, it was not), it would have provided only 225 calories per day for one person. The study found that the mean per capita calories were nearly identical for beneficiaries and nonbeneficiaries, with the sample of 41 elderly beneficiaries consuming 1,403 kilocalories per day compared to 1,453 per day for the 40 elderly nonbeneficiaries. However, there were other program impacts. Reliance on food donations from family and friends and begging declined among beneficiaries as they began to purchase more food in the market (Bazo 1998, as cited in Low, Garrett, and Ginja 1999, 39; Tarp et al. 2002, 108).

In Lesotho, about one-third of pension income, on average, was used for food for the household, often for the purchase of items such as meat, eggs, and sugar. However, pensioners themselves ate only 40 percent of this extra food, on average, so 60 percent of the total additional food benefited other household members (Croome 2006; Beales 2007).

The majority of the cash provided by Malawi's DECT program was spent on food (64 percent, on average), but this share varied over the five-month period, from 70–80 percent between December and February, the most severe months of the food crisis, to 60 percent in March and 30 percent in April, when the maize harvest began, contributing to reductions in both the prices and the demand for maize (Devereux et al. 2007, 33). The transfer was indexed to maize prices to protect beneficiaries against seasonal price fluctuations; however, this adjustment was imperfect, resulting in a disproportionate cut in the transfer value with respect to maize price variation in February. This month represented the lowest maize value relative to the DECT cash in the project period, diminishing households' ability to purchase nonfood items such as healthcare, education, and other goods and services. Notwithstanding this drop in the level of cash, taken as a whole, the project helped households cover their missing food entitlement during a difficult time (Devereux et al. 2007, 34).

As in DECT, FACT beneficiaries exhibited different spending patterns over the life of the project (January–April 2006). From January to February, spending on food increased from 63 to 69 percent, but in March spending on food fell to 45 percent as beneficiaries spent more of the cash on nonfood items (all compared to mean spending on food of 59 percent). The authors note that this could be interpreted as a sign of the flexibility of cash transfers, which allow beneficiaries to meet essential nonfood needs, or it could be a sign of overfunding—providing more than the minimum subsistence needs—on the part of the FACT program. However, because nonessential spending was low (less than 15 percent), it is likely that overfunding was less of a problem than the timing of the receipt of the grant (Devereux, Mvula, and Solomon 2006, 29).

FACT beneficiaries reported that cash acted as an important complement to the food package for two reasons. The food ration contained insufficient supplies to make the typical meal, so beneficiaries used the cash to purchase other necessary food items (for example, vegetables or dried fish). Beneficiaries also used cash to cover the cost of milling maize (either purchased or provided in the food package). Milling represented a sizable share of household expenditures: up to 18 percent (Devereux, Mvula, and Solomon 2006, 30). According to a cluster analysis of household spending strategies among FACT beneficiaries in Malawi, 47 percent of households were categorized as "food first," meaning they spent their transfer almost exclusively on food. More specifically, these households spent 84 percent of their transfer on food, followed by maize milling and other groceries (Devereux, Mvula, and Solomon 2006, 33).

Samson et al. (2004) report the impacts of social grants in South Africa on the share of household expenditures on food items. Receipt of a CSG was associated with increases of 1.5 and 1.2 percentage points in all food items and basic food items, respectively, and receipt of the Disability Grant had a slightly greater impact, with increases of 2.5 and 1.3 percentage points, respectively. Each R1,000 of annual pension received under the OAP was associated with increases of 1.5 and 1.0 percentage points in all food items and in basic food items, respectively (Samson et al. 2004, 79).

In a study focusing on HIV-affected households in Free State Province, Booysen (2004b) found that grant income had a greater impact on household food expenditure than did employment income, suggesting that beneficiaries preferred to use the additional resources of social grants to purchase food. Both the Disability Grant and the OAP were associated with increases in real adult food expenditures (increases of 12.9 and 10.5 percentage points, respectively). The impact of the CSG on food expenditures was slightly negative but statistically insignificant (Booysen 2004b, 22–23).

Hunger and Meal Frequency

Hunger can lead to negative coping strategies, which may increase susceptibility to HIV exposure and infection. At the same time, insufficient food intake can lead to weight loss, which is a strong predictor of morbidity and mortality for HIV-affect individuals (Tabi and Vogel 2006). Cash transfers have been found to increase the number of meals consumed per day and to reduce the number of skipped meals. Case (2001) found that in South African households where pension income is pooled, the presence of a pensioner lowered the probability that an adult in the household had skipped a meal by approximately 25 percent. This finding was supported by open-ended interviews in which pensioners reported that the pension allowed them to purchase enough food (Case 2001, 15). According to Samson et al. (2004), having a female pensioner in the household had a greater impact on child hunger than on adult hunger: the presence of a female pensioner was associated with a 5.8 percent lower probability that a young child in the household experienced hunger and a 4.3 percent lower probability that adults and older children experienced hunger (Samson et al. 2004, 82).

Lesotho's social pension also resulted in fewer skipped meals by beneficiaries. The percentage of beneficiaries indicating that they never have sufficient food to fill them dropped from 20 percent before receiving the pension to 10 percent with the pension, and the percentage reporting that they always had enough food to fill them increased from 36 percent before receiving the pension to 46 percent with the pension (Croome 2006).

An evaluation of Zambia's SCTS indicates that there was a reduction from 19 to 13 percent in the percentage of beneficiary households eating only one meal a day and a reduction from 56 to 34 percent in the number of beneficiaries reporting hunger pangs after a meal, suggesting an increase in the quantity of food consumed. Although the percentage of households eating two meals per day remained constant, the percentage eating three meals per day increased by 6 percentage points (Figure 8.2). This result masked differences between the two agricultural blocks, however. Although beneficiaries in Kalomo agricultural block experienced an increase from 1.89 to 2.13 meals per day, on average, beneficiaries in Kanchele agricultural block barely experienced any change at all, moving from 2.06 to 2.08 meals per day, on average. This may have been due to the proportional decline in food aid in Kanchele from baseline to the evaluation and to the proportional increase in food aid in Kalomo over this same period (Zambia, MCDSS/GTZ 2006, 40–41).

Malawi's DECT program brought about significant increases in the number of meals per day for beneficiaries, from an average of 1.5 meals per day for children and adults at baseline to an average of 2.4 meals per day at evaluation (Devereux et al. 2007, vii). The number of meals per day increased by

Figure 8.2—Household meals per day before and during Zambia's Social Cash Transfer Scheme

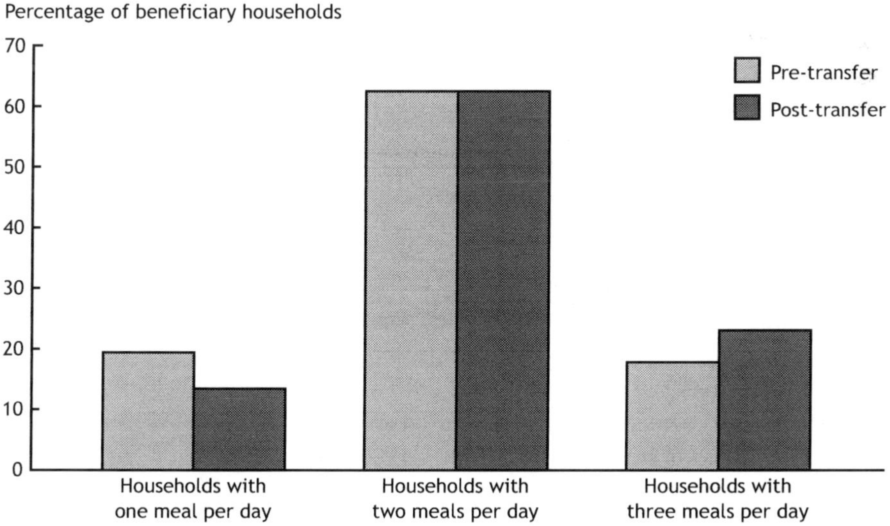

Source: Zambia, MCDSS/GTZ 2006.

as much as 40 percent for adults in female-headed households immediately following the transfer and remained high throughout the duration of the program. This increase in the number of meals per day suggests that DECT protected consumption during the annual hungry season. Also, the gender gap in food consumption between male- and female-headed households was eradicated after receipt of the transfer. However, Devereux et al. (2007) point out that although meals per day is a good indicator of general food security, it is a weak proxy for food intake because families could maintain the same meal frequency while consuming smaller portions. Given the absence of a control group of nonbeneficiaries for the DECT evaluation, it is not possible to conclusively attribute the positive findings on household food security to receipt of DECT transfers (Devereux et al. 2007, 34–35).

The FACT Project in Malawi had a control group, and prior to the provision of FACT transfers there was no statistically significant difference in the average number of meals per day between beneficiary and nonbeneficiary households, although nonbeneficiaries consumed marginally more than beneficiaries. After the transfer was provided and throughout the project period (January–April 2006), the level of food consumption was higher in beneficiary households than in nonbeneficiary households (Figure 8.3). The transfers prevented beneficiary households from suffering the same degree of rationing and hunger that nonbeneficiary households experienced in early 2006 (Devereux, Mvula, and Solomon 2006, 36–37).

Evaluation results from Malawi's Mchinji Cash Transfer program also highlight improvements in food consumption. From March 2007 to March/April 2008, 93 percent of beneficiary households reported improved food consumption compared to 11 percent of comparison households. At the same time, only 1.3 percent of intervention households reported worsened food consumption, whereas 36 percent of comparison households reported this. On the whole, beneficiary households experienced greater satisfaction after meals (23 percentage points higher than comparison households) and were less hungry after meals. Among beneficiary households, only 6.4 percent reported being somewhat hungry and 1.1 percent very hungry after meals compared to 32 percent and 4.8 percent, respectively, of comparison households. On average, comparison households experienced 5.2 days without enough food in the previous month compared to 1.2 days in beneficiary households. There were notable differences in perceptions of whether the household had sufficient food between intervention and comparison groups. Among the intervention group, 80 percent expressed that they had sufficient food for consumption and 10 percent reported that they did not have enough, whereas among the comparison group only 20 percent said they had enough food to

Figure 8.3—Mean household meals per day in Malawi's Food and Cash Transfers Project

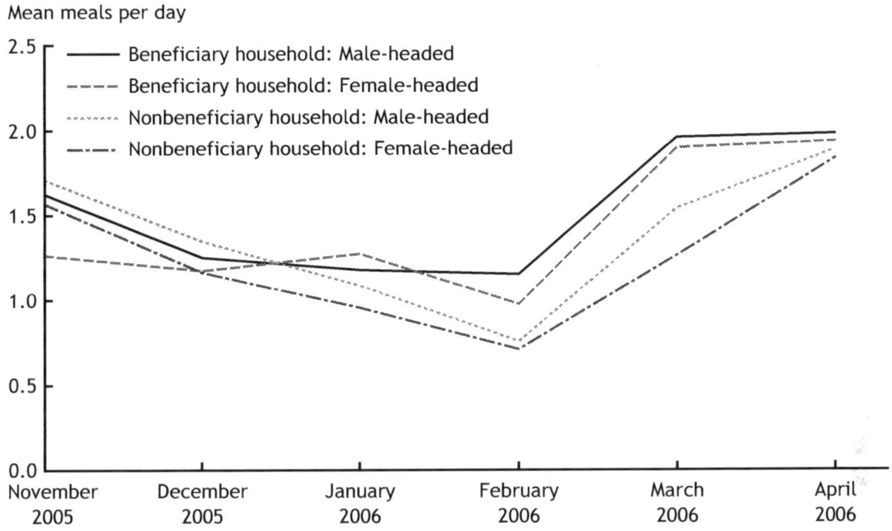

Source: Devereux, Mvula, and Solomon (2006).

eat and 80 percent said they had too little. Nearly half (44 percent) of all household heads from beneficiary households had eaten three meals the day prior to the final follow-up survey compared to 8 percent of comparison household heads (Miller, Tsoka, and Reichert 2008, 34).

According to the 2006 evaluation of Ethiopia's PSNP, three-quarters of beneficiary households reported consuming more and better-quality food after receiving the transfer, and 94 percent of these households attributed the improvement to PSNP. Approximately 60 percent of beneficiaries were able to keep more of the food they produced for their own consumption rather than sell it to meet other needs, and 90 percent of these credited this change to the program. Still, despite these improvements, reports of hunger and rationing continued because the transfers were small and unpredictable (Devereux et al. 2006, 40). The larger 2007 impact evaluation of the PSNP found that households receiving at least half the transfer amount they should have received had (1) a significantly lower probability of having low per capita calorie availability (fewer than 1,800 kilocalories per person per day), 10.6–11.2 percentage points, and (2) an increased mean household calorie availability of 181–183 kilocalories per person per day in the previous 7 days compared to control households (Gilligan, Hoddinott, and Taffesse 2007, 38–42).

Dietary Diversity

Most programs demonstrated positive impacts on dietary diversity, which can provide necessary nutrients for HIV-positive individuals. FACT beneficiary households consumed more diversified diets than did nonbeneficiaries. In late 2005, all households had very low dietary diversity scores, indicating that they were eating foods from an average of two distinct food groups per day. For nonbeneficiary households (and to a lesser degree female-headed beneficiary households), these scores fell during the hungry season (January and February) until March harvests provided staple cereal and root crops, pulses, and vegetables. Beneficiary households, in contrast, experienced consistently higher dietary diversity scores throughout the program period, and by March, the dietary diversity scores for both male- and female-headed beneficiary households surpassed a score of 3 (Figure 8.4). One explanation for this higher score is that FACT provided three food groups in its food package—cereals (maize), pulses (beans), and fat (oil)—which improved both food consumption and dietary diversity for recipient households. In addition to the food transfer, the FACT cash transfer enabled beneficiaries to purchase additional foods, including vegetables, meat, and fish (Devereux, Mvula, and Solomon 2006, 37–38).

During the first four months of the DECT project in Malawi, beneficiaries experienced a slight increase in dietary diversity—from consuming foods from an average of 2.5 food groups in November 2006 to consuming foods from an average of 3 food groups in male-headed households and 2.8 in female-headed households in March 2007. In April 2007, when the spending of the DECT transfer on food was at its lowest, dietary diversity increased by even more, reaching 4 food groups for male-headed households and 3.6 for female-headed households. According to the evaluation of DECT, this makes it difficult to attribute changes in dietary diversity to the cash transfer but does not diminish the impact of DECT on increasing the purchase and consumption of basic food items (Devereux et al. 2007, 36).

Zambia's Social Cash Transfer Scheme improved the dietary diversity of beneficiary households. The average weekly frequency of fat consumption rose from 0.67 days a week to almost 2 days a week, and the percentage of households consuming oil at least once a week rose from 18 to 48 percent. The percentage of households consuming proteins 7 days a week increased from 23 to 35 percent, and the percentage of households consuming vitamins 7 days a week increased from 72 to 84 percent. Program beneficiaries also increased their consumption of cultivated and wild vegetables (66 to 82 percent and 69 to 76 percent, respectively), cultivated fruits (17 to 18 percent), and dried vegetables (1 to 16 percent). Consumption of wild fruits fell from 57 to 26 percent, indicating an improved food situation, because consuming

Figure 8.4—Household diet diversity in Malawi's Food and Cash Transfers Project

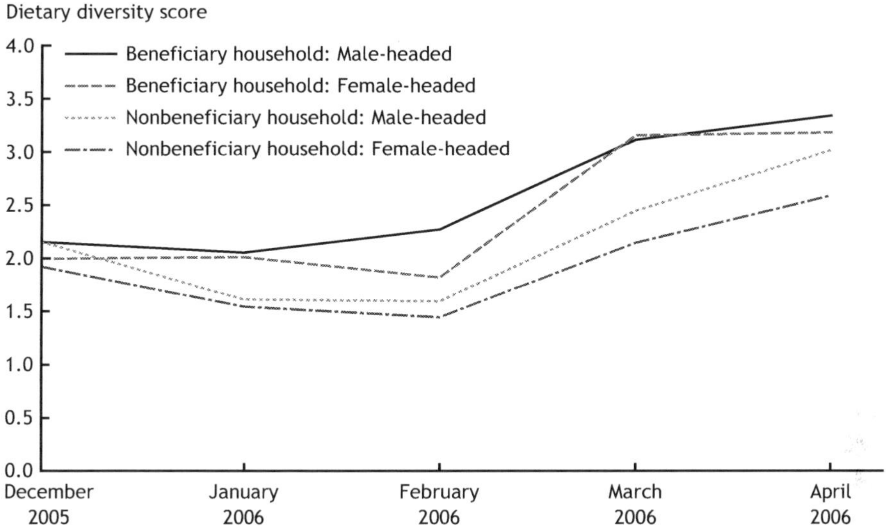

Source: Devereux, Mvula, and Solomon 2006.

wild fruits is often a coping strategy of last resort when no other food is available (Zambia, MCDSS/GTZ 2006, 41).

As of September 2007, approximately 6 months after the transfers began, 92 percent of households that had been receiving Malawi's Mchinji Cash Transfer said that they were more likely to eat higher-quality foods, including fish, chicken, beans, and some vegetables, because of the transfer. Dried fish consumption rose more than five times (from 12 to 63 percent) among beneficiary households, while it nearly doubled (from 5 to 9 percent) among comparison households; fresh fish consumption nearly doubled (from 11 to 19 percent) among beneficiary households and fell by one-third (from 6 to 4 percent) among comparison households; and beef consumption increased fourfold (from 2 to 8 percent) among beneficiary households and fell slightly (from 1 percent to less than 1 percent) among comparison households (Miller et al. 2007). By March/April 2008, beneficiary households were consuming foods from 8.1 food groups, on average, compared to comparison households, which consumed foods from 4.9 groups (Miller, Tsoka, and Reichert 2008, 35).

Nutrition

Food consumption, meal frequency, and dietary diversity—as well as the general health environment and particular caring practices—affect the nutritional status of individuals. Poor nutrition has been shown to be particularly risky for HIV-positive individuals because of the impact of malnutrition on disease progression and transmission (Gillespie and Kadiyala 2005). The best empirical evidence of the impacts of UCTs on nutrition comes from South Africa for both the CSG and the OAP. Using data from KwaZulu-Natal, Agüero, Carter, and Woolard (2007) find that large "dosages" of the CSG in early life increased child height. The impact of the CSG depended on the age of the child upon the introduction of benefits and the regularity of these benefits during what is considered the "nutrition window of opportunity," a child's first three years of age. During this time children are most susceptible to nutritional shortfalls—they are growing very quickly, so they have high nutritional needs and tend to experience disease (especially diarrhea) when they transition from breast milk to adult foods—and any growth faltering is likely to have a permanent effect on their physical and cognitive development. Receipt of the CSG during this "window of opportunity" was found to be critical to the grant's impact on child growth. Indeed, children who first received the CSG transfer after age two or who benefited for less than 20 percent of the nutrition window of opportunity experienced no statistically significant impact. Effects were insignificant for children receiving CSG support for less than 50 percent of the three-year window. However, children who received the transfer before age two and continued to receive benefits for at least two-thirds of the first three years of life experienced a significant improvement in height attainment. These children had HAZ 0.25 higher than children who received benefits for only 1 percent of their first three years of life.[2] Taking a specific case, a male child who received the CSG before age one and received benefits for two-thirds of his first three years of life experienced gains in height for age of 0.4 or approximately 3.5 centimeters, leading to a 2.1 percent gain in adult height. This height gain represents an increase in future earnings estimated to be 1.5–2.0 times, or 60–130 percent, greater than the cost of CSG support (Agüero, Carter, and Woolard 2007, 3, 6, 17–21).[3]

Several studies illustrate impacts of the South Africa OAP on child growth. Duflo (2003) analyzed the impact of the OAP on child nutritional status using data from a national household survey from 1993, when most pension benefi-

[2] The authors use three categories of children as the control group: children who received the CSG after they were three years old, children who applied for the grant but whose applications were rejected or whose benefits had not yet begun, and children for whom applications for the CSG were never made (Agüero, Carter, and Woolard 2007, 8).

[3] Using the estimate of the elasticity of wages for urban males in Brazil of Thomas and Strauss (1997), we can see that the gains in South African wages from an increase in height of 2.1 percent would be between R190 and R262 (Agüero, Carter, and Woolard 2007, 19).

ciaries (men over age sixty-five and women over age sixty) received roughly twice the median per capita income in rural areas (Duflo 2003, 3). Duflo found an improvement in under-five child nutritional status, especially for girls, when the pension recipient was a woman (Duflo 2000, 398). On average, pension income contributed to an increase of 0.68 standard deviations in height for age for girls. Pensions received by women were associated with increased height for age (1.16 standard deviations) and weight for height (1.19 standard deviations) for girls but had a smaller and statistically insignificant effect for boys, whose height for age increased by 0.28 standard deviations (Duflo 2003, 14–16). This was a large effect for girls, considering that the average eligible child had a HAZ of –1.4. Converted into centimeters, these anthropometric improvements represent a 2.23-centimeter increase in girls' height and a 0.88-centimeter increase in boys' height over a two-year period when the pensioner was a woman. Pensions received by men were not associated with improved nutritional status for either girls or boys (Duflo 2000, 398; Duflo 2003, 3). According to Duflo, the differential effect of pension income on child nutrition was a result of female recipients' being younger (their eligibility begins at age sixty compared to age sixty-five for men) and living longer. Duflo hypothesized that, compared to older pension-receiving grandfathers, pension-receiving grandmothers were apt to have stronger incentives to invest in children because they would benefit from their support for a longer period of time in the future (Duflo 2003, 19–20).

Case (2001) found a slightly larger impact of the South Africa OAP. According to her analysis, a pensioner in the household was associated with a 5-centimeter increase in child height and a 1 standard deviation increase in height for age, equivalent to 6 months' worth of growth, for black and colored children from birth to age six (Case 2001, 11).

In Zambia, monitoring reports for the SCTS noted a decrease of 9 percentage points in the proportion of underweight children (from 41 to 32 percent) (Zambia, MCDSS/GTZ 2005). Qualitative data also indicated that households benefited from improved dietary intake and therefore may have experienced improved nutritional outcomes; nevertheless, the survey figures should be interpreted very cautiously. The study reflected a small subset of beneficiary children because not all had growth monitoring cards and only a small number of children were weighed. Furthermore, the anthropometric data may have reflected weight fluctuations due to seasonal food availability and disease (Sridhar and Duffield 2006, 13).

The Mchinji Cash Transfer Scheme demonstrated some impact on child underweight but no impact on mean weight (measured as WAZ). At baseline (March 2007), the percentage of underweight children in both intervention and comparison groups was roughly 35 percent. One year later, 15 percent of intervention children were underweight (a reduction of 20 percentage points), and 26 percent of comparison children were underweight (a reduction of 9 percentage points), representing an impact of 11 percentage points (Miller, Tsoka, and Reichert 2008, 28).

Table 8.1 provides a summary of the impacts of UCTs on food consumption and nutrition.

Impacts of Conditional Cash Transfers on Food Consumption and Nutrition

CCTs can affect nutrition through several pathways. One is the cash transfer itself, which can translate into increased food expenditures and food consumption. In addition, CCTs usually provide counseling about food consumption, dietary diversity, and behavior change for nutrition, often through regular workshops that are required in order to receive the cash transfers. Furthermore, there are often required health and growth promotion visits—which can contribute to improved nutrition—for young children and sometimes mothers. Evidence of CCT impacts indicates that food consumption has improved across programs—in terms of the quantity of food or calories or dietary quality—but the results for nutritional status and anemia are less consistent.

In Mexico, PROGRESA brought about a 10.6 percent increase in the median value of food consumption and a 7.8 percent increase in median caloric acquisition from March 1998 to November 1999 (benefits began in May 1998). Improvements were proportionally greater for the poorest households: food consumption was 13.5 percent higher among beneficiary households in the 25th percentile but only 5.1 percent higher among beneficiary households in the 75th percentile (Hoddinott, Skoufias, and Washburn 2000, 20, 35).

In Turkey, households that received regular cash transfers experienced a 22.6 percent increase in per capita calorie availability compared to the comparison group, but households receiving irregular transfers demonstrated no difference from the comparison group (Ahmed et al. 2007).

Dietary Diversity

In Nicaragua, whereas at baseline all households ate an average of 12.1 different food items, by the end of the two-year evaluation RPS households reported consuming 4 additional food items, on average, compared to control households. Furthermore, beneficiaries consumed food of higher nutritional quality. RPS beneficiaries consumed less of the two staples (grains and beans), which had made up more than half of their pre-program diet, and consumed more nutrient-dense foods, such as meats, vegetables, and fruits, which was encouraged in the RPS education sessions. Expenditures on these

Table 8.1—Summary of impacts of unconditional cash transfer programs on food consumption and nutrition

Country, program	Food consumption	Hunger/meals per day	Dietary diversity	Nutritional status
Ethiopia, PSNP		-10.6 to 11.2 percentage points likelihood that household had low calorie intake +181 to +183 kcal per person		
Lesotho, Old-Age Pension		-10 percentage points never enough to eat +10 percentage points always enough to eat		
Malawi, DECT		+0.9 meals per day +40 percent meals per day (female-headed households)	No impact	
Malawi, FACT		+0.75 mean meals per day (female-headed households) +0.4 mean meals per day (male-headed households)	+1 food category per day, on average	
Malawi, Mchinji Cash Transfer	+83 percentage points food intake improved -35 percentage points food intake worsened	+23 percentage points satisfied after meal -25.5 percentage points somewhat hungry after meal -3.7 percentage points very hungry after meal	+3.2 food groups consumed per day, on average	-11 percentage points child underweight No change in mean weight-for-age z-score
Mozambique, GAPVU		No impact (Low, Garrett, and Ginja 1999)		

(continued)

Table 8.1—Continued

Country, program	Food consumption	Hunger / meals per day	Dietary diversity	Nutritional status
South Africa, CSG	+1.5 percentage points (all food items) +1.2 percentage points (basic food items)			+3.5 cm, on average, if received CSG during first year of life and for at least two-thirds of first three years
South Africa, OAP	+1.5 percentage points (all food items) +1 percentage point (basic food items) +10.5 percentage points in real adult food expenditure (HIV-affected households)	-25 percent chance that adult skipped meal (if pension income pooled) -5.8 percent probability of hunger (young child) -4.3 percent probability of hunger (adults and older children) (if pension received by woman)		+2.23 cm (girls) +0.88 cm (boys) if pension received by woman (national) +5 cm (black and colored children) (Western Cape)
Zambia, SCTS		-6 percentage points households eating one meal per day +6 percentage points households eating three meals per day +30.4 percentage points households consuming oil one time per week	+12 percentage points households consuming vitamins seven times per week +11.6 percentage points households consuming protein seven times per week	Possible reduction in percentage of underweight children

Sources: Low, Garrett, and Ginja (1999); Case (2001); Duflo (2003); Booysen (2004a); Samson et al. (2004); Croome (2006); Devereux, Mvula, and Solomon (2006); Zambia, MCDSS/GTZ (2006); Agüero, Carter, and Woolard (2007); Devereux et al. (2007); Gilligan, Hoddinott, and Taffesse (2007); Miller, Tsoka, and Reichert (2008).

Notes: CSG = Child Support Grant; DECT = Dowa Emergency Cash Transfer; FACT = Food and Cash Transfers Project; GAPVU = Gabinete de Apoio à População Vulnerável; OAP = Old Age Pension; PSNP = Productive Safety Net Programme; SCTS = Social Cash Transfer Scheme. Blank cells indicate that results were not evaluated.

items increased both in absolute terms and as a percentage of total expenditures (Maluccio and Flores 2005, 32). Ethnographic case studies observed people's resistance to consuming unfamiliar foods, however, revealing the difficulties of improving nutrition through "behavior change" components. Program volunteers sometimes organized fairs at which they prepared new foods (such as soy and less familiar vegetables), but the level of enthusiasm was low (Adato and Roopnaraine 2004).

In Colombia, the increase in food consumption was proportional to the increase in total consumption, implying that Familias en Acción did not change the food share among beneficiary households. However, despite the constant share of household budget allocated to food, the increase in protein consumption was proportionally greater than the increase in food consumption, representing an increase in the share of protein consumed (Attanasio and Mesnard 2006, 437). Consumption of meat and dairy increased by 19 percent, fats by 14.3 percent (urban) and 24 percent (rural), and grains by 9.3 percent (urban) and 16.7 percent (rural) (Attanasio and Gomez 2004, 2). These impacts did not appear to depend on program intensity or duration (Attanasio and Mesnard 2006, 438). There was no mention in the evaluation reports of any impact of the nutrition classes provided by the CCT.

Results from an analysis of the impact of Brazil's Bolsa Alimentação on food consumption indicate that there was an increase in dietary diversity of approximately 9 percent. Using a relationship documented by Hoddinott and Yohannes in which a 1 percent increase in dietary diversity is associated with a 0.7 percent increase in per capita caloric availability, the authors expect that Bolsa Alimentação contributed to a 6 percent increase in per capita caloric availability and a 12 percent increase in caloric availability from healthier nonstaples (especially fruits and vegetables) (Olinto et al. 2003).

In Mexico, PROGRESA spurred beneficiary households to consume more calories from vegetables and animal products than control households. Among households interviewed in both 1998 and 1999, there was a 36 percent increase in beneficiary households that reported eating chicken compared with a 19 percent increase in control households. There was less difference between beneficiary and control households in the consumption of staples and other commonly consumed foods (for example, tomatoes, onions, beans, and oil), suggesting that PROGRESA enhanced dietary diversity. Overall, dietary quality improved for beneficiaries through at least one of the following channels: an increase in the variety of foods consumed; an increase in the likelihood that a household consumed fruits, vegetables, or animal products; or an increase in calories acquired from these sources (Hoddinott, Skoufias, and Washburn 2000, 19, 21). There was some evidence that messages provided to women with preschool children in nutrition education sessions (*pláticas*) on such topics as the importance of a diversified diet affected eating habits among beneficiaries and no evidence that the nutritional supplement provided to small children (*papilla*) crowded out the acquisition of calories. There was no evidence of a difference in food prices faced by PROGRESA and control households (Hoddinott, Skoufias, and Washburn 2000, 36).

Several years later, Oportunidades also demonstrated an impact on dietary diversity with increased frequency of consumption of fruits and vegetables for children ages two through four. However, there was no impact on the number of foods consumed (Hernandez-Prado and Hernandez-Avila 2006, 91).

In Honduras, neither demand-side nor supply-side PRAF interventions demonstrated an impact on food consumption or dietary diversity. This is likely to have been due to the small size of the transfer, which represented less than 3.6 percent of average beneficiary expenditure (IFPRI 2003b, 69). However, according to another food consumption analysis using longitudinal data from 2000 to 2002, there was variation in food quality according to the educational level of the household head. In households where the household head had a primary school education, there was an increase in consumption of healthier foods such as meat, fish, eggs, dairy, and fruits. Conversely, in households where the household head had no education, changes in consumption took the form of increased oils, fats, and junk food (Wiesmann and Hoddinott 2007).

Nutrition

The nutritional outcomes of interest measured in CCT evaluations are stunting and iron-deficiency anemia. Two indicators are used to assess stunting: prevalence of stunting among children (usually from birth to age two, sometimes from birth to age five) and mean HAZ, an expression of anthropometric values as a given number of standard deviations below or above the international reference mean or the median value for healthy children. Iron-deficiency anemia is measured as a hemoglobin level under 11 grams per deciliter.

Although some CCT programs have demonstrated success in improving the nutritional status of child beneficiaries in terms of both reduced stunting and reduced anemia, there is considerable variation among programs, with some programs demonstrating no impact or even negative impacts (Figures 8.5 and 8.6).

According to the randomized evaluation comparing treatment and control groups before and after program implementation, conducted from 1997 to 1999, PROGRESA reduced the probability of child stunting by 10 percentage points among children ages twelve through thirty-six months (Hoddinott 2010) and increased average child height by 1–4 percent (Gertler and Boyce 2001). More recent estimates by Hoddinott found a reduction of 7.3 percentage points in stunting prevalence among children under age three and a reduction

Figure 8.5—Conditional cash transfer impacts on stunting

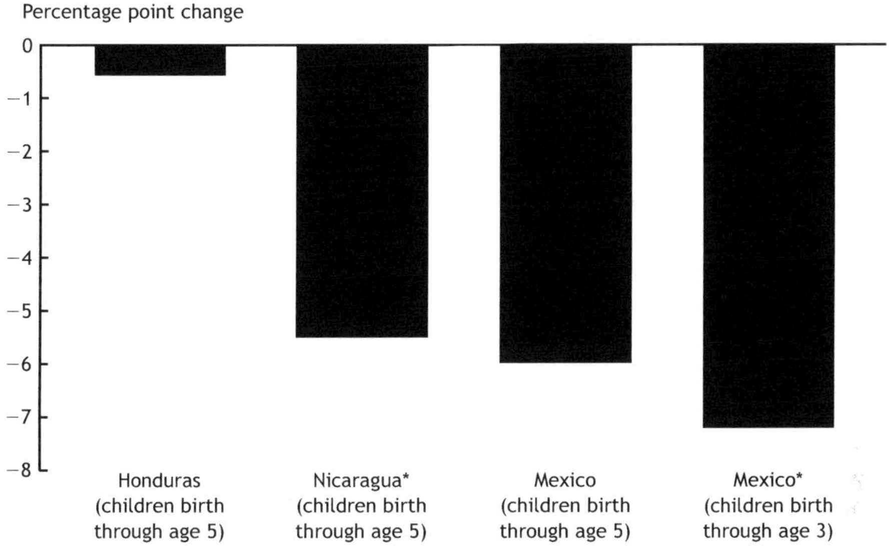

Sources: IFPRI (2003b); Attanasio et al. (2005); Maluccio and Flores (2005); Hoddinott (2010).
Notes: Results from Colombia are not included because they represent an impact on the probability of being stunted, not the prevalence of stunting. * indicates $p < 0.01$.

Figure 8.6—Conditional cash transfer impacts on mean height-for-age z-scores

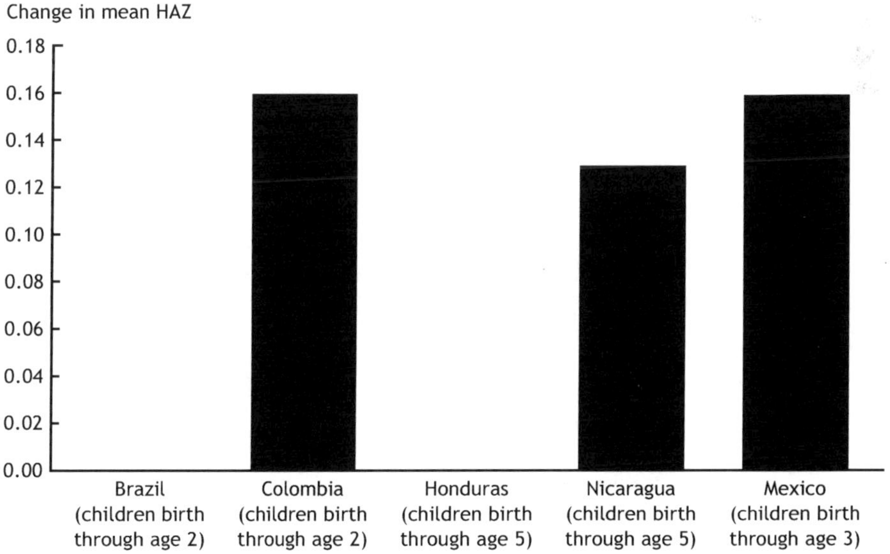

Sources: IFPRI (2003b); Morris et al. (2004); Attanasio et al. (2005); Maluccio and Flores (2005); Hoddinott (2010).

of 6 percentage points among children at age five (Hoddinott 2010). Height-for-age *z*-scores also increased by 0.33. An average child participating in PROGRESA experienced an increase in height of about 1 centimeter per year, or a 1.2 percent increase. The estimated impact of this increase in height alone is a 2.9 percent increase in lifetime earnings (Behrman and Hoddinott 2001). There is evidence that PROGRESA's positive impact on child height is greater in households that received the nutritional supplement (*papilla*); thus it is likely that the supplement plays an important role in these improvements in nutritional status (Hoddinott 2010).

Colombia's Familias en Acción program resulted in a reduction of 6.9 percentage points in the probability that children from birth through age twenty-four months would be stunted, but there was no impact on children older than twenty-four months. Mean HAZ also increased by 0.16. This increase is consistent with the notable increases in health service use of program children under age two: increases in growth and development visits of 16 percentage points in rural areas and 21 percentage points in urban areas and an increase of 23 percentage points in preventive health visits. Additionally, the program provided courses on hygiene, diet, and other topics related to health and nutrition for mothers, but although attendance was encouraged, it was not mandatory (Attanasio et al. 2005, 3).

According to the 2002 impact evaluation, Nicaragua's RPS resulted in a reduction of 5.5 percentage points in the number of stunted children from birth through age five over two years and an increase in mean HAZ of 0.17. This represents a reduction of stunting more than one and a half times faster than the national rate of annual improvement (based on the period 1998-2001). This positive result may have been affected by the transfer size, representing 18 percent of average monthly household expenditure, and the inclusion of multiple nutrition-related conditions, including health checkups for children under age five, participation in community-based growth monitoring for children from birth through age two, and mothers' attendance of health and nutrition education sessions that covered topics such as household sanitation, nutrition, reproductive health, and breastfeeding. RPS also provided iron supplements and deworming medicine to children (Maluccio and Flores 2005).

Honduras's PRAF, on the other hand, had no significant impact on stunting. Although the percentage of stunted children remained essentially unchanged across all three intervention groups and the control group, there was an increase in the percentage of underweight and wasted children, suggesting that PRAF did not protect children against deteriorating nutritional status, caused at least in part by the coffee crisis (Flores et al. 2003). In Honduras there was also no impact on HAZ. Double-difference impacts in mean HAZ fell under the demand-side intervention by 0.02 and under the supply-side intervention by 0.03 but rose slightly under the combined intervention by 0.02 (IFPRI 2003b, 73). This lack of impact is somewhat surprising given that the program required attendance at regular health checkups by children and pregnant women as well as participation by all children under age two in monthly growth-monitoring sessions, which included individualized counseling for mothers on topics such as infant feeding and hygiene practices.[4] However, the monthly transfer size was small, representing only 4 percent of average monthly household expenditures (Maluccio 2004; Schady 2006). Taken together, the small transfer size, sporadic transfer distribution, and insufficient supply-side services may have accounted for PRAF's failure to produce anthropometric results (IFPRI 2003b).

Although CCTs in Colombia, Mexico, and Nicaragua all resulted in a lower prevalence of stunting and higher mean HAZ for young children, the final impact evaluation of Brazil's Bolsa Alimentação found that the program had an adverse effect on nutritional status.[5] A comparison of beneficiary and excluded children showed that even though beneficiary children began to eat a better-quality diet as a result of the program, they experienced *less* weight gain than their nonbeneficiary counterparts—31 grams per month less according to Morris et al. (2004) and 37 grams per month less according to IFPRI (2003a).[6] Furthermore, beneficiary children began to grow *less* rapidly once the transfer became available to the family, even though these children had exhibited a tendency to grow faster than excluded children before they received the transfer (IFPRI 2003a, 29). In sum, as a result of Bolsa Alimentação beneficiary children from birth through age two had lower WAZ by 0.25 and lower HAZ by 0.11 compared to nonbeneficiaries (Morris et al. 2004, 2339).[7] These results—which have subsequently been reversed—were not large, but the possible explanations are instructive with regard to understanding the types of incentives to which one must be attentive in a conditioned program. A previous milk powder distribution program had removed families from the program once children gained weight, and even though this was not the case with Bolsa Alimentação, beneficiary mothers may have assumed that benefits would be discontinued for children exhibiting healthy growth and, hoping to extend the duration of their CCT benefits, may have limited the food intake of their children. Alternatively, health personnel may have manipulated the weight data, again in an effort to increase the proba-

[4] Growth monitoring in PRAF was based on the country's AIN-C program.

[5] Estimates of the program's impact on stunting prevalence are not noted in the literature.

[6] The evaluation compared beneficiaries with a control group of nonbeneficiaries who were selected to receive program benefits but subsequently excluded due to random administrative errors (Morris et al. 2004).

[7] Results were adjusted for household demographic composition and Bolsa Escola beneficiary status (Morris et al. 2004).

bility that children would remain covered by Bolsa Alimentação benefits (IFPRI 2003a; Morris et al. 2004).

Anemia

CCTs have demonstrated mixed results on anemia. PRAF demonstrated no evidence of impact on anemia rates among children ages twelve through twenty-three months in any of the intervention groups (IFPRI 2003b). This is consistent with the lack of impact on any nutritional indicator, but the results do not indicate the specific reason behind the lack of impact.

Even though Nicaragua's RPS provided iron supplements, the program demonstrated no impact on anemia in beneficiary children. This lack of impact may have resulted from inconsistent delivery, shortages, and incomplete doses. The program had a large impact on the percentage of mothers receiving iron supplements for their children in the previous four months. The double-difference average impact was 38 percent, in spite of substantial increases among the control group (Maluccio and Flores 2005, 53). Still, these supplements were not necessarily consumed. The qualitative study in the 2002 evaluation uncovered the fact that some beneficiary mothers did not give the iron supplement to their children because of its perceived bad taste and negative gastrological effects (Adato and Roopnaraine 2004). Finally, if children were already deficient in other micronutrients that limited their hematological response to iron supplementation, they would not exhibit reduced anemia rates (Hoddinott 2010).

Results from PROGRESA/Oportunidades in Mexico show positive impacts on anemia. According to Gertler, PROGRESA resulted in a 25.5 percent reduction in the likelihood that a child age twelve through forty-eight months would be anemic (Gertler 2004, 340). Rivera confirmed this, finding in an experimental study that exposure to PROGRESA had a positive impact on anemia rates (Rivera et al. 2004). According to a 2004 study, Oportunidades was associated with a greater hemoglobin concentration (0.3 grams per deciliter) in children ages twenty-fourth through thirty-five months, resulting in anemia rates 5 percentage points lower for beneficiary children than for nonbeneficiary children in this age group; no impact was noted for older children (ages thirty-six through forty-seven months). These results are not surprising because iron needs are much higher for children ages twenty-four through thirty-five months, and therefore, any additional iron intake would be likely to have a proportionally larger impact for this age group (Hernandez-Prado and Hernandez-Avila 2006, 58).

Oportunidades did not demonstrate an impact on maternal anemia rates (the sample included women over age eighteen who were not pregnant). There are several possible explanations for this lack of impact. First, there was only a small percentage of lactating women who reported consuming the nutritional supplement (which contains iron). Second, the iron content of the supplement was characterized by poor bioavailability, so even if was consumed, it would not improve hemoglobin content as much as expected. Finally, iron requirements are significantly higher during pregnancy. Differences in anemia rates may also have resulted from the study design, in which there were many more women with recent pregnancies (and higher anemia rates) in the first year of evaluation, when the study found higher anemia rates, than in the follow-up evaluation, when the study found lower anemia rates (Hernandez-Prado and Hernandez-Avila 2006, 110).

The success of PROGRESA/Oportunidades in reducing both stunting and anemia among young children may be due to the large transfer size (representing over 20 percent of average monthly household expenditures) and high rate of program coverage (76 percent of households in program areas were selected to participate, and 97 percent of these accepted) (Sridhar and Duffield 2006, 16) as well as the broad range of nutrition-specific conditions targeted to high-risk groups: pregnant and lactating women, children from six through twenty-three months of age, and children ages two through four years old with low weight (Neufeld 2006). In addition to required health checkups and child immunization, mothers must attend health and nutrition education sessions and take their under-five children to be weighed on a monthly basis. The program also provides children with antiparasitcs, multivitamins, and iron supplements and pregnant and lactating women, children between four and twenty-four months and between two and five years old with any signs of malnutrition with a nutrition supplement (called a *papilla*) (Skoufias 2005; Handa and Davis 2006). Oportunidades has not shown a positive impact on breastfeeding practices—in fact, there was a 1.5-month decrease in breastfeeding duration, although not statistically significant—suggesting that the educational component could be strengthened (Hernandez-Prado and Hernandez-Avila 2006, 74).

Understanding the reasons for CCT impacts on nutritional status is difficult, because to date CCT impact evaluations have not been able to disentangle the differential impact of individual program components (that is, income transfer versus additional program activities) or of program conditions in the area of nutrition on observed outcomes. Further analysis comparing different types of nutrition-related activities linked to CCTs and testing any conditionality attached to these would provide much-needed information about the optimal design of CCTs (Bassett 2008). These results would also inform UCT programs and affect decisions about the complementary activities they might include.

Table 8.2 outlines the range of CCT impacts on food consumption and nutrition.

Table 8.2—Impacts of conditional cash transfers on food consumption and nutrition

Country, program	Household food consumption	Stunting prevalence	Mean height-for-age z-scores	Anemia prevalence
Brazil, Bolsa Alimentação	+6 percent in caloric availability +9 percent in dietary diversity +12 percent in caloric availability from healthier nonstaples (especially fruits and vegetables)		-0.11	
Colombia, Familias en Acción	No change in food share but dietary quality improved	-6.9 percentage points probability of being stunted (birth to age two)	+0.16	
	Meat and dairy: +19 percent; fats: +14.3 percent (urban), +24 percent (rural); grains: +9.3 percent (urban), +16.7 percent (rural)	No impact (ages three through seven)		
Honduras, PRAF	No impact on total food consumption	No impact	No impact	No impact
Mexico, PROGRESA	+10.6 percent in mean per capita food consumption	-10 percentage points (ages twelve through thirty-six months)[a] -6 percentage points (birth through age five) -7.3 percentage points (birth through age three)	+0.33	-10.6 percentage points -25.3 percentage points[b]

Mexico, Oportunidades	Increased dietary diversity (especially in vegetables)	-5.5 percentage points (birth through age five)		-5 percentage points (ages twelve through thirty-six months) No impact (ages thirty-six through forty-seven months and women)
Nicaragua, RPS	+4.5 percentage points in food share (as a percentage of household budget) Increased dietary diversity	-5.5 percentage points	+0.17	No impact

Sources: Hoddinott, Skoufias, and Washburn (2000); IFPRI (2003b); Olinto et al. (2003); Attanasio and Gomez (2004); Gertler (2004); Morris et al. (2004); Rivera et al. (2004); Attanasio et al. (2005); Maluccio and Flores (2005); Attanasio and Mesnard (2006); Hernandez-Prado and Hernandez-Avila (2006); Hoddinott (2010).

Notes: PRAF = Programa de Asignación Familiar; PROGRESA = Programa de Educación, Salud y Alimentación; RPS = Red de Protección Social. Blank cells indicate that results were not evaluated.

[a]Taking into account the nonrandom nature of the *papilla* allocation.

[b]Low figure from Rivera et al. (2004); high figure from Gertler (2004).

Complementary Activities for Nutrition

The evidence presented on both CCT and UCT programs shows that these programs can have important effects on food consumption and, in some cases, nutritional status. For HIV-affected families, cash can provide the means to purchase more and better-quality foods. However, there may also be a need for direct nutritional support to meet beneficiaries' particular nutrition needs. For example, an HIV-positive individual may not be able to access adequate foods in the local market and may therefore require special food and micronutrient supplements. Nutrition counseling is also essential to support critical behavioral changes such as appropriate food consumption, diarrhea treatment, and prevention of mother-to-child transmission of HIV. This section describes some additional nutritional activities that could complement cash transfers to benefit HIV-affected households for which cash alone is not enough.

In addition to the increased expenditures on food and improved nutrition that cash assistance alone can lead to, complementary services, such as nutrition education classes, growth monitoring accompanied by counseling, and micronutrient or nutritional supplementation, can further improve dietary and caloric intake while also improving caring and feeding practices associated with healthy infant development—all of which are critical for HIV-affected families. Many food and nutrition programs implemented by NGOs, CBOs, international organizations, and governments provide complementary activities in nutrition that might be integrated with cash transfer programs. These activities can be, but do not necessarily need to be, conditions of receiving the grant. Instead, the grant could be used as a way to facilitate access and participation and to put households in a better financial position to take advantage of new knowledge.

Micronutrient Supplementation

Given the relationship between micronutrient status (particularly vitamin A deficiency) and immunity, ensuring an adequate intake and absorption of micronutrients can be particularly important for HIV-positive individuals (West 2003). There is also some evidence that micronutrient supplementation can be effective in reducing risks associated with mother-to-child transmission (MTCT) of HIV. A study by Filteau in Bangladesh and Tanzania, in which women took antioxidants, particularly vitamin E, late in pregnancy and early in lactation, suggests that this may have contributed to a lower risk of subclinical mastitis, which can affect HIV transmission via breastfeeding (Filteau et al. 1999, cited in Gillespie and Kadiyala 2005, 50). Although trials of vitamin A supplementation among pregnant women in Malawi, South Africa, and Tanzania did not demonstrate reductions in MTCT—and even increased the risk of vertical transmission in Tanzania—multivitamin supplementation (with vitamins C, E, and B) for breastfeeding women in Tanzania moderately reduced HIV transmission in this phase, even for women with poor nutritional status (Coutsoudis et al. 1999; Fawzi et al. 2000, 2002, cited in Gillespie and Kadiyala 2005, 51; Kumwenda et al. 2002). Overall, the evidence suggests that micronutrient supplementation during pregnancy can improve pregnancy and birth outcomes, but it has not been shown to decrease MTCT, except for multivitamin supplementation during lactation, which can reduce transmission during breastfeeding. Vitamin A supplementation for preschool children suffering from HIV has been shown to reduce morbidity and mortality, alleviate persistent diarrhea, and improve height and weight (Coutsoudis et al. 1995; Fawzi et al. 1999; Villamor et al. 2002, cited in Gillespie and Kadiyala 2005, 52, 55).

CCT programs in Mexico and Nicaragua have included the provision of micronutrients (Skoufias 2005; Maluccio and Flores 2005). The conditional component of Kenya's Cash Transfer for OVC requires children ages one through five to attend growth-monitoring sessions at which they receive vitamin A (Kenyam, OVPMHA 2006). Fortified food transfers (see the "Food, Nutrition, and Antiretroviral Therapy" section that follows) and interventions to increase dietary diversity are other ways of increasing micronutrient intake.

Nutrition Counseling

Perhaps the most important intervention to prevent MTCT is counseling about proper infant feeding practices. Because HIV can be transmitted through breast milk, replacement feeding is recommended when it is culturally acceptable, affordable, safe, and sustainable. However, in many places ravaged by the HIV/AIDS epidemic, replacement feeding does not meet these criteria because mothers cannot afford replacement milk and clean water is not available. A recent review of breastfeeding and replacement feeding found that replacement feeding in low-income countries is associated with a higher risk of infant mortality (Coutsoudis and Rollins 2003, cited in Gillespie and Kadiyala 2005, 53). A modeling exercise by Ross and Labbok (2004) shows that for HIV-infected women, exclusive breastfeeding for 6 months is less risky than replacement feeding (with HIV-free survival increased by 32 per 1,000 live births), but after six months, replacement feeding is safer. Given that these recommendations are somewhat complicated and change over time, counseling and follow-up that would help women make appropriate decisions about infant feeding could contribute to improved child outcomes.

More generally, nutrition counseling targeted to HIV-affected individuals can extend the asymptomatic period, stave off opportunistic disease, and prolong lives (Piwoz and Preble 2000, cited in Gillespie and Kadiyala 2005,

53). A study in Ghana by Tabi and Vogel (2006) of the effectiveness of nutrition counseling in improving health outcomes for HIV-affected adults not taking ARVs demonstrated that receiving 7 months of nutrition counseling about protein intake led to significant weight gain among HIV-affected adults. Although the study allowed for detection of a statistically significant increase in weight in the first month, the small sample size (25) made it impossible to detect the smaller increases in weight that occurred after the second month. Tabi and Vogel (2006) recommend individualized nutrition counseling tailored by gender, age, and socioeconomic and cultural background.

Food Supplements

In some cases, nutritional supplements or food transfers may also be necessary to help HIV- and AIDS-affected individuals meet their heightened nutritional needs. Food rations can prevent mild weight loss, and therapeutic foods can help rehabilitate moderately and severely malnourished children and adults who are HIV positive (Gillespie and Kadiyala 2005, 54). Kenya's Cash Transfer for OVC plans to provide UNIMIX, a fortified and enriched nutrient customized for malnourished children (Kenya, OVPMHA 2006, 9). Of concern, however, is the fact that although studies of high-energy and high-protein supplementation have demonstrated that consuming these in additional to the home diet can lead to weight gain (largely fat rather than lean muscle mass), it does not prevent or reverse muscle wasting, a key factor that determines survival (Piwoz and Preble 2000, cited in Gillespie and Kadiyala 2005, 55).

Food, Nutrition, and Antiretroviral Therapy

Food and nutrition are increasingly being associated with the efficacy of ART and patient compliance with drug regimens. There are complex interactions between the consumption of different macro- and micronutrients and the bioavailability and therefore the efficacy of ARVs. For example, a meal high in fat, energy, and protein increases the bioavailability of some types of ARVs (for example, tenofivor), while decreasing the absorption of others (for example, indinavir). Furthermore, some ARVs should be taken with food, while others should be taken on an empty stomach; some should be taken with particular foods; and others are contraindicated with specific foods (Castleman, Seumo-Fosso, and Cogill 2004, 5–6). ART management and nutritional recommendations, therefore, need to be drug specific.

Difficulties in complying with food and nutrition recommendations—often due to inability to access the right foods or absorb them due to existing malnutrition—can lead to poor adherence to ARV regimens. This, in turn, can increase the likelihood of drug resistance, which facilitates opportunistic disease development and the onset of AIDS (Jones and Holloman 2000, cited in Gillespie and Kadiyala 2005, 57). According to a 2005 study conducted by the Consortium for Southern Africa Food Security Emergency in Zambia and Zimbabwe, the provision of corn-soy blend rations resulted in greater acceptability of ARV treatment and better adherence to drug regimens (Greenblott 2007). Cash transfers accompanied by nutritional counseling tied to specific ARV regimens could do the same, although the provision of food and cash transfers in combination may be the most effective means of supporting patients and their families. This is an issue that needs further investigation.

Conclusion

Cash transfer programs, whether UCT or CCT programs, have improved food consumption and dietary diversity and, in some cases, nutritional status. These outcomes are of critical importance to HIV-affected households because they can mitigate the impacts of HIV and maintain an improved quality of life as well as prevent transmission of the disease. As in the case of health impacts, there is insufficient evidence to allow us to determine the effect of conditionality on these outcomes, and we must depend on upcoming results and further testing in different contexts.

Given the importance of food and nutrition to HIV-positive individuals and the constraints to achieving food and nutrition security in the context of poverty, high dependency ratios, and reduced productivity, cash may not be enough, and direct nutritional support may be needed. This chapter outlines some complementary activities, such as nutrition counseling and micronutrient and food supplementation, that could improve outcomes for HIV-positive beneficiaries. Those designing cash transfer programs in communities with a high HIV prevalence should take into account the specific nutritional needs of beneficiaries and consider incorporating complementary activities along with the cash transfer.

CHAPTER 9

Complementary Approaches: Legal and Psychosocial Services, Adult Education and Awareness Programs, Microcredit and Work

AIDS-affected families, like all families, have a diverse array of needs. Cash transfers are not a panacea, and families need other types of economic and social support. Presentations of this review of cash transfers inevitably provoke the argument that cash is not enough, that AIDS-affected families need other kinds of services, such as social welfare services and legal protection, adult education and awareness programs, and opportunities for earning a living through work. In response, we are including a discussion of these different types of activities because (1) we agree that these must constitute a comprehensive strategy for social protection of AIDS-affected families; (2) we recognize that some donors, governments, and NGOs are more comfortable with approaches that potentially make a more direct contribution to labor market participation and economic growth—that is, public works, microcredit, and livelihoods training—and will make their contributions in this form, even if it does not achieve the coverage that a cash transfer would; and (3) we understand that cash transfers can be used to facilitate access to these other services. Linking cash transfers to education, health, and nutrition services, conditional or not, is one set of approaches to facilitating this access, as discussed in the previous sections. Outreach and informational activities, cash disbursements, and other operational processes of the transfer programs present opportunities to involve beneficiaries in other complementary activities. The cash itself can also be used to invest in other activities, depending on the size of the grant; the circumstances of the individual, household, and community; and the nature of supporting services. Other complementary activities offering many forms of care, services, and information can benefit all types of beneficiaries.

There are a number of ways to arrange the provision of complementary services. A first consideration is which services and activities respond to the highest-priority problems and needs. Complementary activities can include, for example, adult literacy classes, credit and job training to address household poverty, immunization drives, health and nutrition education to address child and family health and increase HIV and AIDS awareness, HBC, and referral for ARVs.

A second consideration is who should benefit from the activities. Some activities would be useful for all beneficiaries, while others would target smaller subsets of the beneficiary population. One way to arrange complementary services for key subgroups is to apply a life-cycle approach that involves considering each stage in the life cycle and determining the key interventions in critical periods that can have a positive long-term impact (Tinker, Finn, and Epp 2000, 5). For example, children from birth through age five would have access to nutrition, health, and sanitation services; children ages six through eleven would have access to quality schooling; and children ages twelve through seventeen would receive vocational training as well as health and sex education (Devereux et al. 2005). Other sets of interventions would respond to the needs of adults and the elderly. Similarly complementary services can be tailored to different stages of HIV/AIDS progression. That is, complementary activities can provide specific services to the following groups: HIV-negative, HIV-positive but asymptomatic, people living with AIDS, children living with ill adults, and orphans and other household members left behind when family members die of AIDS (Slater 2004).

The third consideration—and the least developed at this stage—is how complementary activities can be linked with cash transfers. One option is to provide services that can easily be delivered at a cash pay point, following a model used in Integrated Child Development Services Nutrition and Health Days in India. In that program, on days when people come to receive a food transfer, pregnant women and children under age two receive a range of health and nutrition interventions on a single day in a single place, including iron-folic acid and vitamin A supplements, nutritional supplements, immunizations, and nutrition education (Nemer, Gelband, and Jha 2001, 42). This approach is convenient for beneficiaries and may reduce costs for providers due to economies of scale. Another approach is to create specific linkages between the cash transfer program and other organizations that provide services and to connect cash transfer beneficiaries—by means of referrals or personalized visits—with these services. Finding ways to link complementary services with cash transfers without requiring participation (as in a conditional program) remains a challenge, but some interesting examples are emerging. Table 9.1 illustrates a range of complementary activities provided by existing cash transfer programs. Most of these are conditional programs,

Table 9.1—Complementary activities in existing and planned cash transfer programs

Country, program	Conditional cash transfer?	Complementary activities/services
Argentina, Jefes de Hogar	Yes	Professional and other training programs (mainly for principal beneficiaries); labor-related activities and job placement support
Brazil, Bolsa Familia	Yes	Breastfeeding and healthy nourishment programs for mothers (offered by local governments); youth and adult literacy programs; employment and income-generating programs offered by municipalities
Chile, Chile Solidario	Yes	Activities identified as personalized assistance in one of several areas (e.g., health, education, employment, housing, income, family life, legal documentation) that participants enter into by signing and complying with a contract
Colombia, Familias en Acción	Yes	Availability of networks of beneficiary mothers (e.g., women's rights, program management); identification documents; registration; women's empowerment; resource management; encouragement of mothers to attend courses on hygiene, diet, and other topics related to health and nutrition (this is not compulsory)
El Salvador, Red Solidaria	Yes	Support in obtaining identification documents
Honduras, Programa de Asignación Familiar	Yes	Productive training for youth; credit programs directed to adults; training for parents' associations

Jamaica, Programme for Advancement through Health and Education	Yes	Referral of youth who did not qualify for program benefits to social workers who provide advice on accessing benefits from other agencies geared toward youth support; training for beneficiaries and primary agents in schools and health facilities; rehabilitation grants for parents of some beneficiaries (for starting income-generating projects); case management; social worker referral
Kenya, Cash Transfer Program for Orphans and Vulnerable Children	Yes/no	Awareness sessions to promote household skills to deal with health and family issues (nutrition, child and maternal health, social health, prevention and treatment of chronic illness such as malaria, HIV/AIDS, sexually transmitted diseases, etc.)
Mexico, Programa de Educación, Salud y Alimentación / Oportunidades	Yes	Training workshops on health self-care issues; information portals; savings support for retirement; Heritage Component: encouragement of gradual accumulation of economic benefits to which students can gain access when and if they complete middle and higher studies before age twenty-two
Pakistan, Child Support Program	Yes	Preparation of computerized national identification cards; opening of bank accounts
Paraguay, Red de Protección y Promoción Social	Yes	Adult literacy; diagnosis, detection, and attention to children from birth through age five regarding malnutrition problems; identification campaigns directed at undocumented mothers; committees of beneficiaries
Uganda, Community-Led HIV/AIDS Initiatives	Yes/no	Provision of home-based care and food (for regular and orphan-headed households); vocational training materials, fees, and other dues to orphans; HIV/AIDS education through drama and film; shelter construction; basic household items

Sources: Attanasio et al. (2005); Ayala Consulting (2006); Plaatjies (2006); World Bank (2007a).

although some newer programs are mixed, with both unconditional and conditional components. Another challenge is to determine whether uptake of complementary services will work without conditions and, if not, what types of conditionality would be appropriate.

There are many other complementary services and activities that would be appropriate to link to cash transfer programs serving families affected by HIV and AIDS. These are discussed in the sections that follow.

Facilitating Access to Institutions and Documents

One constraint limiting the uptake of social grants is the lack of identification documents, often required for program application and receipt. A number of studies have found that one of the principal reasons that primary caregivers in South Africa do not access the CSG is because they do not have the documents needed to obtain it, such as birth, marriage, and death certificates (Woolard, Carter, and Agüero 2005; Hunter and Adato 2007a, 2007b). According to UNICEF, registering a birth is critical to providing a child the right to a name, nationality, and legal identity (UNICEF 2005). Children who are not registered at birth are vulnerable and experience difficulties establishing their identity and forming family ties. In addition to supporting these fundamental elements of child identity, birth certificates can facilitate children's access to basic services, such as schooling and social assistance, and protect them against many forms of abuse (UNICEF 2007e).

In South Africa, there is a negative correlation between poverty and birth registration, and yet such registration is needed in order to access a cash transfer for the child. In other words, those who most need state support are the least likely to have the documents needed to access that support, and the difficulties of registering births are exacerbated in the context of HIV and AIDS. Birth registration and identification books are needed to access not only cash grants but also housing subsidies, job creation programs, and death benefits (Giese and Smith 2007). The requirement for a birth certificate is a hindrance for accessing cash transfers, but the immediate incentive to register a birth in order to obtain a grant will make that child more likely to have access to other benefits over her lifetime.

Cash transfer programs can also play a role in supporting birth registration and facilitating access to identification documents for beneficiaries (Chapman 2006). For example, in Paraguay a cash transfer program involved identification campaigns directed at undocumented mothers (Ayala Consulting 2006). Another option to overcome the lack of birth documentation is to give midwives birth registration forms to fill in when babies are born (van Dijk 2007).

In Turkey, the CCT program requires that applicants provide marriage certificates or divorce papers to apply for benefits for their children and that parents and children have citizen cards and numbers.[1] In an evaluation of the CCT program, officials and beneficiaries said that for a large number of women, this resulted in their formalizing their marriages and obtaining birth certificates for their children and that these requirements have allowed poor families to obtain citizenship cards and numbers, facilitating the processing of their requests from a range of state institutions (Kudat et al. 2006).

Information and Awareness Campaigns

A growing number of cash transfer programs disseminate information about health, nutrition, HIV, and other topics related to promoting human capital. For example, Kenya's Cash Transfer for OVC provides lectures on child and maternal health and nutrition and on prevention and treatment of chronic illnesses (malaria, HIV, STDs) for beneficiaries receiving both CCTs and UCTs. These awareness sessions are based on UNICEF modules used for community health and nutrition training and are coordinated by UNICEF and the Government of Kenya (Kenya, OVPMHA 2006, 6).

Malawi's DECT program included a well-developed system of sensitization messages delivered on paydays. While beneficiaries were waiting for their turn to collect the cash payment, the DECT program disseminated messages using teachers and facilitators, as well as local music and drama groups that shared messages via songs and plays. Often trained government staff delivered messages, but when no one of this level was available, Concern field officers stepped in. The provision of messages varied across DECT locations, based on staff availability and timing. If a field team arrived late to the pay point, they did not provide messages (Devereux et al. 2007, 8).

The key messages provided to DECT beneficiaries were related to the primary, secondary, and complementary objectives of the program. They included use of the transfer for family food consumption and farming (coupled with nutrition messages on the last two paydays), HIV/AIDS prevention, and use of smart cards. Concern Worldwide community liaison staff conveyed behavioral messages about HIV and AIDS, taking aside chiefs and elders to teach them separately in an effort to inform more men about this sensitive issue. Beneficiaries recalled messages about condoms and HIV testing. However, because of the variation in the coverage of sensitization messages, some beneficiaries reporting never or rarely having heard such messages. Program evaluators surmised that HIV/AIDS information may have been presented before some beneficiaries arrived at the pay point, while they were involved in the administrative activities of picking up the transfer, or after

[1] In Turkey, single, never-married parents are rare among the poorest 6 percent of the population eligible for CCT benefits.

they departed from the pay point (Devereux et al. 2007, 9–10). In general, beneficiaries' impressions of the sensitization campaign were largely positive. The use of local musicians and actors, as well as the dancing that often accompanied the music, mitigated the boredom of waiting in line for the cash transfer. And beneficiaries often found the teachers and facilitators effective and funny (Devereux et al. 2007, 11).

Information campaigns alone may not be sufficient to significantly affect health outcomes, however, particularly with respect to HIV transmission. According to Malawi's 2004 Demographic and Health Survey, despite overall advanced knowledge about HIV transmission and infection vectors, HIV prevalence remains high. This suggests that Malawians may understand the causes of HIV/AIDS but have not adapted their behavior. Information campaigns, then, are unlikely to be successful without other services that help overcome key constraints to behavior change, such as the provision of free condoms, VCT, or ARVs (McCord 2005). (See the "Psychosocial Support" section.)

Psychosocial Support

Children living in households affected by HIV and AIDS can experience a range of hardships, from poverty and ill health to social instability and grief, all of which affect their physical, cognitive, and psychological development. Psychosocial needs—"to be happy, creative, to belong in social groups, and to have hope for the future"—can be addressed at home by strengthening children's daily routines and seeking opportunities for normal childhood behavior (for example, playing) or through programs or activities beyond what children receive in their home environment (Richter, Foster, and Sherr 2006, 9, 16–17).

Richter, Foster, and Sherr (2006) argue that psychosocial support, care, and rehabilitation are best provided by the family or the community because children who experience lasting supportive, stimulating, and affectionate relationships are more likely to feel hope for the future as well as to develop resources for coping with the challenges of HIV and AIDS. The authors recommend involving local CBOs and prioritize placing and keeping children in settings with supportive family or other caregivers before looking to outside interventions. For children who suffer from extreme mental or behavioral disorders, the support of trained professionals may be necessary (Richter, Foster, and Sherr 2006, 11).

Cash transfers could be linked to psychosocial support services. One such example is Mozambique's National Institute for Social Action program, which itself provides psychosocial support (Devereux et al. 2005). In Malawi's SCTS, CBOs, extension workers, and child protection workers collaborate to link cash transfer beneficiaries to psychosocial support services (UNICEF 2007).

Psychosocial services would be particularly helpful and can be tailored for groups affected by HIV and AIDS in specific ways, such as orphans and girls experiencing abuse.

Social Welfare Services, Child Protection, and Other Legal Protections and Entitlements

A growing interest has emerged among a number of international organizations in examining the potential for increasing the role of social welfare services (SWS) in the context of social protection. SWS include family support services such as ECD, assistance with access to services and transfers, parenting support, substance abuse counseling, legal support, and home-based care. SWS also include child protection services provided to abused, neglected, or exploited children, including early detection and response, policy enforcement, and case management. Social protection is seen as an access point through which SWS can play an increased role, and SWS are seen as a means of complementing and improving transfer programs. Among the issues discussed at an international meeting on this topic in 2007 was the need to investigate means of building linkages between SWS and cash transfers. Ideas included potentially using the targeting process, by which families or individuals are screened for benefit eligibility, to identify their social service needs. Follow-up could then occur, whether or not the family qualified for transfers. Another opportunity for linkages would be to use pay points (where people collect their transfers) for making contact with a large number of families to gather information on social welfare needs and provide information on available SWS (UNICEF 2008).

Cash transfer programs provide the benefit of increasing legal protections and entitlements through some of their documentation requirements. As noted earlier, they provide incentives for families to obtain documents such as birth certificates and marriage and divorce certifications that can also provide a range of legal protections over time. Linkages with cash transfer programs could also potentially be facilitated for other forms of legal protection with special relevance to AIDS-affected families and individuals, such as child protection, inheritance protection, and other legal services. Children may need special attention in the context of changing household structures, as well as the new vulnerabilities created by the illness and death of parents and other relatives and increased levels of poverty in their households and communities. Women may also need special attention because they face a variety of abusive circumstances, including vulnerability to asset loss in the case of the death of a spouse. In Zimbabwe, a program called Linkages for the Economic Advancement of the Disadvantaged (LEAD) helps protect the assets of low-income AIDS-affected households by providing vouchers for legal services (for example, drawing up wills, handling guardianship and maintenance claims for orphans). The voucher ensures that a beneficiary can select and consult with a lawyer from a firm participating in the LEAD program free of charge (AED 2003, cited in Gillespie and Kadiyala 2005, 73). A Save the Children report about the inheritance problems of vulnerable members of society, including orphans (especially girls) and widows, suggests that community workers be trained to disseminate information about legal rights, wills, and other legal issues via radio, theater, brochures and leaflets, posters, and discussion groups (*IRIN News* 2007).

As cash transfer programs expand, it is important to pay attention to how these may be affecting the need for child protection and other social welfare services in unanticipated ways. For example, in South Africa at least a few cases have been reported of conflicts between family members over who will take charge of children who have lost their parents related to the opportunity presented for access to the large FCG (about three times the size of the CSG). The result may be that relatives who are more powerful but worse caregivers will take charge of the children (Meintjes and Giese 2006, 420; Giese 2007/08, 18). There has been no documentation of the extent to which this is a problem, but these cases highlight the importance of effectively functioning social services that can detect and respond to these situations when they arise, particularly in cases of abuse. A related problem in the South African case is that the DSD is responsible for the administration of both the social security grants and social services, so the impressive rollout of the grants has resulted in a "crowding out" of social welfare services. According to a DSD document, the crowding-out effect has resulted in the severe curtailment and neglect of other services (South Africa, Department of Social Development 2007).

Microcredit, Access to Finance, and Productive Activities

As discussed in Chapter 2, there are both hopes and doubts about the potential for microfinance to play a significant role in assisting HIV-affected individuals and communities. Although HIV-affected households, and particularly foster families and single parents widowed by AIDS, could certainly benefit from income and productive investments, there are risks to targeting high-risk groups with microcredit programs (World Bank 2005). Households affected by HIV and AIDS are likely to experience more difficulty in repaying loans due to the combination of increased household expenses (for example, for medicine) and loss of income providers in the household. The diversion of loans from productive uses to immediate HIV/AIDS-related expenses (for example, for medicines, caretakers, and funeral costs) and the possible lack of availability of both productive members of the household and members with knowledge about running businesses, can exacerbate repayment difficulties and lead to higher default rates. Borrowers affected by HIV and AIDS may also be less able to attend meetings. In many cases, when a family member is diagnosed with HIV or AIDS, the borrower stops repaying the loan due to diminished motivation and psychological trauma (Wilkinson 1999; Bondevik 2003).

Despite these risks, there are innovations to make microfinance viable for HIV/AIDS-affected clients. From the perspective of microfinance institutions (MFIs), maintaining a diverse portfolio—a mixture of HIV-affected and non-affected beneficiaries—can preserve profitability (UNCDF/SUM 2003; Nyamandi 2005). From the perspective of households, microfinance can play a role in mitigating the impact of HIV by providing cash that has protective and preventive functions (Nyamandi 2005). Arguments for additional roles that microfinance can play are based on the facilitating role that MFIs and implementing partners tend to play in the course of program operations. These include organizers of community gatherings, which are opportunities for sharing information and implementing prevention activities (for example, using nonformal education techniques to promote behavior change and linking clients to other prevention services) at low cost (Nyamandi 2005). For example, by relying on existing financial staff to deliver preventive HIV/AIDS messages to large numbers of microfinance clients during monthly microfinance gatherings, the NGO Credit with Education can provide these important additional services at low cost (Bondevik 2003). The Intervention with Microfinance for AIDS and Gender Equity (IMAGE) program in South Africa also linked poverty-targeted microfinance with participatory adult learning on topics such as sexual behaviors, gender-based violence, and HIV prevention (IMAGE 2002, cited in Gillespie and Kadiyala 2005, 72). As suggested earlier, these kinds of adult education and awareness campaigns can be carried out in the context of a cash grant as well as a loan, but microcredit can take advantage of the infrastructure and staff of existing loan dispersal programs.

In addition to linking microfinance with health information, awareness raising, and education, several design elements have been suggested for microfinance programs in an HIV/AIDS context. The United Nations recommends that microfinance services be targeted to clients who are HIV-positive but still productive family members and to surviving family members (UNCDF/SUM 2003). Loans can be designed with built-in flexible terms that provide a "rest" for clients between loan cycles and do not require that clients necessarily move to larger loans (Nyamandi 2005). MFIs can incorporate innovative financial products, including health insurance covering costs involved with dealing with opportunistic disease, burial and funeral insurance, insurance of outstanding loan balances against the client's death, or emergency loans (Bondevik 2003; Nyamandi 2005).

An example with some of these features is the Zambuko Trust in Zimbabwe. The program lent money only to HIV-affected clients who were economically active, and it included several requirements: a mandatory 1 percent insurance fee that would cover the loan if the client died, obligatory savings, and strict enforcement of group responsibility for loans. The Trust's HIV-affected clients had a higher percentage of school enrollment among boys ages six through sixteen and more savings accounts than did non-HIV-affected clients (Barnes et al. 2001, cited in Gillespie and Kadiyala 2005, 72).

There are some examples of cash transfer programs with links to microcredit and income-earning opportunities. Mozambique's INAS program (which followed the GAPVU cash transfer program) provided support for income-generating projects (Devereux et al. 2005). In a few countries in Latin America, there are plans in development for linking cash transfers with savings and loan programs. El Salvador's Red Solidaria had as one of its planned interventions a Sustainability Network for Families that would promote and fund productive projects and microcredit to support the CCT beneficiaries, particularly small farmers (El Salvador 2007). However, in the very poorest regions, a straight CCT is being rolled out on a large scale, with the microcredit to follow later, and the reach of the program is uncertain; certainly it is likely to be far more limited than the scale of the CCT. This all returns us to the point made earlier: although microfinance and livelihoods activities have the potential to help poor, AIDS-affected families secure livelihoods, and such programs should be promoted and adapted to reach these families at the pace and scale possible, it is likely that the most destitute will not be well positioned to benefit, and a cash transfer should be available as a safety net.

Apart from microfinance, cash transfers provide other types of opportunities for poor people to access finance and to save. Cash transfer programs that transfer funds through bank accounts have allowed people who have never had an account to open one. In Mexico, Oportunidades began depositing its cash transfers in bank accounts for some beneficiaries, and by 2006 about 1.2 million beneficiary families received their transfers this way. This opened up their access to other financial services (Oportunidades 2006b). In socially conservative regions of Turkey, female CCT beneficiaries' interactions with banks and government departments have a particular significance, empowering women who have never before had any contact with a bank as they now deal with bank officials, ATMs, and deposit books (Kudat et al. 2006; Adato et al. 2007).

Public Works

Public works programs provide payment in cash or in kind in return for labor. There is no consensus among governments, donors, and NGOs about the appropriateness of these programs for HIV/AIDS-infected and affected households, which often face labor constraints. Some argue that public works are never suitable for HIV/AIDS-affected households, while others assert that asymptomatic HIV-positive individuals, who may be "vulnerable but viable," can participate in public works schemes and that their inclusion in such programs is an important way to minimize stigma (Harvey 2004, 35). As in the case of microcredit and livelihoods programs, public works can provide cash with valuable spin-offs, including those specific to the needs of people affected by AIDS, but they will serve the subset of the better off. Also, the more intensive and integrated the activities in a public works program, the fewer people can be covered (Adato et al. 1999).

Targeting in public works programs may not be optimal for HIV/AIDS-affected households. Self-targeting—based on an offer of low wages—is frequently used to ensure that only poor households participate in public works projects. However, for HIV-positive individuals who have particularly high nutritional needs, self-targeting processes that induce households to either lower consumption (due to low wages) or take on physically challenging work without sufficient caloric intake could accelerate the onset of AIDS (Slater 2004).

Appropriate employment for HIV/AIDS-affected households usually differs from that for a healthy population, which can undertake physically demanding labor. HIV-positive individuals may need programs offering a reduced workload, low-input activities (for example, beekeeping, low-intensity horticulture), and labor-saving techniques. These arrangements can allow beneficiaries to continue work even after some illness has set in (Slater 2004; McCord 2005). A CARE Food-for-Work program in Zimbabwe made separate arrangements for ill beneficiaries, such as light work duties (for example, childcare for children whose mothers were working on the project) and restricted demands (for example, smaller bucket sizes or reduced work norms). The Zibambele Program in KwaZulu-Natal targeted extremely vulnerable labor-constrained households affected by HIV/AIDS. It offered flexible work time (for example, 8 days per month) and flexible hours to allow beneficiaries to cover their caring duties in the home (McCord 2005). The Mashuro Small Scale Irrigation Project in Gutu, Zimbabwe, applied light productivity work norms to PLWA who participated in earthwork, nursery management, and development of canals (Kayira, Greenaway, and Greenblott 2004, 10).

Instead of providing employment exclusively to individuals, some programs have used household contracts, which allow households to substitute a different worker if the primary public works beneficiary falls ill or dies. Household contracts can also allow for the diversification of household income because the primary public works program beneficiary can take another job while the secondary beneficiary continues to work in the public works project

(McCord 2005). The Working for Water program in South Africa, which used teams of exclusively HIV-positive workers, trained two workers for every one worker needed. This enabled both the work and the beneficiary household income to continue uninterrupted, although it also doubled training costs (McCord 2005). The Zibambele Program also provided household contracts. According to recent research on the program, despite the low monthly income—due to the low wage and the fact that most workers were working part time—the Zibambele Program had a significant impact on education and food consumption outcomes for children in public works households. The percentage of households that reported regularly reducing children's meal sizes because they could not afford food fell from 34 percent to 1 percent, and regular school attendance increased from 67 to 90 percent. At the same time, beneficiaries reported engaging in fewer activities that caused them to feel shame (for example, a need to beg), experiencing a lesser psychosocial burden and becoming more likely to carry out ceremonies to mark the anniversary of family deaths (McCord 2005, 36–37).

Even with limited work responsibilities and household contracts, demands on caretakers in households with a public works beneficiary and other sick household members may increase significantly. In these conditions, public works programs that pull the remaining viable household member(s) away may detract from household well-being unless other services, such as support for OVC, are provided (Slater 2004; McCord 2005).

Another approach that offers a partial solution to this problem is a form of public works program that involves the direct provision of social services for those affected by HIV and AIDS. This can include paying beneficiaries to work in HBC, ARV roll-out, ECD, voluntary counseling and testing, and birth registration, among other services (McCord 2005). For example, the Zimbabwe Red Cross HBC program has provided work for more than 2,000 HBC facilitators selected by their communities. These facilitators were generally unemployed, minimally educated women who had been affected by HIV/AIDS in some way: many were HIV positive themselves, while others were caring for an ill family member or had experienced the loss of a family member. Therefore, the facilitators understood on a personal level the challenges of living with HIV and AIDS and the stigma associated with it. Facilitators were trained (for a total of about two months) in both the theoretical underpinning of HBC and the practical tasks and were tested for competence before starting work independently. Once working, they trained family members in appropriate care, monitored patient conditions, and offered basic nursing and referral, identified children affected by HIV/AIDS, disseminated information about drug side effects and compliance, and networked with other service providers (McCord 2005, 42). In Mozambique, a program of the World Food

Programme (WFP) has provided food as an incentive to HBC workers since 2002. By providing one-third of the ration that chronically ill beneficiaries receive, the program brought about improved quality of HBC care, enabling HBC workers to meet their own food needs and fulfill their HBC responsibilities (Kayira, Greenaway, and Greenblott 2004, 17).

Public works programs can also target youth, who may be losing knowledge passed down through generations as parents die of AIDS. The Junior Farmer Field and Life Schools, run by the Food and Agriculture Organization of the United Nations (FAO) and WFP in Mozambique, provided food for training to out-of-school youth, especially teen orphans, who learned technical and entrepreneurial skills. OVC ages twelve through seventeen were trained for one year in both traditional and modern agricultural techniques. To complement the technical training, participatory educational drama helped the youth groups explore sensitive issues around HIV/AIDS, psychosocial problems, gender roles, and health and nutrition (Kayira, Greenaway, and Greenblott 2004, 16).

Experience from a number of public works programs illustrates that such programs are conducive to linkages with IEC components. For example, some food for training programs have paid community activists to learn about HIV/AIDS prevention and care and then teach these concepts to the broader community. Other programs have targeted truck drivers transporting food and workers at food or wage distribution points with HIV prevention messages (McCord 2005).

Using public works beneficiaries to provide key services for HIV/AIDS-affected households (for example, HBC and ECD) raises the concern that, if poorly trained, these workers could harm rather than help households affected by HIV/AIDS and OVC. Proper coordination, training, and supervision are needed to provide quality services (McCord 2005; Altman 2007). This raises a trade-off, however, between scale and quality of training—in that the number of people who can be reached will be a small fraction of those in need—similar to that faced by South Africa's National Public Works Programme, which aimed to provide formal qualifications as well as significantly reduce unemployment, a difficult combination (Adato et al. 1999).

South Africa's Expanded Public Works Programme (EPWP) is emphasizing new forms of training. Its current program includes a social sector involving home- and community-based care (HCBC) ECD programs. These are a response to both unemployment, providing a form of social protection, and to the AIDS epidemic, because the programs are designed to benefit those providing services (mainly women, who normally do this work without training or payment), as well as those adults and children receiving care. The HCBC component has emphasized stipends for volunteers and provision of accredited training. The ECD component has thus far focused mainly on skills provision for care providers. In addition to care providers, the ECD plan also envisions work for gardeners, cooks, and administrators as part of ECD provision. South Africa's Department of Health and Department of Education also have HCBC and ECD programs, respectively, which are linked in varying ways with the EPWP. The social-sector component of the EPWP has moved slowly and not yet received the priority that was envisioned (Parenzee and Budlender 2007). However, it has important potential as a model for HIV/AIDS-responsive social protection in South Africa and elsewhere.

Beyond providing services tailored to HIV-affected households, public works programs can support the creation of private assets for households affected by HIV/AIDS, such as simple kitchen gardens and school gardens (McCord 2005, 20). Kitchen gardens, generally placed near homesteads, can boost household consumption of fruits and vegetables and, in times of surplus, can generate additional household income. Community gardens run by HIV-positive self-help groups and those caring for children affected by HIV/AIDS can provide similar benefits, and school gardens can produce food for school-based consumption and generate income to support vulnerable school children. Home gardens in Ethiopia, Uganda, and Zimbabwe focused on increasing crop diversity, planting vegetables with high protein and micronutrient value and medicinal herbs, and teaching food storage and processing techniques. PLWA have received food rations for participating in training to start their own home gardens, and targeted community members have received food rations for working on trench, kitchen, and community gardens for labor-constrained HIV/AIDS-affected households. Similarly, households have also received payment for participation in training about home sanitation, water treatment (for drinking water and wastewater management), composting, developing wood fuel briquettes from home waste, maintenance and treatment of water supply facilities and pit latrines, and behavior change (Kayira, Greenaway, and Greenblott 2004, 13).

Conclusion

AIDS-affected families, like all families, have diverse profiles and a diverse array of needs, and cash transfers do not respond to all of these needs. Indeed, there must be a comprehensive social protection system to allow families affected by HIV and AIDS to meet these needs. Several key issues must be considered when arranging the provision of complementary services: (1) which services respond to priority needs; (2) who should benefit from the activities, all beneficiaries or a subset (for example, those at a specific stage of the life cycle or those experiencing a specific stage of HIV or AIDS illness); and (3) how complementary activities can be linked with cash transfer programs. Cash transfer programs can facilitate access to other critical services provided at cash pay points. Thus far this approach is more theoretical than proven, but it would be convenient and efficient for beneficiaries and providers, reducing costs due to economies of scale and using referrals or personalized visits to connect cash transfer beneficiaries to services.

There are many complementary services and activities that would be appropriate to link to cash transfer programs serving families affected by HIV and AIDS. Facilitating access to documents such as birth registration and marriage certificates can, in turn, increase access to services. Information and awareness campaigns can provide important information on HIV prevention and mitigation. Information alone, however, may not be enough to effect behavioral change. Instead, other products and services may be necessary, such as free condoms, VCT, or ARVs. Psychosocial support services already provided by some cash transfer programs or linked to them can be particularly beneficial to AIDS-affected families facing stigma and the loss of loved ones and breadwinners. Social welfare services and child protection are particularly important because children may need special attention in the context of changing household structures, new vulnerabilities created by illness and death of parents and other relatives, and increased levels of poverty in their households and communities.

Although households affected by HIV and AIDS are likely to experience more difficulty repaying loans due to the combination of increased household expenses and loss of income providers in the household, microcredit can be tailored to meet the needs of these households through the provision of flexible loan terms that allow clients to "rest" between loans as well as participatory adult learning on topics such as sexual behaviors, gender-based violence, and HIV prevention. These should be approached carefully, however, for if misguided they could do more harm to families than good.

Public works programs can be designed to meet the needs of HIV-affected households by offering lighter workloads, flexible hours, and household contracts, which allow an additional person from a household to participate in the program. Public works can also involve the direct provision of social services for those affected by HIV and AIDS (HBC, ARV roll-out, ECD, and VCT) and the creation of private assets for households affected by HIV/AIDS, such as simple kitchen gardens and school gardens. Still, it is important to note that although microfinance and public works programs have the potential to help poor AIDS-affected families secure livelihoods, it is likely that the most destitute will not be well positioned to benefit, and a cash transfer program should be available as a safety net.

CHAPTER 10

Conclusions

Social protection plays an important role as part of a comprehensive response to HIV and AIDS. It is needed to break the vicious circle of HIV/AIDS and food insecurity and to stem the loss of human capital among AIDS-affected families. Cash transfers have demonstrated a strong potential to reduce poverty and strengthen children's education, health, and nutrition, and thus they can form a central part of a social protection strategy for families affected by HIV and AIDS. This conclusion is based on evidence from (1) studies of several large-scale, well-established transfer programs in southern Africa; (2) studies from newer, smaller cash transfer programs in southern and eastern Africa; (3) modeling of impacts of cash transfers in Sub-Saharan Africa; and (4) studies of CCTs in Latin America and Asia.

Impacts of Cash Transfers

CCT programs have demonstrated large, statistically significant impacts on poverty and on education, health, and nutrition outcomes, mainly for children. This research is from Asian and Latin American countries, where HIV prevalence is very low and impacts on families affected by AIDS are thus neither measured nor a policy objective. However, the impacts of CCTs are reviewed in this monograph because they offer the best evidence to date of the potential of cash transfers to protect and improve the human capital of poor children. With respect to education indicators, most CCTs have significantly increased school enrollment and attendance, and some have affected other indicators such as grade progression and dropout rates. There is variation between the magnitude of impacts across countries, types of indicators measured, and target groups, for example, between primary and secondary schools, girls and boys, and rural and urban, but most programs show consistent, significant, and substantial impacts, particularly where indicators are low at baseline. There has been less demonstration of impacts on achievement, calling for more attention to the quality of schools—a challenge that will be even greater when CCTs move to Sub-Saharan Africa. In terms of health and nutrition, CCT programs have increased health service use and reduced the incidence of illness, although evidence of the latter is weaker than that of the former. CCTs have achieved strong results with respect to increases in the quantity and quality of food consumption and improvements in nutritional status, although the latter varies considerably across countries and types of indicators. Like education, health service quality, particularly for certain kinds of services such as prenatal care, is a huge challenge and limits impacts (Morris 2010). Again the challenge will be even greater in Sub-Saharan Africa.

Although most of the Latin American countries producing the reported CCT impacts have better infrastructure, services, and administrative capacities than do most countries in Sub-Saharan Africa, strong CCT impacts have been achieved in some very poor countries with low levels of infrastructure and implementation capacities, such as Bangladesh and Nicaragua. Design and implementation approaches have been adapted to different country conditions, capacities, and objectives.

UCTs, with a growing presence in eastern and southern Africa, have also demonstrated substantial positive impacts on the well-being of families and children. These results come from modeling using large national datasets in South Africa and empirical studies at the provincial, district, or subdistrict level in several countries. The main impacts demonstrated in South Africa have been on school enrollment. Significant gender discrimination in schooling decisions in some countries indicate that it is critical to pay attention to gender issues in designing programs. One approach is through a hard or soft conditionality for girls' schooling, although this must be considered in light of whether other contextual factors make conditionality feasible or appropriate. One option might be to offer a supplemental grant if all girls are in school.

There may also be some impacts on schooling via the spending of cash transfers on school expenses. In all southern African countries in this review, the largest grant expenditures by far were on food, which could also have an indirect effect on schooling via nutrition and health improvements, although these studies did not examine this impact pathway. OAP spending on education in several countries, modeling exercises comparing grant modalities, and evidence of pension-driven enrollment effects found in South Africa suggest OAPs are one way of supporting children's education. Evidence from South Africa also suggests that cash transfer programs targeted to the elderly (particularly women) can have a positive impact on children's nutritional status. However, pensions will miss children in households without elderly residents and will be lost if the recipient passes away. A grant for households with children will better ensure that children have grant access. There is no evidence yet, however, establishing what type of grant income ultimately leads to children's well-being across different measures.

UCTs have had some impacts on self-reported health status in several countries. There is also some limited evidence of impacts of UCTs on nutritional status, though they were not directly assessed in most evaluations—a gap that should be addressed in future cash transfer evaluations. The fact that an impact on child height in South Africa was found only where the CSG was received sufficiently early in a child's life and covered the majority of the first three years of his life demonstrates the importance of cash transfers for very young children, and also that of guaranteeing continued receipt during this critical period of child growth and development. Impacts on health and nutrition from other country studies are inferred only from health expenditures, although these amounts were mostly very small. Health spending could imply improved health but not necessarily; lower health spending among households with cash transfers could also represent a diminished need to spend on healthcare resulting from better health.

UCTs were largely spent on food and led to increased food consumption in beneficiary households. In most of the programs evaluated, grants were associated with self-reported reduction in hunger and an increase in the average number of meals per day, except when the transfer size was too small. In some countries the transfer was also associated with an increase in dietary diversity. The role of factors such as seasonality or nutrition education is sometimes unclear, but cash transfers are boosting household food intake, resulting in less hunger.

Analyses of existing cash transfer programs and country simulations demonstrate that these programs have the potential to reduce poverty, particularly the poverty gap and the severity of poverty, if they are targeted to poor households, households with children, households without able-bodied members, or the elderly. The impacts on headcount poverty tend to be smaller, showing that the poor are generally not pushed above the poverty line, but the fact that the poverty gap and the severity of poverty measures improve as a result of cash transfer programs illustrates that the very poor would benefit.

These impact findings collectively present a convincing case that cash transfers not only reduce poverty and increase food consumption but can improve certain education, health, and nutrition indicators. No other social protection mechanism has yet demonstrated these impacts through well-designed impact evaluations. At the time of this writing, only a few rigorous evaluations of UCTs in southern and East Africa were available; other studies had smaller sample sizes or weaker control groups, but additional well-designed, large-scale evaluations were under way, and they will add to the evidence base in the coming years. Still, given the urgent needs of AIDS-affected families, there is sufficient evidence to conclude that cash transfers can play an important role in the mitigation of HIV/AIDS impacts, as well as in prevention.

Targeting

Targeting transfers in the context of HIV and AIDS involves decisions around who most needs benefits, whether to target AIDS-affected families or very poor families and how to reach both, and what criteria and processes will best reach them. There is ample evidence that HIV/AIDS drives many processes that undermine food security and increase poverty. Targeting through indicators that capture the poor *and* proxies for AIDS-affected households can most effectively reach those who are the most vulnerable and least resilient in the face of HIV and AIDS. In a country like South Africa, where cash transfers are not rationed, poverty criteria alone are sufficient to reach AIDS-affected households (although only those with children, which is problematic). In countries such as Malawi and Zambia, where the grants are rationed to 10 percent of a given community, reaching AIDS-affected households requires overlaying poverty criteria with proxy indicators of AIDS-affected households: labor constraints, illnesses, and high dependency ratios have been effectively used thus far.

An alternative approach is to use categorical targeting of the elderly. More than half of the orphans living in six countries in southern and East Africa were living with grandparents, and there is considerable evidence of the positive impact of OAPs on children. An OAP could be targeted based on means testing (depending on costs and benefits), or additional criteria such as dependency ratios could be applied where narrower targeting was necessary. However, this approach would miss adults and children in households without elderly members and would leave others vulnerable to the death of the elderly member. If the goal is to reach children, a per-child designated grant is probably the most effective means, although evidence based on comparative impact assessments is lacking in this debate. Political considerations will also be relevant—what types of grants are most likely to garner political support.

An important process of political mobilization for social protection in the context of HIV and AIDS has convened largely around OVC, but this has proved problematic. Questions have arisen as to how to define a vulnerable child, whether orphans are disadvantaged in relation to nonorphans—including children with ill parents as well as those suffering other forms of deprivation and trauma—and whether children affected by AIDS are more in need of material assistance than poor children affected by other misfortunes, for example, other diseases, conflicts, or conditions making their families chronically unable to secure a livelihood. The evidence is complex. Orphans are in very poor households and also in better-off households that can afford to take them in. Some studies find that orphans are disadvantaged with respect to food security, nutrition, health, and education; other studies find that they are not. These findings are not necessarily contradictory but rather are contingent on variables such as the relationships between children and caregivers, their poverty or wealth status, and household demographics and structure. Targeting to respond to these variations at a household level would be infeasible. In light of concerns around accuracy, equity, and stigma, a consensus is building around targeting cash transfers based on poverty and multiple vulnerability criteria rather than targeting orphans or families living with AIDS.

A more difficult ethical quandary surrounds people on ART. Evidence of the importance of nutrition to the effectiveness of ART has motivated programs providing food transfers to clients, and more recently there have been suggestions that cash transfers be targeted similarly. However, food is likely to be a better form of transfer for those on ART given the primary nutritional objective of the transfer and the immediate need for food support as well as food with particular nutritional properties. But cash provides flexibility to meet other needs of patients, such as transportation to pick up their drugs. There is no research to date comparing food versus cash transfers for ART patients, and such research would be helpful. However, cash and food transfers have different objectives: administered in conjunction with ART, the latter provide not so much social protection as nutritional rehabilitation, and many programming guidelines require cutting off the food when the patient has improved (to a certain BMI). In this light, a direct food transfer for ART patients received in conjunction with their treatment, coupled with a cash transfer for households or children, would be optimum.

Another set of targeting issues relates to the methods best suited to target AIDS-affected families within the context of administrative capacities. There are currently three main systems that predominate with respect to targeting cash transfers. In Latin America, where there is administrative and financial capacity to carry out data-intensive proxy means test surveys and analysis, these programs tend to perform well in targeting extreme poverty. This method is probably not practical or cost efficient in the context of low administrative capacity and sparsely populated areas and would also likely be politically problematic if there was no community involvement in decisions in which as little as 10 percent of a community received transfers. The system used in South Africa, applying an application-based means test, has worked reasonably well as long as the burden of proof for the means test has not been unreasonable in the socioeconomic context: in the past, when documentation was required that people could not access, there were very large exclusion errors. Targeting has improved since these requirements were relaxed in practice. The fact that the level of coverage is so high in South Africa means that there are far fewer exclusions that have to be negotiated at the community level.

In Kenya, Malawi, and Zambia, regional and local committees supervise community-based targeting systems, applying a set of common criteria and processes. Although not without their flaws, these community-based processes are reported to generally work smoothly and provide a basis for consensus rather than conflict; this is important when just a small portion of the population will receive assistance. These processes appear to have performed reasonably well with respect to identifying AIDS-affected households to receive benefits. However, concerns remain that they are missing some of the very poor and that they may not be sufficiently effective and cost-efficient. They involve a substantial amount of transaction costs and capacity building to implement, which is a challenge as programs scale up to a national level. Nonetheless, given the variation in household conditions and the complex configurations of deprivation and dependency, a generic targeting formula using standard poverty proxy indicators applied uniformly would probably produce errors. Complexity is better managed at a local level, with communities better positioned to judge circumstances and give such attention to detail—as long as the committees are strong and impartial and checks and balances are functioning. A study comparing different targeting methods in Zambia (Watkins 2008) concludes that categorical targeting is less expensive than a proxy means test but that additional criteria are needed to identify the poor. The study found that in two out of three districts, community-based methods (compared with poverty deciles) were effective in identifying the poorest households, whereas in one they were not. The poorly performing district had less easily identifiable ultra poor and more clustering around the mean. The study authors therefore recommended that methods be selected based on local conditions, moving from geographic targeting to community-based targeting to proxy means tests as the prevalence and severity of poverty decrease.

Several additional conclusions emerge from recent experience with targeting. First, the right balance must be found between using an equitable, uniform process of applying the criteria and a qualitative assessment that catches errors of application or what the other criteria miss. Second, programs should consider giving the transfer primarily to women or the designated primary caregivers of children, as in the Latin American and South African models; this contributes to improvements in women's status and that of children. It would also ensure that women in polygamous households are not disadvantaged. Third, special design features, or other forms of assistance altogether, are needed to reach hard-to-reach children, such as street children and those in child-headed households. Fourth, all of the alternative targeting methods, from proxy means tests to community-based methods, carry risks of missing certain kinds of households and individuals, for example, remote households living in difficult terrain, migrants, and people who self-exclude or face discrimination by other community members due to race, ethnicity, caste, disability, HIV/AIDS status, or other factors. Ways to reach these groups, through eligibility criteria and targeting methods, should be carefully designed into the process. Fifth, given the impacts of HIV and AIDS, the human costs of errors of exclusion are graver than the financial costs of inclusion errors, assuming that the latter are not so high as to make the program nonviable. It is worth allowing some inclusion errors in order to reduce exclusions.

Conditionality

This monograph has focused heavily on the implications of cash transfers for protecting human capital because of the threats that HIV and AIDS pose to the human capital of families, including the health, nutrition, and education of children. These threats result from a vicious downward spiral involving illness, loss of income and assets, decreased food security, the need for children to care for the ill or otherwise work, inability to afford healthcare and school expenses, and stigma and emotional distress that reduce children's participation or performance in school. A concern over the ability of cash transfers to affect human capital is also driven by the evidence on the interactions among early childhood nutrition, health, and education and the effect of these interactions on long-term income-earning potential and thus long-term intergenerational transmission of poverty or emergence from it. In other words, many children who are not protected from the effects of HIV and AIDS on their families now will never recover.

For these reasons, we examine not only UCTs in southern and eastern Africa but also CCTs in Asia and Latin America, which are designed primarily to strengthen nutrition, health, and education and may thus provide lessons for progressing toward these goals in Africa. CCTs have shown much promise globally but also raise many concerns as they are introduced in new contexts—and heavily AIDS-affected contexts are certainly one such type. This monograph has reviewed the debates around conditionality and the key issues that policymakers should weigh in considering them. For Sub-Saharan African countries concerned with mitigating the impacts of AIDS, these include, first, the importance of designing them to carefully address priority issues rather than adopting a blueprint from Latin America. For example, if in South Africa AIDS risk is reduced specifically where girls graduate from high school, CCTs should be designed specifically with the objective of increasing high school matriculation rates rather than adopting a generic primary school attendance design if the attendance level is already high. Furthermore, although cash transfers may help children stay in school by substituting for children's contribution to subsistence production or by paying for school expenses, they may not meet the need for girls to take care of ill relatives or small children (in which case an alternative or complementary program of HBC or ECD might be more effective). Conditionality is a form of incentive and can be designed to encourage participation in, for example, secondary school or health awareness (including HIV prevention) services. Conditionality may be appropriate for particular geographic areas under particular combinations of circumstances—for example, high numbers of orphans, low attendance rates, and evidence of discrimination against girls in schooling—or availability of health services but low levels of participation.

The second key policy issue is whether a CCT produces added value (for example, in school enrollment) beyond an UCT; if not, the purpose of conditioning should be questioned. Answering this question requires more evidence than is yet available. The few analyses looking at this question with respect to education in Latin America have found significant impacts attributed to conditionality; the one study in Africa did not. But these are not sufficient to be definitive. The third issue is whether conditional transfers will be more politically popular and thus fiscally sustainable than unconditional transfers. Currently the idea is controversial and far more unpopular among social protection advocates than is the case in Latin America. However, some other policymakers and many among the middle classes are more comfortable providing money with obligations, or they prefer health and education programs to transfers; but conditionality helps get cash transfers in the door.

Fourth, and of greatest significance, is whether a country has the administrative capacity, service availability, and budgets necessary to run a CCT. A related issue is the urgency with which transfers are needed and how long it would take to build up the needed capacity. Although answers to all these questions will vary by country, the overall conclusion that we reach at this time is that UCTs are more appropriate to respond to the immediate needs of severely AIDS-affected communities and households in low-income countries in southern and East Africa. Some poor countries in Asia and Latin America have had very successful CCTs, and many have used their program as an impetus to improve education and health services, bringing in NGOs to support government provision where needed. NGOs already provide many services in Africa where government does not. Given the importance of improving services, regardless of whether there are cash transfers, it would be worth considering whether the current interest in CCTs could be used to accelerate service improvements. However, supply improvements will be very slow at best. For this reason, UCTs are more appropriate for the near term for severely AIDS-affected communities in need of immediate support. Conditionalities should be tested on a small scale to determine their impact on carefully selected outcomes and where appropriate services are available.

In this regard, there are services and activities—from productive economic activities and early childhood development to adult education and health awareness—that can be linked to cash transfer programs, with participation in these activities encouraged but not required. This new area needs experimentation in terms of modalities and mechanisms for linkages.

Social Protection in the Context of AIDS: Cash Transfers versus Alternative Interventions

A final key policy debate addressed in this monograph concerns the relative advantages of cash transfers vis-à-vis alternative social protection interventions for families affected by HIV and AIDS. Criticisms of a cash transfer approach are driven, on the one side, by concerns about meeting urgent nutritional needs via food and nutrition interventions, and, on the other side, by the preference for building sustainable livelihood opportunities through promoting economic activities. Furthermore, some argue that cash transfers are simply not sufficient to meet the diverse psychosocial, social welfare, and legal needs of families and individuals affected by HIV and AIDS. These are all valid arguments, and for this reason we have included a discussion of food-based interventions in Chapter 8 (on nutrition) and Chapter 9 (on psychosocial, social welfare, legal support, public works, microcredit, and livelihoods interventions), which can be implemented alongside, independent of, as an alternative to, or in concert with cash transfer programs. Chapter 2 provided a conceptual framework for understanding the objectives of social protection and the types of interventions available for achieving them. The argument for cash as the most appropriate approach for a government-administered national system of social protection for households that are the very poorest and most severely AIDS affected is illustrated in this framework in terms of where they fall on the capacities-inputs-scalability continuum: cash transfers tend to require fewer capacities and inputs, are faster to scale up, and are more likely to achieve wider coverage than are alternative approaches.

This does not mean that cash transfers are the only approach. On the contrary, a mix of interventions is needed, appropriate to the priority needs and capacities of beneficiaries and implemented by different institutions. As seen in Chapter 8, a critical part of this mix involves food and nutrition programs. An HIV-positive individual may not be able to access or identify adequate foods in the local market and may therefore require special food and micronutrient supplements. A beneficiary may be so ill that she can consume only special foods due to mouth sores or nausea, for example. Nutrition counseling is also essential to support critical behavioral changes such as appropriate food consumption, diarrhea treatment, and prevention of mother-to-child transmission of HIV. Food and nutrition programs are likely to be particularly useful for subgroups of AIDS-affected families, for example, people on ART and children in need of nutrition rehabilitation. There is a developing literature on food versus cash transfers, but these studies need to be carried out looking through an HIV/AIDS lens, in high-prevalence areas. Food assistance will continue to play an important protective role. However, logistics, volatility of food prices, and the political economy at the international and national levels make it unlikely that food transfers would be scaled up as a national strategy of social protection. Furthermore, many international agencies and NGOs providing food-based support for HIV programs have policies that require ending the transfer once nutritional rehabilitation has taken place. This is very different from a cash transfer, which should be a dependable regular source of income for very poor families.

Chapter 9 presented options for economic strengthening through public works, microcredit, and livelihoods activities and how these can be adapted to the conditions of households and communities affected by HIV and AIDS. These are also important parts of a strategy for AIDS-responsive social protection. These approaches will be more effective for families that are "less affected"—less labor constrained, less destitute, and possibly better off in terms of various asset endowments. Given the level of inputs and capacities required, livelihoods support activities will simply not be able to reach as many people as cash transfers. They can be designed to be pushed toward the middle of that capacities-inputs continuum to be more AIDS appropriate—for example, toward public works involving less physically demanding work and livelihoods support activities involving home gardens or small livestock. Many NGOs are successfully implementing these kinds of programs for AIDS-affected families. They will remain, however, less amenable to being scaled up to meet the urgent and huge need that currently exists—a demand that will only continue to grow as disease stages progress and the regional impacts approach their peak.

A useful framework for determining the types of interventions needed by different categories of people (including the AIDS-affected poor) is offered by Malawi (2009) for the 40 percent of the population considered to be poor. For the 10 percent who are "ultra poor and incapacitated" and whose primary social support needs are survival and human capital investment, cash transfers and school feeding are recommended. For the 5 percent who are "ultra poor with labor capacity"—whose needs involve survival, productive assets, and employment—public works, school feeding, and cash and food for assets and consumption, combined with skill building, are recommended. For the 25 percent who are "moderately poor"—whose needs are for employment, skills, capital, productive assets, and protection from asset erosion—agricultural input subsidies, public works, insurance, and microfinance are needed.

"AIDS-affected families" do not constitute a homogenous category; they embody many variations with respect to wealth or poverty, education, household structure, stage of illness progression, dependency ratios, social status, and access to assets. This argues for a mix of social protection approaches rather than a single approach. However, pursuing a mix does not conflict with a national strategy of scaling up cash transfers for the most vulnerable families. Cash transfers are featured here because they offer an effective strategy for relatively quickly reaching AIDS-affected families who are the very poorest, most constrained, and at risk with respect to human capital. These are important considerations given the extent and nature of deprivation, the long-term risk to human capital, and the current international and national political willingness to act surrounding HIV and AIDS.

Additional knowledge gaps remain. These include gaps on operational issues such as the appropriate size of the cash transfer and how to give it flexibility under changing circumstances (for example, prices, markets); the number of transfers per household; whether, when, and how to transition households out of a program and into what to transition it; and how to scale up a program and the roles for government, NGOs, and CBOs in program implementation and service delivery.[1] Other questions pertain to human capital objectives and service delivery: what is the current status of services, what is the potential for improving them, and how can these constraints be overcome? Although poor infrastructure and low levels of administrative capacity are real constraints to the functioning of social protection programs, these have been overcome in some very poor countries and can be mitigated by careful program design and oversight and by the use of NGOs where government services are insufficient. Still other questions pertain to political economy: how much will the program cost, is this "affordable," who will pay for it, and how can this strategy be made politically viable? The last question is perhaps the most critical; ambitious plans to scale up in some countries have not received the follow-through anticipated, in substantial part due to political ambivalence.

Another concern is the relative cost-effectiveness of different social protection mechanisms, such as cash transfer programs versus free healthcare.

[1] See Fiszbein and Schady et al. (2009) and Samson, van Niekerk, and MacQuene (2006) for reviews of other cash transfer design issues.

Unfortunately, there are no cost-benefit analyses of different programs, and certainly not in HIV/AIDS-affected countries (Hagemejer and Behrendt 2008). We can, however, look at the estimated cost, represented as a percentage of GDP, to provide child benefits. According to an International Labour Organization study, a basic universal child benefit providing a maximum of 50 cents per day for two children under age fourteen per woman would cost from 1.0 to 3.5 percent of GDP for selected countries in Africa and Asia (about 3.5 percent in the countries in southern and eastern Africa, such as Kenya and Tanzania). In general, these costs will decrease over time. The study therefore concludes that low-income countries can afford to implement a basic package of social protection, especially when this is undertaken in partnerships between countries and donors. A full social protection package may not be feasible all at once; instead, a sequential approach may be more appropriate (Hagemejer and Behrendt 2008).

Social assistance and social security are often seen as luxuries available only to rich countries; however, they can also be seen as necessities for poor countries. These are all issues relevant to a wider antipoverty and social protection agenda but require further analysis through an HIV/AIDS lens. Such analysis can be done in the course of action as part of the efforts currently under way to scale up cash transfer programs and political processes currently under way to work for social protection as an integral part of the response to HIV and AIDS.

APPENDIX

Research Methods and Data

The first stage of preparing this monograph involved identification of the key focal issues: first the decision to focus on cash transfers, then a selection of the issues pertaining to cash transfers. A vast number of issues are related to cash transfers that potentially could be reviewed—including their impacts, technical aspects of program design, administrative and institutional issues, political economy, costs, and others—not all of which could be included in one monograph. Prioritization was based on prior knowledge and a preliminary review of the literature on social protection in general, especially in the context of HIV and AIDS, followed by consultation with stakeholders, including a presentation of the proposal to the Joint Learning Initiative on Children and HIV/AIDS (JLICA) Learning Group on Strengthening Families, discussion at a meeting of the UN Inter-Agency Task Team on Children and HIV and AIDS Working Group on Social Protection, and further discussions between members of JLICA and other stakeholders. These discussions took into account the focus of other papers and the significance of the questions discussed to the broader objectives of JLICA and its stakeholders.

The second stage involved a search of databases for peer-reviewed literature. The databases searched included the following: Agora-Cab 1; Agricola; CAB Direct; the Directory of Open Access Journals; Econlit; Eldis; PubMed; Highwire Press; Ingentaconnect.com; OAlster; PAIS International; Political Science: A Sage full-text collection; Scelio: Scientific Electronic Library Online; Scirius; Sociological Abstracts; Sociology: A Sage full-text collection; and Worldwide Political Science Abstracts. The publications selected from these searches were then entered into the program reference manager.

The third stage involved a broader literature search and review—the main research method used in the monograph—including a review of published and gray literature. This included a review of peer-reviewed journal articles, qualitative and quantitative program evaluations, program design documents and manuals of operation, published and unpublished working papers, and reports. The documents reviewed led us to more relevant documents, which we found on the web, through literature databases, or through email or telephone requests to authors or organizations that commissioned the studies. The gray literature was particularly important to this monograph because most of the research done on cash transfer programs in Africa is in this form, with little yet published in journals (this does not apply to the Latin America literature, for which we used both original project reports and subsequent journal articles). In total, over 300 documents were reviewed for this monograph.

The fourth stage involved analysis of the literature. This process began with a review of different types of cash transfer programs implemented in different contexts and ways in which they are or can be responsive to the needs of AIDS-affected families. A subset of programs was selected for in-depth review, including all those for which some evaluation or impact research had been done, where some data were available on education, health, nutrition, or poverty impacts (see Table 1.1 for descriptions of the programs selected). We did not include (1) programs without impact data, (2) programs such as disability grants with very narrow targeting criteria, or (3) programs that included work requirements.[1] A total of 20 cash transfer programs were analyzed in the monograph, along with 10 unconditional programs in East and southern Africa and 10 conditional programs (from Latin America, the Caribbean, and Asia).[2] Table 1.1 shows the unconditional cash transfer programs in Sub-Saharan Africa that we reviewed in this study, plus others that were extensions of earlier programs or current expansions or were otherwise mentioned in the monograph. We also included poverty impact results from empirical studies of 6 existing cash transfer programs (4 unconditional in South Africa and 4 conditional in Latin America) and simulation models for 18 African countries. Table A.1 shows the main evaluations from which data were drawn.

The analysis continued with a careful review of each document, collecting and summarizing each finding that provided information relevant to a wide range of issues (wider than those reported in this monograph). A large database was constructed in Microsoft Access, with approximately 65 variables (including descriptive characteristics and others related to issues of primary and secondary interest to the monograph). Data on these variables from the documents were entered into the database for all programs to the extent that the data were available on each issue. The table created a "case-ordered meta-matrix," organizing data by case (each country-based cash transfer pro-

[1] The one exception was the PSNP in Ethiopia, which had components with and without work requirements because of the large scale of this program and the quality of the evaluation, with outcomes of direct relevance to the focuses of this review.

[2] The exception among the 10 unconditional programs was the Ethiopian PSNP, which is partly conditioned on work.

Table A.1—Unconditional cash transfer program evaluations reviewed for program impacts

Country	Program	Study area	Study sample
Ethiopia	Productive Safety Net Program (PSNP)	8 *woredas*	960 households
Ethiopia	PSNP	262 *woredas*	3,700 households
Kenya	Cash Transfer Program for Orphans and Vulnerable Children	3 districts (Garissa, Kwale, and Nairobi)	500 beneficiary households; 250 control households
Malawi	Dowa Emergency Cash Transfer (DECT)	Dowa District	31 households (DECT and excluded); 37 key informants; 2 pay points
Malawi	Food and Cash Transfers Project	3 districts (Dowa, Lilongwe, and Nkhotakota)	1,000 households (500 beneficiary and 500 control)
Malawi	Social Cash Transfer Pilot Scheme	4 Traditional Authorities (Nyoka, Kapondo, Dambe, and Mduwa) within Mchinji District	819 households (round 1) 789 households (round 2) 766 households (round 3)
Mozambique	Gabinete de Apoio à População Vulnerável	Maputo	41 beneficiaries 40 non-beneficiaries (meet eligibility criteria)
South Africa	Social grants	Free State Province	163 HIV-affected households; 72 affected households that experienced morbidity or mortality in 3 or 4 periods; 108 households that did not experience morbidity or mortality
South Africa	Social grants	National	30,000 households (2000 Income and Expenditure Survey); 30,000 households (September 2000 Labour Force Survey); 20,000 (1998), 30,000 (1999) (October Household Surveys)
South Africa	Child Support Grant (CSG)	KwaZulu-Natal Province	245 children receiving the CSG before age three (from the KwaZulu-Natal Income Dynamics Study)

Time period	Methods	Comments
April-June 2006	Household and community questionnaires; key informant interviews; market survey	Sample not representative of all of Ethiopia or of all communities where PSNP was implemented
June-September 2006	Household and community questionnaires	Data collected more than one year after program began, so recall period was long; control group formed using matching methods
December 15-29, 2006	Household questionnaire; key informant interviews	No control group; long recall period (6 months)
April 2007	Secondary data review; qualitative fieldwork (focus groups, interviews, observation at pay points)	No control group
November 2005-May 2006	Monitoring data; household and market surveys; qualitative fieldwork	
March 2007-March/April 2008	Household questionnaire; qualitative fieldwork (focus groups, key informant interviews)	No strict control group but a comparison group was used
December 1997	Single-visit 24-hour recall for food consumption	Small sample size; exclusive focus on elderly beneficiaries in capital city
May 2001-December 2002	Household questionnaire	Small purposive sample
2000	Household questionnaire; poverty simulations, analysis of administrative data from the Department of Social Development	
1993, 1998, 2004	Household questionnaire	

(continued)

Table A.1—Continued

Country	Program	Study area	Study sample
South Africa	Child Support Grant	Umkhanyakude District, KwaZulu-Natal Province	11,178 households (data from the Africa Centre for Health and Population Studies longitudinal demographic surveillance system)
South Africa	Old-Age Pension	Langeberg Health District, Western Cape	1,300 individuals in 300 households
South Africa	Old-Age Pension	National	9,000 households
Zambia	Social Cash Transfer Scheme	2 agricultural blocks in Kalomo District	Randomized sample of 303 households (274 at end line)[a]

Sources: Bazo (1998); Duflo (2000, 2003); Case (2001); Tarp et al. (2002); Booysen (2004a); Samson et al. (2004); Case, Hosegood, and Lund (2005); Devereux, Mvula, and Solomon (2006); Devereux et al. (2006, 2007); Zambia, MCDSS/GTZ (2006); Acacia Consultants (2007); Agüero, Carter, and Woolard (2007); Gilligan, Hoddinott, and Taffesse (2007); Miller, Tsoka, and the Mchinji Evaluation Team (2007).

[a]Kalomo central agricultural block: baseline, 146 households; end line, 128 households; Kanchele central agricultural block: baseline, 157 households; end line, 146 households.

gram) on one axis and variables on the other (representing the key research themes and questions).

The next stage of the analysis focused on a narrower set of cross-cutting themes, comparing them across all programs for which data were available at the time the research for this monograph was done. The central cross-cutting themes of the monograph are (1) targeting, (2) conditionality, (3) impacts on poverty, (4) impacts on education, (5) impacts on health, and (6) impacts on nutrition. Gender is also brought out as a cross-cutting subtheme within each broader theme.

Findings on impacts come mostly from quantitative data to the extent that they were available. Findings on targeting and conditionality draw on quantitative and qualitative research. Where quantitative studies were conducted in such a way as to report on statistical significance (for example, in all of the CCT evaluations), we report only significant findings.[3] It is important to note that there is wide variation across the studies in research design, research and analytic methods, control groups, sample sizes, time frames,

[3] In the tables where we report impact findings, blank cells normally mean that the indicator was not evaluated.

Time period	Methods	Comments
2002-2004	Household questionnaire	No strict control group; used older siblings
1999	Household questionnaire; anthropometry; some open-ended questions	Self-reported health status (continued)
August-December 1993	Household questionnaire; anthropometry (children birth through age seven)	Kalomo: September 2004-September 2005
Kanchele: December 2004-December 2005	Household questionnaire; focus groups; key informant interviews with stakeholders	No control group

and so forth. The studies on CCT programs used the most rigorous methods from the discipline of economics, whereas the quantitative methods used in some of the UCT program evaluations vary substantially with respect to rigor (Table A.1 explains these variations). It is also important to note that at the time that this monograph was written, more rigorous impact evaluations of cash transfer programs were under way in several African countries, but the results of most were not available before this monograph was finalized; we have reported those that were available.

Table A.1 provides information on the design of the UCT programs reviewed or mentioned in this study. It also includes information on the newer planned program.

References

Acacia Consultants. 2007. Evaluation of cash transfer program in Nairobi, Kwale, and Garissa districts: Final report. Acacia Consultants / UNICEF, Nairobi, Kenya.

Adato, M. 2000. The impact of PROGRESA on community social relationships: Final report to PROGRESA. International Food Policy Research Institute, Washington, D.C.

Adato, M., and S. Gillespie. 2006. State and community in promoting resilience: Rethinking social protection for adults and children in the context of HIV and AIDS: A new research agenda. Concept note, International Food Policy Research Institute, Washington, D.C.

Adato, M., and L. Haddad. 2002. Targeting poverty through community-based public works programmes: Experience from South Africa. *Journal of Development Studies* 38 (3): 1–36.

Adato, M., and J. Hoddinott. 2007. *Conditional cash transfer programs: A magic bullet for reducing poverty?* 2020 Focus Brief on the World's Poor and Hungry People. Washington, D.C.: International Food Policy Research Institute.

Adato, M., and J. Hoddinott 2010. Conditional cash transfers in the second decade: Current debates and new frontiers. In *Conditional cash transfers in Latin America*, ed. M. Adato and J. Hoddinott. Baltimore: Johns Hopkins University Press.

Adato, M., and D. Mindek. 2000. PROGRESA and women's empowerment: Evidence from six Mexican states. In The impact of PROGRESA on women's status and intrahousehold relations, ed. M. Adato, B. de la Brière, D. Mindek, and A. Quisumbing. Final Report to PROGRESA, Government of Mexico. International Food Policy Research Institute, Washington, D.C.

Adato, M., and T. Roopnaraine. 2004. Un analysis social de la 'Red de Protección Social' (RPS) en Nicaragua. International Food Policy Research Institute, Washington, D.C.

———. 2010a. Conditional cash transfer programs: Participation and power. In *Conditional cash transfers in Latin America*, ed. M. Adato and J. Hoddinott. Baltimore: Johns Hopkins University Press.

———. 2010b. Women's status, gender relations, and conditional cash transfers. In *Conditional cash transfers in Latin America*, ed. M. Adato and J. Hoddinott. Baltimore: Johns Hopkins University Press.

Adato, M., A. Ahmed, and F. Lund. 2004. *Linking safety nets, social protection, and poverty reduction: Directions for Africa.* 2020 Africa Conference Brief 12. Washington, D.C.: International Food Policy Research Institute.

Adato, M., and S. Feldman with Z. Karelina. 2009. Understanding how gender relations shape outcomes of conditional cash transfer programs: Findings from Bangladesh and Turkey on gender-focused investment and policy reform in education. Photocopy, International Food Policy Research Institute, Washington, D.C.

Adato, M., T. Roopnaraine, and E. Becker. 2011. Understanding use of health services in conditional cash transfer programs: Insights from qualitative research in Latin America and Turkey. *Social Science and Medicine* 72 (12): 1921–1929.

Adato, M., L. Haddad, D. Horner, N. Ravjee, and R. Haywood. 1999. From works to public works: Labor-intensive public works in Western Cape Province, South Africa. International Food Policy Research Institute, Washington, D.C.

Adato, M., S. Kadiyala, T. Roopnaraine, P. Biermayr-Jenzano, and A. Norman. 2005. *Children in the shadow of AIDS: Studies of vulnerable children and orphans in three provinces in South Africa*. RENEWAL Discussion Paper. Washington, D.C.: International Food Policy Research Institute.

Adato, M., T. Roopnaraine, N. Smith, E. Altinok, N. Çelebioğlu, and S. Cemal. 2007. An evaluation of the conditional cash transfer program in Turkey: Second qualitative and anthropological study. Final report submitted to the General Directorate of Social Assistance and Solidarity, Prime Ministry, Republic of Turkey. International Food Policy Research Institute, Washington, D.C.

AED (Academy for Educational Development). 2003. *Multisectoral responses to HIV/AIDS: A compendium of promising practices from Africa*. Washington, D.C.

Agüero, J., M. Carter, and I. Woolard. 2007. *The impact of unconditional cash transfers on nutrition: The South African Child Support Grant*. Working Paper 39. Brasilia: International Poverty Research Center.

Ahmed, A. U. 2004. Assessing the performance of conditional cash transfer programs for girls and boys in primary and secondary schools in Bangladesh. International Food Policy Research Institute, Washington, D.C.

———. 2005. *Comparing food and cash incentives for schooling in Bangladesh*. Washington, D.C., and Rome: International Food Policy Research Institute and World Food Programme.

———. 2006. Evaluating the Reaching Out-of-School Children Project in Bangladesh: A baseline study. International Food Policy Research Institute, Washington, D.C.

Ahmed, A., M. Adato, A. Kudat, D. Gilligan, T. Roopnaraine, and R. Colasan. 2007. Impact evaluation of the conditional cash transfer program in Turkey: Final report. International Food Policy Research Institute, Washington, D.C.

Ainsworth, M., and D. Filmer. 2006. Inequalities in children's schooling: AIDS, orphanhood, poverty, and gender. *World Development* 34 (6): 1099–1128.

Ainsworth, M., and I. Semali. 2000. *The impact of adult deaths on children's health in northwestern Tanzania*. World Bank Policy Research Working Paper Series. Washington, D.C.: World Bank.

Alderman, H., J. Hoddinott, and B. Kinsey. 2003. *Long-term consequences of early childhood malnutrition*. Food Consumption and Nutrition Division Discussion Paper 168. Washington, D.C.: International Food Policy Research Institute.

Alderman, H., J. Behrman, D. Ross, and R. Sabo. 1996. The results of endogenous human capital in Pakistan's rural wage labor market. *Oxford Bulletin of Economics and Statistics* 58 (1): 29–55.

Alderman, H., J. Behrman, V. Lavy, and R. Menon. 2001. Child health and school enrollment: A longitudinal analysis. *Journal of Human Resources* 36 (1): 185–205.

Altman, M. 2007. Early childhood development (0–4) project. Presentation to the RENEWAL Workshop, Human Sciences Research Council, Washington, D.C., March 12–13.

Ashley, C., and D. Carney. 1999. *Sustainable livelihoods: Lessons from early experience.* London: Department for International Development.

Attanasio, O., and L. C. Gomez. 2004. *Evaluacion de impacto del programa familias en accion: Subsidios condicionados en la Red de Apoyo Social.* London: Institute of Fiscal Studies.

Attanasio, O., and A. Mesnard. 2006. The impact of a conditional cash transfer program on consumption in Colombia. *Fiscal Studies* 27 (4): 421–442.

Attanasio, O., L. C. Gomez, P. Heredia, and M. Vera-Hernandez. 2005. *The short-term impact of a conditional cash subsidy on child health and nutrition in Colombia.* London: Institute of Fiscal Studies.

Attanasio, O., E. Fitzsimons, A. Gomez, D. Lopez, C. Meghir, and A. Mesnard. 2006. *Child education and work choices in the presence of a conditional cash transfer program in rural Colombia.* London: Institute for Fiscal Studies.

Auvert, B., A. Buvé, B. Ferry, M. Caraël, L. Morison, E. Lagarde, N. J. Robinson, M. Kahindo, J. Chege, N. Rutenberg, R. Musonda, M. Laourou, and E. Akam. 2001. Ecological and individual-level analysis of risk factors for HIV infection in four urban populations in Sub-Saharan Africa with different levels of HIV infection. *AIDS* 15 (Supplement 4): 15–30.

Ayala Consulting. 2006. Country program profiles. Background document prepared for the Third International Conference on Conditional Cash Transfers, Istanbul, June 26–30.

Baird, S., C. McInstosh, and B. Özler. 2009. *Designing cost-effective cash transfer programs to boost schooling among young women in Sub-Saharan Africa.* Policy Research Working Paper 5090. Washington, D.C.: World Bank.

——. 2010. *Cash or condition?* Impact Evaluation Series 45. Policy Research Working Paper 5259. Washington, D.C.: World Bank.

Baird, S., E. Chirwa, C. McIntosh, and B. Özler. 2009. *The short-term impacts of a schooling conditional cash transfer program on the sexual behavior of young women.* Impact Evaluation Series 40. Policy Research Working Paper 5089. Washington, D.C.: World Bank.

Bakari, J. P., S. McKenna, A. Myrick, K. Mwinga, G. J. Bhat, and S. Allen. 2000. Rapid voluntary testing and counseling for HIV: Acceptability and feasibility in Zambian antenatal care clinics. *Annals of the New York Academy of Sciences* 918 (November): 64–76.

Barnes, C., E. Keogh, N. Nemarundwe, and L. Nyikahadzoi. 2001. *Microfinance and households coping with illness and death in Zimbabwe: An exploratory study.* Washington, D.C.: Management Systems International.

Barnett, T., and P. Blaikie. 1992. *AIDS in Africa: Its present and future impacts.* New York: Guilford.

Barrientos, A. 2003. *What is the impact of noncontributory pensions on poverty? Estimates from Brazil and South Africa.* Manchester, U.K.: Institute for Development Policy and Management, School of Environment and Development, University of Manchester.

———. 2004. Cash transfers for older people reduce poverty and inequality. Background paper. In *World Development Report 2006*. Washington, D.C.: World Bank.

Bassett, L. 2008. *Can conditional cash transfer programs play a greater role in reducing child undernutrition?* World Bank Social Protection Discussion Paper 0835. Washington, D.C.: World Bank.

Bazo, G. A. 1998. The impact of the food subsidy program on the vulnerable elderly in the city of Maputo: A comparison of consumption levels between participants and nonparticipants. Thesis, Eduardo Mondlane University, Maputo, Mozambique.

Beales, S. 2007. How older people spend their pensions. HelpAge International, London.

Behrman, J. R. 2000. *Literature review on interactions between health, education, and nutrition and the potential benefits of intervening simultaneously in all three.* International Food Policy Research Institute, Washington, D.C.

Behrman, J., and J. Hoddinott. 2000. *An evaluation of the impact of PROGRESA on preschool child height.* International Food Policy Research Institute, Washington, D.C.

———. 2001. *An evaluation of the impact of PROGRESA on preschool child height.* FCND Discussion Paper 104. Washington, D.C.: Food Consumption and Nutrition Division, International Food Policy Research Institute.

Behrman, J., H. Alderman, and J. Hoddinott. 2004. Hunger and malnutrition. In *Global crises, global solutions,* ed. B. Lomborg. Cambridge, U.K.: Cambridge University Press.

Behrman, J. R., S. W. Parker, and P. E. Todd. 2009. Medium-term impacts of the *Oportunidades* conditional cash transfer program on rural youth in Mexico. In *Poverty, inequality, and policy in Latin America,* ed. S. Klasen and F. Nowak-Lehmann. Cambridge, Mass., U.S.A.: Massachusetts Institute of Technology Press.

Behrman, J., P. Sengupta, and P. Todd. 2000. The impact of PROGRESA on achievement test scores in the first year. Final report. International Food Policy Research Institute, Washington, D.C.

———. 2001. *Progressing through PROGRESA: An impact assessment of a school subsidy experiment.* International Food Policy Research Institute, Washington, D.C.

Behrman, J., J. Hoddinott, J. Maluccio, A. Quisumbing, R. Martorell, and A. Stein. 2003. The impact of experimental nutritional interventions on education into adulthood in rural Guatemala: Preliminary longitudinal analysis. Photocopy, University of Pennsylvania, Philadelphia, Penn., U.S.A.; International Food Policy Research Institute, Washington, D.C.; and Emory University, Atlanta, Ga., U.S.A.

Bennell, P. 2005. The impact of the AIDS epidemic on the schooling of orphans and other directly affected children in Sub-Saharan Africa. *Journal of Development Studies* 41 (3): 467–488.

Besley, T., and R. Kanbur. 1993. The principle of targeting. In *Including the poor,* ed. M. Lipton and J. van der Gaag. Washington, D.C.: World Bank.

Bicego, G., S. Rutstein, and K. Johnson. 2003. Dimensions of the emerging orphan crisis in Sub-Saharan Africa. *Social Science and Medicine* 56 (6): 1235–1247.

Bloom, S., M. Urassa, J. Ng'wesshemi, and J. T. Boerma. 2002. Community effects on the risk of HIV infection in rural Tanzania. *Sexually Transmitted Infections* 78 (4): 261–266.

Boerma, J., S. Gregson, C. Nyamukapa, and M. Urassa. 2003. Understanding the uneven spread of HIV within Africa: Comparative study of biologic, behavioral, and contextual factors in rural populations in Tanzania and Zimbabwe. *Sexually Transmitted Infections* 30 (10): 779–787.

Bondevik, P. 2003. *Microfinance: A selective introduction with special focus on HIV/AIDS*. Occasional Paper 5/03. Oslo: Norwegian Church Aid.

Booysen, F. 2004a. The role of social grants in mitigating the socio-economic impact of HIV/AIDS. Paper presented at the Centre for the Study of African Economies Conference on Growth, Poverty Reduction, and Human Development in Africa, St. Catherine's College, Oxford, U.K., March 21–22.

——. 2004b. Social grants as safety net for HIV/AIDS-affected households in South Africa. *Journal of Social Aspects of HIV/AIDS Research Alliance* 1 (1): 45–56.

Booysen, F., and M. Bachmann. 2002. HIV/AIDS, poverty, and growth: Evidence from a household impact study conducted in the Free State Province, South Africa. Paper presented at the Annual Conference of the Centre for the Study of African Economies, Oxford, U.K., March 18–19.

Booysen, F., M. Bachmann, Z. Matebesi, and J. Meyer. 2004. *The socio-economic impact of HIV/AIDS on households in South Africa: Pilot study in Welkom and Qwaqwa, Free State Province*. Bloemfontein, South Africa: University of the Free State Centre for Health Systems Research and Development.

Bourguignon, F., F. Ferreira, and P. Leite. 2003. Conditional cash transfer, schooling, and child labour: Micro-simulating Brazil's Bolsa Escola program. *World Bank Economic Review* 17 (2): 229–254.

Brewin, M. 2006. *Dowa Emergency Cash Transfer (DECT) project: Baseline survey report*. Lilongwe, Malawi: Concern Worldwide.

Brook, D. W., N. K. Morojele, C. Zhang, and J. S. Brook. 2006. South African adolescents: Pathways to risky sexual behavior. *AIDS Education and Prevention* 18 (3): 259–272.

Bryceson, D., and J. Fonseca. 2006. An enduring or dying peasantry: Interactive impact of famine and HIV/AIDS in rural Malawi. In *AIDS, poverty, and hunger: Challenges and responses*, ed. S. R. Gillespie. Washington, D.C.: International Food Policy Research Institute.

Budlender, D. 2007. Affidavit in the High Court of South Africa (Transvaal Provincial Division), Case Number 025754/05, July.

Budlender, D., S. Rosa, and K. Hall. 2005. *At all costs? Applying the means test for the Child Support Grant*. Cape Town, South Africa: Children's Institute and Centre for Actuarial Research, University of Cape Town.

Burtless, G. 1995. The case for randomized field trials in economic and policy research. *Journal of Economic Perspectives* 9 (2): 63–84.

Byron, E., S. Gillespie, and M. Nangami. 2006. *Integrating nutrition security with treatment of people living with HIV: Lessons being learned in Kenya*. RENEWAL Working Paper. Washington, D.C.: International Food Policy Research Institute.

Caldés, N., D. Coady, and J. Maluccio. 2006. The cost of poverty alleviation transfer programs: A comparative analysis of three programs in Latin America. *World Development* 34 (5): 818–837.

Caldwell, R. 2005. Food aid and chronic illness: Insights from the Community Household Surveillance surveys. Tango International on behalf of WFP and C-SAFE. Paper presented at IFPRI's International Conference on HIV/AIDS and Food and Nutrition Security, Durban, South Africa, April 14–16.

Campbell, A. K., P. Chatterjee, S. Ismail, R. Pearson, and M. Renshaw. 2007. *Can the Kenyan State put the 300,000 most vulnerable children in the country on a cash transfer programme by the end of 2010?* Working paper. New York: UNICEF.

Cardoso, E., and A. P. Souza. 2003. *The impact of cash transfers on child labor and school attendance in Brazil.* Nashville, Tenn., U.S.A.: Department of Economics, Vanderbilt University.

Carter, M., and C. Barrett. 2006. The economics of poverty traps and persistent poverty: An asset-based approach. *Journal of Development Studies* 42 (2): 178–199.

Case, A. 2001. *Does money protect health status? Evidence from South African pensions.* Princeton, N.J., U.S.A.: Woodrow Wilson School of Public and International Affairs, Center for Health and Well-being, Princeton University.

Case, A., and C. Ardington. 2006. The impact of parental death on school outcomes: Longitudinal evidence from South Africa. *Demography* 43 (3): 401–420.

Case, A., and A. Deaton. 1998. Large cash transfers to the elderly in South Africa. *Economic Journal* 108 (450): 1330–1361.

Case, A., V. Hosegood, and F. Lund. 2005. The reach and impact of child support grants: Evidence from KwaZulu-Natal. *Development Southern Africa* 22 (4): 467–482.

Case, A., C. Paxson, and J. Ableidinger. 2003. *The education of African orphans.* Princeton, N.J., U.S.A.: Center for Health and Well-being Research Program in Development, Princeton University.

Castleman, T., E. Seumo-Fosso, and B. Cogill. 2004. *Food and nutrition implications of antiretroviral therapy in resource limited settings.* Washington, D.C.: Food and Nutrition Technical Assistance (FANTA), Academy for Educational Development.

Chapman, K. 2006. Using social transfers to scale up equitable access to education and health services. Photocopy, Department for International Development, London.

Chaudhury, N. 2007. Gender and CCTs in South Asia education sector. PowerPoint presentation at the seminar CCTs and Gender Gaps, World Bank, Washington, D.C., May.

CIA (Central Intelligence Agency of the United States). 2010. *World factbook.* Accessed January 15, 2010. www.cia.gov/library/publications/the-world-factbook/rankorder/2155rank.html.

Coady, D., M. Grosh, and J. Hoddinott. 2004. *Targeting of transfers in developing countries: Review of lessons and experience.* Washington, D.C.: World Bank.

Coudel, A., J. Hentschel, and Q. Wodon. 2002. *Poverty measurement and analysis in the PRSP sourcebook.* Washington, D.C.: World Bank.

Coutsoudis, A., and N. Rollins. 2003. Breast feeding and HIV transmission: The jury is still out. *Journal of Pediatric Gastroenterology and Nutrition* 36 (4): 434–442.

Coutsoudis, A., R. Bobat, H. Coovadia, L. Kuhn, W. Tsai, and Z. Stein. 1995. The effects of vitamin A supplementation on the morbidity of children born to HIV-infected mothers. *American Journal of Public Health* 85 (8): 1076–1081.

Coutsoudis, A., K. Pillay, E. Spooner, L. Kuhn, and H. M. Coovadia. 1999. Randomized trial testing the effect of vitamin A supplementation on pregnancy outcomes and early mother-to-child HIV-1 transmission in Durban, South Africa. South Africa Vitamin A Study Group. *AIDS* 13 (12): 1517–1524.

CRIN (Child Rights Information Network). 2005. Cash subsidies for children affected by HIV/AIDS: Background paper on the pre-pilot and pilot initiatives. London.

Croome, D. 2006. Lesotho pensions. Impact Project presentation, Lisbon, October.

Cruz, C., R. de la Torre, and C. Velásquez. 2006. *Evaluación externa de impacto del Programa Oportunidades, 2001-2006.* Cuernavaca, Mexico: Instituto Nacional de Salud Pública.

C-SAFE and WFP (Centre for Sustainability: Agriculture, Food, Energy, Environment and World Food Programme). 2005. C-SAFE regional analysis: Household vulnerability and the impact of food aid. Prepared by Tango International.

Datt, G., E. Payongayong, J. Garrett, and M. Ruel. 1997. *The GAPVU cash transfer program in Mozambique: An assessment.* FCND Discussion Paper 36. Washington, D.C.: Food Consumption and Nutrition Division, International Food Policy Research Institute.

de Brauw, A., and J. Hoddinott. 2008. *Must conditional cash transfer programs be conditioned to be effective? The impact of conditioning transfers on school enrollment in Mexico.* IFPRI Discussion Paper 00757. Washington, D.C.: International Food Policy Research Institute.

Deininger, K., M. Garcia, and K. Subbarao. 2003. AIDS-induced orphanhood as a systemic shock: Magnitude, impact, and program interventions in Africa. *World Development* 31 (7): 1201–1220.

de Janvry, A., and E. Sadoulet. 2006. When to use a CCT versus a CT approach? Notes prepared for the Third Annual Conference on Conditional Cash Transfers, Istanbul, Turkey, by the University of California at Berkeley and DECRG (Development Research Group), World Bank, Washington, D.C.

de Janvry, A., F. Finan, and E. Sadoulet. 2006. *Evaluating Brazil's Bolsa Escola Program: Impact on schooling and municipal roles.* Berkeley, Calif., U.S.A.: University of California at Berkeley.

de Janvry, A., E. Sadoulet, P. Solomon, and R. Vakis. 2006. *Uninsured risk and asset protection: Can conditional cash transfer programs serve as safety nets?* Social Protection Working Paper. Washington, D.C.: World Bank.

Demombynes, G. 2005. *A poverty profile for Zambia: Based on the 2002-3 living conditions monitoring survey.* World Bank, Washington, DC.

Devereux, S. 2001. *Social pensions in Namibia and South Africa.* Discussion Paper 379. Brighton, U.K.: Institute of Development Studies, University of Sussex.

———. 2002. Can social safety nets reduce chronic poverty? *Development Policy Review* 20 (5): 657–675.

Devereux, S., and R. Sabates-Wheeler. 2004. *Transformative social protection.* Working Paper 232. Brighton, U.K.: Institute of Development Studies, University of Sussex.

Devereux, S., P. Mvula, and C. Solomon. 2006. *After the FACT: An evaluation of Concern Worldwide's Food and Cash Transfers Project in three districts of Malawi.*

Brighton, U.K., and Lilongwe, Malawi: Institute of Development Studies, University of Sussex, and Concern Worldwide, Malawi.

Devereux, S., J. Marshall, J. MacAskill, and L. Pelham. 2005. *Making cash count: Lessons from cash transfer schemes in east and southern Africa for supporting the most vulnerable children and households*. London: Save the Children, HelpAge International, and Institute of Development Studies, University of Sussex.

Devereux, S., R. Sabates-Wheeler, M. Tefera, and H. Taye. 2006. *Ethiopia's Productive Safety Net Programme (PSNP): Trends in PSNP transfers within targeted households*. Brighton, U.K., and Addis Ababa, Ethiopia: Institute of Development Studies and Indak International.

Devereux, S., C. Mthinda, F. Power, P. Sakala, and A. Suka. 2007. *An evaluation of Concern Worldwide's Dowa Emergency Cash Transfer Project (DECT) in Malawi, 2006/07*. Lilongwe, Malawi: Concern Worldwide.

DfID (Department for International Development). 2005. *Social transfers and chronic poverty: Emerging evidence and the challenge ahead*. A DfID Practice Paper. London.

Donovan, D., L. Bailey, E. Mpyisi, and M. Weber. 2003. *Prime-age adult morbidity and mortality in rural Rwanda: Effects in household income, agricultural production, and food security strategies*. Research Report. Kilgali, Rwanda: Ministry of Agriculture, Animal Resources, and Forestry, Food Security Support Project. www.aec.msu.edu/agecon/fs2/rwanda/index.htm.

Duflo, E. 2000. Child health and household resources in South Africa: Evidence from the Old Age Pension program. *American Economic Review* 90 (2): 393–398.

——. 2003. Grandmothers and granddaughters: Old-age pensions and intrahousehold allocation in South Africa. *World Bank Economic Review* 17 (1): 1–25.

Duflo, E., P. Dupas, M. Kremer, and S. Samuel. 2006. *Education and HIV/AIDS prevention: Evidence from a randomized evaluation in Western Kenya*. Policy Research Working Paper 4024. Washington, D.C.: World Bank.

Ellis, F. 2007. *Social transfer case study no. 7*. Food Subsidies Programme, Mozambique. Regional Hunger and Vulnerability Program. Norwich, U.K.: University of East Anglia.

El Salvador. 2007. *Red Solidaria Programa social de atencion a la pobreza: Documento tecnico*. San Salvador: Government of El Salvador.

Evans, D., and E. Miguel. 2007. Orphans and schooling in Africa: A longitudinal analysis. *Demography* 44 (1): 35–57.

Farrington, J., and R. Slater. 2006. Introduction: Cash transfers: Panacea for poverty reduction or money down the drain? *Development Policy Review* 24 (5): 499–511.

Fawzi, W. W., R. L. Mbise, E. Hertzmark, M. R. Fataki, M. G. Herrera, G. Ndossi, and D. Spiegelman. 1999. A randomized trial of vitamin A in relation to mortality among human immunodeficiency virus-infected and -uninfected children in Tanzania. *Pediatric Infectious Disease Journal* 18 (2): 127–133.

Fawzi, W., G. Msamanga, D. Hunter, E. Urassa, B. Renjifo, D. Mwakagile, E. Hertzmark, J. Coley, M. Garland, S. Kapiga, G. Antelman, M. Essex, and D. Spiegelman. 2000. Randomized trial of vitamin supplements in relation to vertical transmission of HIV-1 among Tanzania. *Journal of Acquired Immune Deficiency Syndromes* 23 (3): 246–254.

Fawzi, W., G. Msamanga, D. Hunter, B. Renjifo, G. Antelman, H. Bang, K. Manji, S. Kapiga, D. Mwakagile, M. Essex, and D. Spiegelman. 2002. Randomized trial of vitamin supplements in relation to transmission of HIV-1 through breastfeeding and early child mortality. *AIDS* 16 (14): 1935–1944.

Filmer, D., and N. Schady. 2006. *Getting girls into school: Evidence from a scholarship program in Cambodia*. Policy Research Working Paper 3910. Washington, D.C.: World Bank.

Filteau, S. M., G. Lietz, G. Mulokozi, S. Bilotta, C. J. Henry, and A. M. Tomkins. 1999. Milk cytokines and subclinical breast inflammation in Tanzanian women: Effects of dietary red palm oil or sunflower oil supplementation. *Immunology* 97 (4): 595–600.

Fiszbein, A., and N. Schady with F. H. G. Ferreira, M. Grosh, N. Kelleher, P. Olinto, and E. Skoufias. 2009. *Conditional cash transfers: Reducing present and future poverty.* Washington, D.C.: World Bank.

Flores, R., S. Morris, P. Olinto, J. Medina, and O. Neidecker. 2003. *Evaluation of the Family Allowance Program (PRAF) in Honduras: Health and nutrition impacts.* Washington, D.C.: Social Policy Monitoring Network, Inter-American Development Bank.

Foster, J., J. Greer, and E. Thorbecke. 1984. A class of decomposable poverty measures. *Econometrica* 52 (3): 761–766.

Galler, J. R. 1984. Behavioral consequences of malnutrition in early life. In *Nutrition and Behavior,* ed. J. R. Gailer. New York: Plenum.

Galler, J., F. Ramsey, G. Solimano, and W. Lowell. 1983. The influence of early malnutrition on subsequent behavioral development and classroom behavior. *Journal of the American Academy of Child Psychiatry* 22 (1): 16–22.

Gassmann, F., and C. Behrendt. 2006. *Cash benefits in low-income countries: Simulating the effects on poverty reduction for Senegal and Tanzania.* Discussion Paper 15. Social Security Department, International Labour Organization, Rome.

Gentilini, U. 2007. *Cash and food transfers: A primer.* Rome: World Food Programme.

Gertler, P. J. 2000. The impact of PROGRESA on health. Photocopy, International Food Policy Research Institute, Washington, D.C.

——. 2004. Do conditional cash transfers improve child health? Evidence from PROGRESA's control randomized experiment. *American Economic Review* 94 (2): 336–341.

Gertler, P. J., and S. Boyce. 2001. An experiment in incentive-based welfare: The impact of PROGRESA on health in Mexico. Royal Economic Society Series on the Royal Economic Society Annual Conference, April 7–9, University of Warwick, Coventry, U.K.

Giese, S. 2007/08. Setting the scene for social services: The gap between service need and delivery. In *South African child gauge, 2007/2008*, ed. P. Proudlock, M. Dutschke, L. Jamieson, J. Monson, and C. Smith. Cape Town, South Africa: Children's Institute, University of Cape Town.

Giese, S., and L. Smith. 2007. *Rapid appraisal of home affairs policy and practice affecting children in South Africa.* Cape Town, South Africa: Alliance for Children's Entitlement to Social Security.

Gilborn, L., R. Nyonyintono, R. Kabumbuli, and G. Jagwe-Wadda. 2001. *Making a differ-*

ence for children affected by AIDS: Baseline findings from operations research in Uganda. New York: Population Council.

Gillespie, S. 2008. *Food prices and the AIDS response: How they are linked, and what can be done*. HIV, Livelihoods, Food and Nutrition Security: Findings from RENEWAL Research (2007–2008), Brief 1. Washington, D.C.: International Food Policy Research Institute.

Gillespie, S., and S. Kadiyala. 2005. *HIV/AIDS and food and nutrition security: From evidence to action*. Food Policy Review 7. Washington, D.C.: International Food Policy Research Institute.

Gillespie, S., L. Haddad, and R. Jackson. 2001. HIV/AIDS, food and nutrition security: Impacts and actions. In *Nutrition and HIV/AIDS*. Nutrition Policy Discussion Paper 20. Geneva: United Nations Standing Committee on Nutrition.

Gillespie, S., S. Kadiyala, and R. Greener. 2007. Is poverty or wealth driving HIV transmission? *AIDS* 21 (7): S5–S16.

Gilligan, D., J. Hoddinott, and A. S. Taffesse. 2007. *The impact of Ethiopia's food security program on household food security and well-being: An interim assessment*. Washington, D.C.: International Food Policy Research Institute.

Glewwe, P., H. Jacoby, and E. King. 2001. Early childhood nutrition and academic achievement: A longitudinal analysis. *Journal of Public Economics* 81 (3): 345–368.

Gorman, M. 2004. *Age and security: How social pensions can deliver effective aid to poor older people and their families*. London: HelpAge International.

Goudge, J., T. Gumede, S. Russell, L. Gilson, and A. Mills. 2007. Costs and other barriers to health care (the SACOCO study). PowerPoint presentation, Centre for Health Policy, MRC/WITS Rural Public Health and Health Transitions Research Unit, School of Public Health, University of Witwatersrand, and University of East Anglia, London School of Hygiene and Tropical Medicine, June.

Goudge, J., S. Russell, L. Gilson, T. Gumede, S. Tollman, and A. Mills. 2009. Illness-related impoverishment in rural South Africa: Why does social protection work for some and not others? *Journal of International Development* 21 (2): 231–251.

Gouws, E., K. A. Stanecki, R. Lyerla, and P. D. Ghys. 2008. The epidemiology of HIV infection among young people aged 15–24 years in southern Africa. *AIDS* 22 (Supplement 4): S5–S16.

Grantham-McGregor, S., Y. B. Cheung, S. Cuerto, P. Glewwe, L. Richter, and B. Strupp. 2007. Developmental potential in the first 5 years for children in developing countries. *Lancet* 369 (9555): 60–70.

Greenblott, K. 2007. *Social protection in the era of HIV and AIDS: Examining the role of food-based interventions*. Occasional Paper 17. Rome: World Food Programme.

Greenblott, K., and K. Greenaway. 2007. Food security and nutrition: Meeting the needs of orphans and other children affected by HIV and AIDS in Africa. Report prepared for the World Food Programme and UNICEF. World Food Programme, Rome.

Guhan, S. 1994. Social security options for developing countries. *International Labour Review* 133 (1): 36–53.

Haarman, D. 1998. *From the maintenance grant to a new child support*. Cape Town, South Africa: University of the Western Cape.

Haddad, L., and S. Gillespie. 2001. Effective food and nutrition policy responses to HIV/AIDS: What we know and what we need to know. *Journal of International Development* 13 (4): 487–511.

Hagemejer, K., and C. Behrendt. 2008. *Can low-income countries afford basic social security?* Social Security Policy Briefings Paper 3. Geneva: Social Security Department, International Labour Organization.

Halder, S., and A. Hussain. 1999. Identification of the poorest and the impact of credit on them: The case of BRAC. Photocopy, BRAC Research and Evaluation Division, Dhaka.

Hallman, K. 2004. *Socioeconomic disadvantage and unsafe sexual behaviors among young women and men in South Africa.* Policy Research Division Working Paper 190. New York: Population Council.

Handa, S., and B. Davis. 2006. The experience of conditional cash transfers in Latin America and the Caribbean. *Development Policy Review* 24 (5): 513–536.

Hargreaves, J. R., L. A. Morison, J. C. Kim, C. P. Bonell, J. D. H. Porter, C. Watts, J. Busza, G. Phetla, and P. M. Pronyk. 2008. The association between school attendance, HIV infection and sexual behavior among young people in rural South Africa. *Journal of Epidemiology and Community Health* 62 (2): 113–119.

Harvey, P. 2004. *HIV/AIDS and humanitarian action.* Research Report 16. London: Humanitarian Policy Group, Overseas Development Institute.

Harvey, P., and N. Marongwe. 2006. Independent evaluation of Oxfam GB Zambia's Emergency Cash-Transfer Programme. Photocopy, Overseas Development Institute, London.

Hashemi, S. 1997. Those left behind: A note on targeting the hard-core poor. In *Who needs credit? Poverty and finance in Bangladesh,* ed. G. D. Wood and I. Sharif. Dhaka, Bangladesh: Dhaka University Press.

Heckman, J., and J. Smith. 1995. Assessing the case for social experiments. *Journal of Economic Perspectives* 9 (2): 85–110.

HelpAge International. 2002. *State of the world's older people, 2002.* London.

——. 2007. Website. www.helpage.org/Home.

Hernández, B., D. Ramírez, H. Moreno, and N. Laird. 2004. Evaluación del impacto de Oportunidades en la mortalidad materna e infantile. In *Resultados de la Evaluación Externa del Programa de Desarrollo Humano Oportunidades.* Cuernavaca, México: Instituto Nacional de Salud Publica / Oportunidades / CIESAS (Centro de Investigaciónes y Estudios Superiores en Antropologia Social).

Hernandez-Prado, B., and M. Hernandez-Avila, eds. 2006. *Evaluacion externa de impacto del Programa Oportunidades.* Tomo II, *Alimentacion.* Cuernavaca, Mexico: Instituto Nacional de Salud Pública.

Hoddinott, J. 2010. Conditional cash transfers and nutrition. In *Conditional cash transfers in Latin America,* ed. M. Adato and J. Hoddinott. Baltimore: Johns Hopkins University Press.

Hoddinott, J., E. Skoufias, and R. Washburn. 2000. The impact of PROGRESA on consumption: A final report. International Food Policy Research Institute, Washington, D.C.

Hoddinott, J., J. Maluccio, J. Behrman, R. Flores, and R. Martorell. 2008. Effect of a nutrition intervention during early childhood on economic productivity in Guatemalan adults. *Lancet* 371 (9610): 411–416.

Hulme, D., and P. Mosley. 1997. Finance for the poor or poorest? Financial innovation, poverty, and vulnerability. In *Who needs credit? Poverty and finance in Bangladesh*, ed. G. D. Wood and I. Sharif. Dhaka, Bangladesh: Dhaka University Press.

Hunter, N., and M. Adato. 2007a. *The Child Support Grant in KwaZulu-Natal: Perceptions and experience inside the household.* Research Report 73. Durban, South Africa: School of Development Studies, University of KwaZulu-Natal.

———. 2007b. *The Child Support Grant in Kwazulu-Natal: Understanding administration and household access.* Research Report 72. Durban, South Africa: School of Development Studies, University of KwaZulu-Natal.

IFPRI (International Food Policy Research Institute). 2003a. Estudo de avaliação de impacto para o Programa Bolsa Alimentação Relatorio 3: Analise de impacto final. Photocopy, Washington, D.C.

———. 2003b. PRAF/IBD Project Phase II: Intermediary impact. Photocopy, Washington, D.C.

IMAGE (Intervention with Microfinance for AIDS and Gender Equity). 2002. *Social interventions for HIV/AIDS: Intervention with micro-finance for AIDS and gender equity.* Evaluation Monograph 1. Acornhoek, South Africa: Rural AIDS Development Action Research (RADAR) Programme.

IMF (International Monetary Fund). 1996. *International financial statistics* (January). Washington, D.C.

International Poverty Center. 2007. Interview with Stephen Kasaija from the Ministry of Gender, Labour and Social Development, Uganda, September 6. Brasilia, Brazil.

IRIN News. 2007. Mozambique: Left with nothing. June 25.

Jensen, R. 2003. Do private transfers "displace" the benefits of public transfers? Evidence from South Africa. *Journal of Public Economics* 88 (1): 89–112.

JLICA (Joint Learning Initiative on Children and AIDS). 2007. Website. www.jlica.org/.

———. 2009. *Home truths: Facing the facts on children, AIDS, and poverty.* Final report of the Joint Learning Initiative on Children and HIV/AIDS. Boston.

Jones, S. G., and F. Holloman. 2000. Continuous quality improvement project: Decreasing the potential for the development in the inpatient setting of drug resistance by improving nursing practice for HAART administration. *Journal of the Association of Nurses in AIDS Care* 11 (2): 76–86.

Jukes, M., S. Simmons, and D. Bundy. 2008. Education and vulnerability: The role of schools in protecting young women and girls from HIV in southern Africa. *AIDS* 22 (4): S41–S46.

Kabeer, N. 2002. Safety nets and opportunity ladders: Addressing vulnerability and enhancing productivity in South Asia. *Development Policy Review* 20 (5): 589–614.

Kakwani, N., and K. Subbarao. 2005. *Ageing and poverty in Africa and the role of social pensions.* Brasilia: International Poverty Centre, United Nations Development Programme.

Kakwani, N., F. V. Soares, and H. H. Son. 2005. *Conditional cash transfers in African countries*. Brasilia, Brazil: International Poverty Centre, United Nations Development Programme.

——. 2006. Cash transfers for school-age children in African countries: Simulation of impacts on poverty and school attendance. *Development Policy Review* 24 (5): 553–569.

Kamb, M. L., F. Rhodes, T. Hoxworth, J. Rogers, A. Lentz, C. Kent, R. MacGowen, and T. A. Peterman. 1998. What about money? Effect of small monetary incentives on enrollment, retention, and motivation to change behaviour in an HIV/STD prevention counselling intervention. The Project RESPECT Study Group. *Sexually Transmitted Infections* 74 (4): 253–255.

Kaufman, C., S. Clark, N. Manzini, and J. May. 2004. Communities, opportunities, and adolescents' sexual behavior in KwaZulu-Natal, South Africa. *Studies in Family Planning* 35 (4): 261–274.

Kayira, K., K. Greenaway, and K. Greenblott. 2004. *Food for assets: Adapting programming to an HIV/AIDS context*. Johannesburg, South Africa: Consortium for Southern Africa Food Security Emergency Learning Center.

Kenya, OVPMHA (Office of the Vice President and Ministry of Home Affairs). 2006. *Cash transfers for orphan and vulnerable children (OVC)*. Nairobi.

Khandker, S. R., M. M. Pitt, and N. Fuwa. 2003. *Subsidy to promote girls' secondary education: The female stipend program in Bangladesh*. World Bank, Washington, D.C.

Kimuna, S., and Y. Djamba. 2005. Wealth and extramarital sex among men in Zambia. *International Family Planning Perspectives* 31 (2): 83–89.

Kudat, A., with contributions from H. Tatlidil, B. Ozbilgin, C. Baykal, M. Adato, and A. Ahmed. 2006. Evaluating the conditional cash transfer program in Turkey: A qualitative assessment. Project report. International Food Policy Research Institute, Washington, D.C.

Kumwenda, N., P. G. Miotti, T. E. Taha, R. Broadhead, R. J. Biggar, J. B. Jackson, G. Melikian, and R. D. Semba. 2002. Antenatal vitamin A supplementation increases birth weight and decreases anemia among infants born to human immunodeficiency virus-infected women in Malawi. *Clinical Infectious Diseases* 35 (5): 618–624.

Kwaramba, P. 1997. *The socio-economic impact of AIDS on commercial agricultural production in Zimbabwe*. Working Paper 19, Economic Advisory Project. Harare, Zimbabwe: Zimbabwe Farmer's Union and Friedrich Ebert Stiftung.

Lagarde, E., M. Schim van der Loeff, C. Enel, B. Holmgren, R. Dray-Spira, G. Pison, J. P. Piau, V. Delaunay, S. M'Boup, I. Ndaye, M. Cœuret-Pellicer, H. Whittle, and P. Aaby. 2003. Mobility and the spread of human immunodeficiency virus into rural areas of West Africa. *International Journal of Epidemiology* 32 (5): 744–752.

Leatt, A., and D. Budlender. 2006. Under what conditions? Social security for children in South Africa. University of Cape Town, South Africa.

Levy, D., and J. Ohls. 2007. Evaluation of Jamaica's PATH Program: Final report. Mathematica Policy Research, Princeton, N.J., U.S.A.

Lindblade, K. A., F. Odhiambo, D. H. Rosen, and K. M. DeCock. 2003. Health and nutritional status of orphans < 6 years old cared for by relatives in western Kenya. *Tropical Medicine and International Health* 8 (1): 67–72.

Loevinsohn, M., and S. Gillespie. 2003. *HIV/AIDS, food security, and rural livelihoods: Understanding and responding*. Food Consumption and Nutrition Division Discussion Paper 157. Washington, D.C.: International Food Policy Research Institute.

Low, J., J. Garrett, and V. Ginja. 1999. *Can cash transfer programs work in resource-poor countries? The experience of Mozambique*. Food Consumption and Nutrition Division Discussion Paper 74. Washington, D.C.: International Food Policy Research Institute.

Lundberg, M., and M. Over. 2000. Sources of financial assistance for households suffering an adult death in Kagera, Tanzania. *South African Journal of Economics* 68 (5): 1–39.

Malawi. 2009. Draft outline Social Support Programme. Photocopy, Government of Malawi, Lilongwe.

Malawi, Ministry of Economic Planning and Development / World Bank. 2005. *Second Integrated Household Survey 2005: An extract of findings*. Lilongwe, Malawi, and Washington, D.C.: Ministry of Economic Planning and Development, National Statistics Office, and World Bank.

Maluccio, J. A. 2004. Effects of conditional cash transfer programs on current poverty, consumption, and nutrition. Paper presented at the Second International Workshop on Conditional Cash Transfer Programs, São Paulo, Brazil, April.

——. 2005. *Coping with the "coffee crisis" in Central America: The role of the Nicaraguan Red de Protección Social*. Food Consumption and Nutrition Division Discussion Paper 188. Washington, D.C.: International Food Policy Research Institute.

——. 2009. Household targeting in practice: The Nicaraguan Red de Protección Social. *Journal of International Development* 21 (1): 1–23.

Maluccio, J., and R. Flores. 2005. *Impact evaluation of a conditional cash transfer program: The Nicaraguan Red de Protección Social*. Research Report 141. Washington, D.C.: International Food Policy Research Institute.

Maluccio, J., A. Murphy, and F. Regalia. 2006. Does supply matter? Initial supply conditions and the effectiveness of conditional cash transfers for schooling in Nicaragua. Photocopy, Inter-American Development Bank, Washington, D.C.

Martorell, R. 1995. Results and implications of the INCAP Follow-up Study. *Journal of Nutrition* 125 (Supplement): S1127–S1138.

——. 1999. The nature of child malnutrition and its long-term implications. *Food and Nutrition Bulletin* 20 (3): 288–292.

Martorell, R., K. L. Khan, and D. G. Schroeder. 1994. Reversibility of stunting: Epidemiological findings in children from developing countries. *European Journal of Clinical Nutrition* 48 (Supplement 1): S45–S57.

Mason, J. B., P. Musgrove, and J.-P. Habicht. 2003. At least one-third of poor countries' disease burden is due to malnutrition. Disease Control Priorities Project, World Bank, World Health Organization, John Fogarty International Center, Population Reference Bureau, National Library of Medicine, and the Bill and Melinda Gates Foundation, Washington, D.C.

Mather, D., D. Donovan, M. Weber, H. Marrule, and A. Alage. 2004. Prime-age adult mortality and household livelihood in rural Mozambique: Preliminary results and implications for HIV/AIDS mitigation efforts. Paper prepared for the Annual Conference of the Centre for the Study of African Economies, Oxford.

Mauldon, J. G. 2003. Providing subsidies and incentives for Norplant, sterilization and other contraception: Allowing economic theory to inform ethical analysis. *Journal of Law, Medicine, and Ethics* 31 (3): 351–364.

McCord, A. 2005. *Public works in the context of HIV/AIDS*. Cape Town, South Africa: Public Works Research Project, Southern Africa Labour and Development Research Unit.

Medlin, C., and D. de Walque. 2008. *Potential applications of conditional cash transfers for prevention of sexually transmitted infections and HIV in Sub-Saharan Africa*. Policy Research Working Paper 4673. Washington, D.C.: World Bank.

Meintjes, H., and S. Giese. 2006. Spinning the epidemic: The making of mythologies of orphanhood in the context of AIDS. *Childhood* 13 (3): 407–430.

Meintjes, H., D. Budlender, S. Giese, and L. Johnson. 2003. *Children "in need of care" or in need of cash? Questioning social security provisions for orphans in the context of the South African AIDS pandemic*. Joint working paper. Cape Town, South Africa: Children's Institute and the Centre for Actuarial Research, University of Cape Town.

Menon, R., J. M. Wawer, K. J. Konde-Lule, N. K. Sewankembo, and L. Chuanjun. 1998. The economic impact of adult mortality on households in Rakai District, Uganda. In *Confronting AIDS: Evidence from the developing world*, ed. M. Ainsworth, L. Fransen, and M. Over. Brussels, Belgium: European Commission.

Miller, C., M. Tsoka, and the Mchinji Evaluation Team. 2007. $13 a month for half a year: Round 2 impact of the Mchinji Cash Transfer. PowerPoint presentation to the National Social Protection Steering Committee, Government of Malawi, Lilongwe, December 11.

Miller, C., M. Tsoka, and K. Reichert. 2008. Impact evaluation report: External evaluation of the Mchinji Social Cash Transfer Pilot. Draft, Center for International Health and Development, Boston University, Boston, and Center for Social Research, University of Malawi, Lilongwe.

Moller, V., and M. Ferreira. 2003. Noncontributory pensions and poverty study. South African survey report. Rhodes University and University of Cape Town, South Africa.

Molyneux, M. 2006. Mothers at the service of the new poverty agenda: Progresa/Oportunidades, Mexico's Conditional Cash Transfer programme. *Social Policy and Administration* 40 (4): 425–449.

Morris, S. 2010. Conditional cash transfers and health. In *Conditional cash transfers in Latin America*, ed. M. Adato and J. Hoddinott. Baltimore: Johns Hopkins University Press.

Morris, S. S., P. Olinto, R. Flores, E. A. F. Nilson, and A. C. Figueiro. 2004. Conditional cash transfers are associated with a small reduction in the rate of weight gain of preschool children in northeast Brazil. *Journal of Nutrition* 134 (9): 2336–2341.

Muwanga, F. 2002. *Impact of HIV/AIDS on agriculture and the private sector in Swaziland: The demographic, social, and economic impact in subsistence agriculture, com-*

mercial agriculture. Mbabane, Swaziland: Ministry of Agriculture and Co-operatives and Business.

Nampanya-Serpell, N. 2000. Social and economic risk factors for HIV/AIDS affected families in Zambia. Paper presented at the AIDS and Economic Symposium, Durban, South Africa, July 7–8.

Nemer, L., H. Gelband, and P. Jha. 2001. *The evidence base for interventions to reduce malnutrition in children under five and school-age children in low and middle-income countries*. Commission on Macroeconomics and Health Working Paper WG5:11. Geneva: World Health Organization.

Neufeld, L. 2006. Nutrition in the Oportunidades conditional cash transfer program: Strengths and challenges. Paper presented at the Third International Conference on Conditional Cash Transfers, Istanbul, Turkey, June 26–30.

Nii-Amoo Dodoo, F., E. M. Zulu, and A. C. Ezeh. 2007. Urban–rural differences in the socioeconomic deprivation—Sexual behavior link in Kenya. *Social Science and Medicine* 64 (5): 1019–1031.

Nsutebu, E. F., J. D. Walley, E. Mataka, and C. F. Simon. 2001. Scaling-up HIV/AIDS and TB home-based care: Lessons from Zambia. *Health Policy and Planning* 16 (3): 240–247.

Nyamandi, C. 2005. How can micro finance products reach out to HIV/AIDS infected or affected communities? The Microfinance Gateway. www.microfinancegateway.org/p/site/m/template.rc/1.9.25570/.

Olinto, P., R. Flores, S. Morris, and A. Viega. 2003. The impact of the Bolsa Alimentação program on food consumption. Paper presented at the annual meetings of the International Association of Agricultural Economists, Durban, South Africa, August.

Oni, S. A., C. L. Obi, A. Okorie, D. Thabede, and A. Jordaan. 2002. The economic impact of HIV/AIDS on rural households in Limpopo Province. *South African Journal of Economics* 70 (7): 1173–1192.

Oportunidades (Programa de Desarrollo Humano Oportunidades). 2003. *Programa Institucional Oportunidades, 2002-2006*. Mexico City, D.F.

———. 2006a. Comités de Promoción Comunitaria. In *Manual operativo de los Comités de Promoción Comunitaria*. Mexico City, D.F.: Subdirección de Enlace Comunitario.

———. 2006b. *Oportunidades: Un programa de resultados*. Mexico City, D.F.

Ortiz, J. 2007. Social cash transfer from pilot to scaling up, Malawi. PowerPoint presentation at the Global Consultation on ECD in Social Policies, New York, August 29–31.

Özler, B., and D. de Walque. 2009. Financial incentives and HIV prevention in Sub-Saharan Africa: Evidence from three experimental interventions. PowerPoint presentation to the Development Research Group (DECRG) of the World Bank, New York, November 10.

Palacios, R., and O. Sluchynsky. 2006. *Social pensions, Part I: Their role in the overall pension system*. Washington, D.C.: World Bank.

Parenzee, P., and D. Budlender. 2007. *South Africa's Expanded Public Works Programme: Exploratory research of the social sector*. Cape Town, South Africa: ON PAR Development and CASE.

Parker, J., I. Singh, and K. Hattel. 2000. *The role of microfinance in the fight against HIV/AIDS*. Bethesda, Md., U.S.A.: Development Alternatives.

Parker, S. 2004. Evaluación del impacto de Oportunidades sobre la inscripción, reprobación y abandono escolar. In *Resultados de la evaluación externa del Programa de Desarrollo Humano Oportunidades*. Mexico City, D.F.: Instituto Nacional de Salud Publica / Oportunidades / CIESAS.

Parker, S., and E. Skoufias. 2000. *The impact of PROGRESA on work, leisure, and time allocation*. Washington, D.C.: International Food Policy Research Institute.

Paton, N., S. Sangeetha, A. Earnest, and R. Bellamy. 2006. The impact of malnutrition on survival and the CD4 count response in HIV-infected patients starting antiretroviral therapy. *HIV Medicine* 7 (5): 323–330.

Pearson, R., C. Alviar, and A. Hussein. n.d. The evolution of the Government of Kenya Cash Transfer Programme for vulnerable children between 2002 to 2006 and prospects. UNICEF, Kenya.

Petry, N. M., B. Martin, and C. Finocche. 2001. Contingency management in group treatment: A demonstration project in an HIV drop-in center. *Journal of Substance Abuse Treatment* 21 (2): 89–96

Pettifor, A., and C. MacPhail. 2009. Girls and education: CCT study. Presentation at the Investigator Meeting, Johannesburg, South Africa, June 25.

Pettifor A., B. Levandowski, C. MacPhail, N. Padian, M. Cohen, and H. Rees. 2008. Keep them in school: The importance of education as a protective factor against HIV infection among young South African women. *International Journal of Epidemiology* 37 (6): 1266–1273.

Piwoz, E., and E. Preble. 2000. *HIV/AIDS and nutrition: A review of the literature and recommendations for nutritional care and support in Sub-Saharan Africa*. SARA Project discussion paper. Washington, D.C.: US Agency for International Development.

Plaatjies, D. 2006. Conditional cash transfer programs in South Africa. Presentation made at the Third International Conference on Conditional Cash Transfers, Istanbul, Turkey, June 26–30.

Pollitt, E., K. Gorman, and E. Metallinos-Katasaras. 1991. Long-term developmental consequences of intrauterine and postnatal growth retardation in rural Guatemala. In *Future directions in infant development research*, ed. G. Suci and S. Robertson. Cornell Symposium Series. New York: Springer.

Pollitt, E., M. S. Gorman, P. L. Engle, J. A. Rivera, and R. Martorell. 1995. Nutrition in early life and the fulfillment of intellectual potential. *Journal of Nutrition* 125 (4) (Supplement 4): S1111–S1118.

Ponce, J. 2006. The impact of a conditional cash transfer program on students' cognitive achievements: The case of the "Bono de Desarrollo Humano" of Ecuador. www.flacso.org.ec/docs/desa_humano.pdf.

PROGRESA (Programa de Educación, Salud y Alimentación). 1997. PROGRESA: Education, health, and nutrition program. Photocopy, Mexico City, D.F.

Rahman, H., and M. Hossain, eds. 1995. *Rethinking rural poverty: Bangladesh as a case-study*. Thousand Oaks, Calif., U.S.A.: Sage.

RHVP (Regional Hunger and Vulnerability Programme). 2007. *Wahenga policy briefs: Social transfers*. Hampshire, U.K.: Masdar.

Richardson, S., H. Birch, and C. Ragbeer. 1975. The behavior of children at home who were severely malnourished in the first 2 years of life. *Journal of Biosocial Science* 7 (3): 255–267.

Richter, L., G. Foster, and L. Sherr. 2006. *Where the heart is: Meeting the psychosocial needs of young children in the context of HIV/AIDS*. The Hague, the Netherlands: Bernard van leer Foundation.

Rivera, J. A., D. Sotres-Alvarez, J.-P. Habicht, T. Shamah, and S. Villalpando. 2004. Impact of the Mexican Program for Education, Health, and Nutrition (PROGRESA) on rates of growth and anemia in infants and young children. *Journal of the American Medical Association* 291 (21): 2563–2570.

Rivers, J., E. Silvestre, and J. Mason. 2004. *Nutritional and food security status of orphans and vulnerable children*. New Orleans, La., U.S.A.: Department of International Health and Development, Tulane University School of Public Health and Tropical Medicine.

Rosa, S., A. Leatt, and K. Hall. 2005. *Does the means justify the end?* Cape Town, South Africa: Children's Institute, University of Cape Town.

Ross, J. S., and M. H. Labbok. 2004. Modeling the effects of different infant feeding strategies on infant survival and mother to child transmission of HIV. *American Journal of Public Health* 94 (7): 1174–1180.

SAARC (South Asian Association for Regional Cooperation). 2007. *SAARC Regional Strategic Framework for the protection, care, and support of children affected by HIV/AIDS*. Kathmandu, Nepal.

Sabates-Wheeler, R., and L. Pelham. 2005. A country-by-country review of the social protection content of national plans of action for orphans and vulnerable children. University of Sussex, Brighton, U.K.

Samson, M. 2006. Are conditionalities necessary for human development? PowerPoint presentation made at the Third International Conference on Conditional Cash Transfers, Istanbul, Turkey, June 26–30.

Samson, M., K. MacQuene, and I. van Niekerk. 2006. *Social grants: South Africa*. London: Overseas Development Institute.

Samson, M., I. van Niekerk, and K. MacQuene. 2006. *Designing and implementing social transfer programmes*. Cape Town, South Africa: Economic Policy Research Institute.

Samson, M., U. Lee, A. Ndlebe, K. MacQuene, I. van Niekerk, V. Gandhi, T. Harigaya, and C. Abrahams. 2004. *The social and economic impact of South Africa's social security system*. Final report. Research Paper 37. Cape Town, South Africa: Economic Policy Research Institute.

SASSA (South African Social Security Agency). 2007. Website. www.sassa.gov.za/content.asp.

Savage, K., and E. Umar. 2006. *Independent evaluation of Oxfam GB Malawi's Cash-Transfer Programme*. London: Overseas Development Institute.

Schady, N. 2006. Conditional cash transfer programs: Reviewing the evidence. Paper presented at the Third International Conference on Conditional Cash Transfers, Istanbul, Turkey, June 26–30.

Schady, N., and M. C. Araujo. 2006. *Cash transfers, conditions, school enrollment, and child work: Evidence from a randomized experiment in Ecuador*. World Bank Policy Research Working Paper 3930. Washington, D.C.: World Bank.

Schady, N., and A. Fiszbein. 2007. Ayudando a reducir la pobreza en el corto y mediano plazo: Los programas de transferencias monetarias condicionadas (TMC). Paper presented at the World Bank seminar Comunidad CCTs en América Latina y el Caribe, Washington, D.C., September.

Schubert, B. 2004a. Scaling up—Extending social cash transfers beyond the pilot area. Sixth report. German Technical Assistance, Lusaka, Zambia.

——. 2004b. Test phase results of the Pilot Social Cash Transfer Scheme, Kalomo District. Fourth report. German Technical Assistance, Kalomo, Zambia.

——. 2005. *The Pilot Social Cash Transfer Scheme: Kalomo District, Zambia*. Manchester, U.K.: Chronic Poverty Research Center.

——. 2006. Implementing the Malawi Social Cash Transfer Pilot Scheme. Report on a consultancy for the Department of Poverty and Disaster Management Affairs, Malawi. UNICEF, Lilongwe, Malawi.

——. 2007. Update on piloting the scale-up of the Malawi Social Cash Transfer Scheme. Sixth report, November-December. UNICEF, Lilongwe, Malawi.

Schubert, B., and M. Huijbregts. 2006. The Malawi Social Cash Transfer Pilot Scheme: Preliminary lessons learned. Paper presented at the Conference Social Protection Initiatives for Children, Women and Families: An Analysis of Recent Experiences, New York, October 30-31. UNICEF, New York.

Schubert, B., and R. Mwiinga. 2005. The feasibility of conditional social cash transfers for destitute households in the municipality of Chipata, Zambia. CARE International, Lusaka, Zambia.

Schubert, B., and R. Slater. 2006. Social cash transfers in low-income African countries: Conditional or unconditional? *Development Policy Review* 24 (5): 571-578.

Schubert, B., D. Webb, M. Temin, and P. Masabane. 2007. *The impact of social cash transfers on children affected by HIV and AIDS: Evidence from Zambia, Malawi, and South Africa*. Lilongwe, Malawi: UNICEF, Eastern and Southern Africa Regional Office.

Schultz, T. P. 2001. *School subsidies for the poor: Evaluating a Mexican strategy for reducing poverty*. FCND Discussion Paper 102. Washington, D.C.: International Food Policy Research Institute,

——. 2004. School subsidies for the poor: Evaluating the Mexican PROGRESA poverty program. *Journal of Development Economics* 74 (1): 199-250.

Schwenk, A., A. Beisenherz, G. Kremer, V. Diehl, B. Salzberger, and G. Fätkenheuer. 1999. Bioelectrical impedance analysis in HIV-infected patients treated with triple antiretroviral treatment. *American Journal of Clinical Nutrition* 70 (5): 867-873.

Semba, R. D., and A. M. Tang. 1999. Micronutrients and the pathogenesis of human immunodeficiency virus infection. *British Journal of Nutrition* 81 (3): 181-189.

Semba, R. D., N. Shah, and D. Vlahov. 2001. Improvement of anemia among HIV-infected injection drug users receiving highly active antiretroviral therapy. *Journal of Acquired Immune Deficiency Syndromes* 26 (4): 315-319.

Shah, M. K., N. Osborne, M. Mbilizi, and G. Vilili. 2001. *Impact of HIV/AIDS on agriculture productivity and rural livelihoods in the central region of Malawi*. Lilongwe, Malawi: CARE International.

Sharma, M., M. Zeller, C. Henry, C. Lapenu, and B. Helms. 2000. Assessing the relative poverty level of MFI clients synthesis report based on four case studies. Photocopy, International Food Policy Research Institute for the Consultative Group to Assist the Poorest, Washington, D.C.

Silva, M., P. R. Skolnik, S. L. Gorbach, D. Spiegelman, I. B. Wilson, M. G. Fernandez-DiFranco, and T. A. Knox. 1998. The effect of protease inhibitors on weight and body composition in HIV-infected patients. *AIDS* 12 (13): 1645–1651.

Skoufias, E. 2005. *PROGRESA and its impacts on the welfare of rural households in Mexico.* IFPRI Research Report 139. Washington, D.C.: International Food Policy Research Institute.

Skoufias, E., B. Davis, and S. de la Vega. 2001. Targeting the poor in Mexico: An evaluation of the selection of households into PROGRESA. *World Development* 29 (10): 1769–1784.

Slater, R. 2004. *The implications of HIV/AIDS for social protection.* London: Overseas Development International.

Soul City Khomanani and CDC (Centers for Disease Control). 2007. HIV and AIDS prevention, care and treatment. Cited in Alliance for Childrens' Access to Social Security, Promoting a comprehensive approach to social security to meet the needs of children made vulnerable by HIV/AIDS in South Africa. PowerPoint presentation, International Expert Meeting on Social Protection Systems, Utrecht, the Netherlands, February 15.

South Africa, Department of Social Development. 2004. Minister and MECs to give priority to the removal of children from prison as well as the provision of more protection for other vulnerable children. Media release, Department of Social Development, Pretoria, South Africa, October 6.

——. 2007. *Strategic plan, 2007-2010.* Pretoria: Department of Social Development.

Sridhar, D., and A. Duffield. 2006. *A review of the impact of cash transfer programmes on child nutritional status and some implications for Save the Children UK Programmes.* London: Save the Children U.K.

Stewart, S. 2007. No worse than their peers? Orphans' nutritional status in five Eastern and Southern African countries. UNICEF.

Stokes, C. S. 2002. *Measuring impacts of HIV/AIDS on rural livelihoods and food security.* Rome: Gender and Population Division, Food and Agriculture Organization of the United Nations.

Streak, J. 2008. The rise of the conditional cash transfer programme for children affected by poverty: Should South Africa follow the trend? Photocopy.

Subbarao, K., and D. Coury. 2004. *Reaching out to Africa's orphans: A framework for public action.* Washington, D.C.: World Bank.

Subbarao, K., A. Mattimore, and K. Plangemann. 2001. *Social protection of Africa's orphans and vulnerable children: Issues and good practices program options.* Africa Region Human Development Working Paper. Washington, D.C.: World Bank.

Subbarao, K., A. Bonnerjee, J. Braithwaite, S. Carvalho, K. Ezemenari, C. Graham, and A. Thompson. 1997. *Safety net programs and poverty reduction: Lessons from cross-country experience.* Washington, D.C.: World Bank.

Tabi, M., and R. L. Vogel. 2006. Nutritional counselling: An intervention for HIV-positive patients. *Journal of Advanced Nursing* 54 (6): 676–682.

Tarp, F., K. Simler, C. Matusse, R. Heltberg, and G. Dava. 2002. The robustness of poverty profiles reconsidered. *Economic Development and Cultural Change* 51 (1): 77–108.

Thomas, D., and J. Strauss. 1997. Health and wages: Evidence on men and women in urban Brazil. *Journal of Econometrics* 77 (1): 159–185.

Thornton, R. L. 2008. The demand for, and impact of, learning HIV Status. *American Economic Review*, 98 (5): 1829–1863.

Tinker, A., K. Finn, and J. Epp. 2000. *Improving women's health: Issues and interventions*. Washington, D.C.: World Bank.

Tladi, L. S. 2006. Poverty and HIV/AIDS in South Africa: An empirical contribution. *Journal of Social Aspects of HIV/AIDS Research Alliance* 3 (1): 369–381.

Todd, P., and K. I. Wolpin. 2003. Using a social experiment to validate a dynamic behavioral model of child schooling and fertility: Assessing the impact of a school subsidy program in Mexico. Manuscript, University of Pennsylvania, Philadelphia, U.S.A.

Ueyama, M. 2007. *Mortality, mobility, and schooling outcomes among orphans: Evidence from Malawi*. Discussion Paper 00710. Washington, D.C.: International Food Policy Research Institute.

Uganda, MGLSD (Uganda, Ministry of Gender, Labour, and Social Development). 2007. *Design of a cash transfer pilot for Uganda: Final report*. Kampala, Uganda: Uganda Social Protection Task Force.

UNAIDS (Joint United Nations Programme on HIV/AIDS). 2010. *Global report: UNAIDS report on the global AIDS epidemic*. Geneva.

UNAIDS/UNICEF/WHO (United Nations Programme on HIV/AIDS / UNICEF / World Health Organization). 2007. *Children and AIDS: A stocktaking report*. New York.

UNCDF/SUM (United Nations Capital Development Fund / Special Unit for Microfinance). 2003. *Microfinance and HIV/AIDS*. Donor Brief 14. Washington, D.C.: Consultative Group to Assist the Poor.

UNGASS (United Nations General Assembly Special Session). 2001. *Declaration of commitment on HIV/AIDS*. Resolution S/26-2 adopted by the General Assembly. New York. www.un.org/ga/aids/coverage/FinalDeclarationHIVAIDS.html.

UNICEF. 2003. *Africa's orphaned generations*. New York.

——. 2005. The "rights" start to life: A statistical analysis of birth registration. Accessed December 2011. www.unicef.org/protection/BirthReg10a_rev.pdf.

——. 2006. *Africa's orphaned and vulnerable generations: Children affected by AIDS*. New York.

——. 2007a. *UNICEF Malawi annual report 2006*. New York.

——. 2007b. *QandA: The Malawi Social Cash Transfer Pilot*. New York. www.unicef.org/malawi/MLW_resources_qasocialcashpilot.pdf.

——. 2007c. Global Partners Forum seeks to build support for children affected by HIV/AIDS. New York. www.unicef.org/aids/index_30958.

——. 2007d. Inter-Agency Task Team on Children and HIV and AIDS. New York. www.unicef.org/aids/.

——. 2007e. *Enhanced protection for children affected by AIDS*. New York.

——. 2008. The role of social welfare services in social protection: Toward a policy-relevant research agenda. Report presented at a meeting of Save the Children U.K., London, November 29–30.

——. 2009. *Children and AIDS: Fourth stocktaking report, 2009*. New York.

UNICEF/Kenya. 2007a. What value of cash transfer will have an impact on outcomes for the Poorest Kenyan Children? Lessons from Latin America. Nairobi.

——. 2007b. Facing the crisis together: The Government of Kenya's Cash Transfer Programme for Orphans and Vulnerable Children. Draft (March). Nairobi.

USAID (U.S. Agency for International Development). 2002. *How does HIV/AIDS affect African businesses?* Washington, D.C.: Population, Health and Nutrition Information Project.

van Damme, W., and G. Kegels. 2006. Health system strengthening and scaling up antiretroviral therapy: The need for context-specific delivery models. Comment on Schneider et al. *Reproductive Health Matters* 14 (27): 24–26.

van Dijk, D. 2007. Social protection for children affected by AIDS, including social cash transfers. Report of the International Meeting of Stop Aids Now, Utrecht, the Netherlands, February 15–16.

Verweel, G., A. M. Van Rossum, N. G. Hartwig, T. F. Wolfs, H. J. Scherpbier, and R. de Groot. 2002. Treatment with highly active antiretroviral therapy in human immunodeficiency virus type 1-infected children is associated with a sustained effect on growth. *Pediatrics* 109 (2): E25–E31.

Villamor, E., R. Mbise, D. Spiegelman, E. Hertzmark, M. Fataki, K. E. Peterson, G. Ndossi, and W. W. Fawzi. 2002. Vitamin A supplements ameliorate the adverse effect of HIV-1, malaria, and diarrheal infections on child growth. *Pediatrics* 109 (1): E6.

Voluntary Service Overseas. 2006. *Reducing the burden of HIV and AIDS care on women and girls*. VSO policy brief. London.

Watkins, B. 2008. *Alternative methods for targeting social assistance to highly vulnerable groups*. Report submitted to the Technical Working Group on Social Assistance, Zambia, February 4. Washington, D.C.: Kimetrica International.

Weidle, P. J., N. Wamai, P. Solberg, C. Liechty, S. Sendagala, W. Were, J. Mermin, K. Buchacz, P. Behumbiize, R. L. Ransom, and R. Bunnell. 2006. Adherence to antiretroviral therapy in a home-based AIDS care programme in rural Uganda. *Lancet* 368 (9547): 1587–1594.

Weiser, S. D., K. Leiter, D. R. Bangsberg, L. M. Butler, F. Percy-de Korte, Z. Hlanze, N. Phaladze, V. Iacopino, and M. Heisler. 2007. Food insufficiency is associated with high-risk sexual behavior among women in Botswana and Swaziland. *PLoS Medicine* 4 (10): e260.

West, K. P. Jr. 2003. Vitamin A deficiency disorders in children and women. *Food and Nutrition Bulletin* 24 (4) (Supplement): S78–S90.

WHO (World Health Organization). 2002. Community home-based care in resource-limited settings: A framework for action. World Health Organization, Geneva.

Wiesmann, D., and J. Hoddinott. 2007. The impact of a conditional cash transfer program on food consumption: The Honduras family allowance program (PRAF). Paper presented at the Experimental Biology Conference, International Food Policy Research Institute, Washington, D.C., April 29.

Wilkinson, B. 1999. Field notes for considering microfinance services in the context of AIDS orphans. Prepared for USAID/Zambia. IRIS Center, University of Maryland, College Park, Md., U.S.A.

Woolard, I., M. Carter, and J. Agüero. 2005. Analysis of the child support grant: Evidence from the KwaZulu-Natal income dynamics study, 1993–2004. Report to the Department of Social Development, Republic of South Africa.

World Bank. 1990. *World development report 1990: Poverty.* New York: Oxford University Press.

———. 2004. Global Partners Forum for Orphans and Vulnerable Children Living in a World with HIV and AIDS. December 15–16. http://info.worldbank.org/etools/bspan/PresentationView.asp?PID=1390&EID=67.

———. 2005. The OVC Toolkit for SSA: A toolkit on how to support orphans and other vulnerable children (OVC) in Sub-Saharan Africa (SSA). Washington, D.C.

———. 2006a. Third International Conditional Cash Transfers Conference. Conference proceedings. Washington, D.C.

———. 2006b. Repositioning nutrition as central to development: A strategy for large-scale action. Washington, D.C.

———. 2007a. Tackling poverty in the short and long run: An assessment of the experience of conditional cash transfer programs. Washington, D.C.

———. 2007b. Impact evaluation design: Cash transfer pilot in Zambia. Concept note, Washington, D.C.

Yamano, T., and T. Jayne. 2004. Measuring the impact of working-age adult mortality on small-scale farm households in Kenya. *World Development* 32 (1): 91–119.

Yaschine, I. 1999. The changing anti-poverty agenda: What can the Mexican case tell us? *IDS Bulletin* 30 (2): 47–60.

Zachariah, R., M. Fitzgerald, M. Massaquoi, O. Pasulani, L. Arnould, S. Makombe, and A. D. Harries. 2006. Risk factors for high early mortality in patients on antiretroviral treatment in a rural district of Malawi. *AIDS* 20 (18): 2355–2360.

Zambia, MCDSS/GTZ (Zambia, Ministry of Community Development and Social Services / German Technical Cooperation). 2005. *Monitoring report,* 2nd ed.: *Pilot Social Cash Transfer Scheme, Kalomo District, Zambia.* Lusaka, Zambia.

———. 2006. Evaluation report: Kalomo Social Cash Transfer Scheme. Lusaka, Zambia.

Zambia, MCDSS/TWG (Zambia, Ministry of Community Development and Social Services / Technical Working Group on Social Assistance). 2007a. Kalomo evaluation—Way forward? Photocopy, Lusaka, Zambia.

———. 2007b. Implementation framework for scaling up to a national system of social transfers in Zambia. Photocopy, Lusaka, Zambia.

About the Authors

Michelle Adato is director of social and gender assessment at the Millennium Challenge Corporation. At the time she wrote this research monograph, she was a senior research fellow with the Poverty, Health, and Nutrition Division of the International Food Policy Research Institute, Washington, DC.

Lucy Bassett is a social protection specialist at the World Bank. At the time she wrote this research monograph, she was a research assistant with the Poverty, Health, and Nutrition Division of the International Food Policy Research Institute, Washington, DC.

Index

Page numbers for entries occurring in figures are suffixed by *f;* those for entries in notes by *n;* and those for entries in tables by *t.*

Made in United States
Troutdale, OR
11/03/2026

56844465R00133